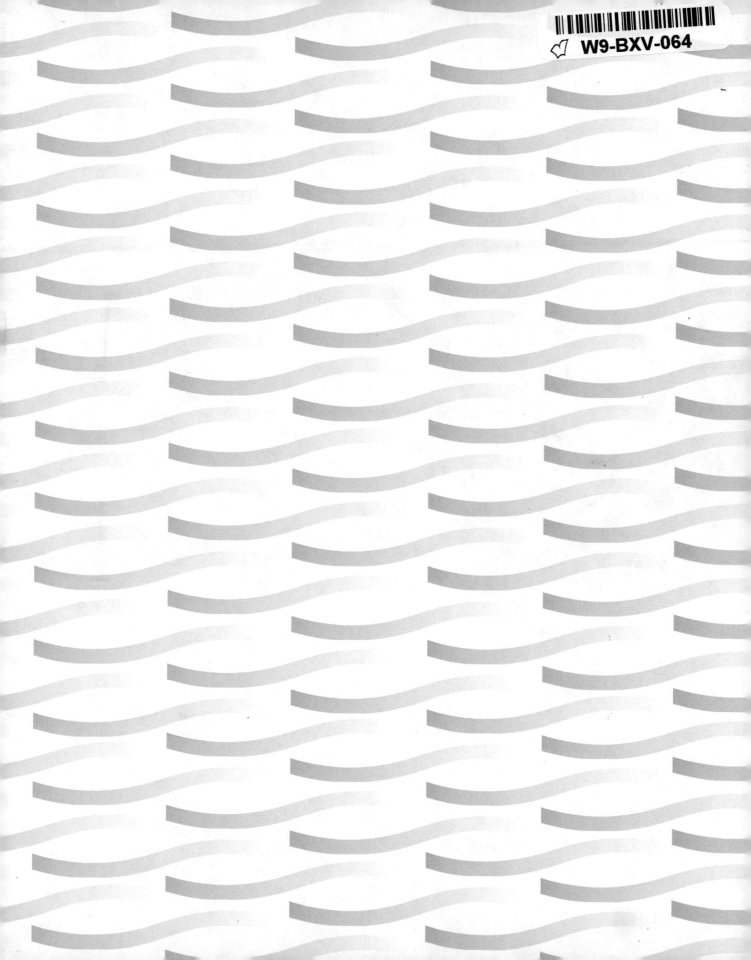

Gourmet's SWEETS

Gourmet's SWEETS

From the Editors of Gourmet

PHOTOGRAPHS BY ROMULO A. YANES

CONDÉ NAST BOOKS   RANDOM HOUSE

NEW YORK

LIBRARY OF CONGRESS
CATALOGING-IN-PUBLICATION DATA

Main entry under title:
Gourmet's Sweets: desserts for every occasion /
    from the editors of Gourmet; food photographs
    by Romulo A. Yanes.
                p. cm.
      Includes index.
        ISBN 0-375-50200-9 (alk. paper)
        1. Desserts.   I. Gourmet.
   TX773.G672   1998
   641.8'6—dc21   98-3750

Random House website address:
www.randomhouse.com

Some of the recipes in this work were published
previously in Gourmet Magazine.

Printed in the United States of America
on acid-free paper.

98765432
First Edition

All informative text in this book was written by
Diane Keitt and Caroline A. Schleifer.

Front Jacket: Profiteroles with Burnt Orange Ice Cream
and Hot Fudge Sauce, page 98.

Back Jacket: Little Chocolate Cherry Cake, page 168; Grapefruit
and Campari Granita, page 71; Kumquat, Grape, and Kiwifruit Soup,
page 137; Chocolate Raspberry Ganache Cake, page 108.

Frontispiece: Old-Fashioned Cherry Vanilla Pie, page 50.

For Condé Nast Books

Jill Cohen, *President*
Ellen Maria Bruzelius, *Division Vice President*
Lucille Friedman, *Fulfillment Manager*
Tom Downing, *Direct Marketing Manager*
Paul DiNardo, *Direct Marketing Assistant*
Serafino J. Cambareri, *Quality Control Manager*

For *Gourmet* Books

Diane Keitt, *Director*
Caroline A. Schleifer, *Editor*

For *Gourmet* Magazine

Gail Zweigenthal, *Editor-in-Chief*

Zanne Early Stewart, *Executive Food Editor*
Kemp Miles Minifie, *Senior Food Editor*
Alexis M. Touchet, *Associate Food Editor*
Lori Walther, *Food Editor*
Elizabeth Vought, *Food Editor*
Katy Massam, *Food Editor*
Shelton Wiseman, *Food Editor*
Alix Palley, *Food Editor*

Romulo A. Yanes, *Photographer*
Marjorie H. Webb, *Style Director*
Nancy Purdum, *Senior Style Editor*

Produced in association with
Media Projects Incorporated

Carter Smith, *Executive Editor*
Anne B. Wright, *Project Editor*
John W. Kern, *Production Editor*
Marilyn Flaig, *Indexer*

Joel Avirom, *Jacket and Book Design*
Jason Snyder, *Design Assistant*

The text of this book was set in Twentieth Century by Joel Avirom and
Jason Snyder. The four-color separations were done by American Color,
Seiple Lithographers, and Applied Graphic Technologies. The book was
printed and bound at R. R. Donnelley and Sons. Stock is Citation Web
Gloss, Westvāco.

ACKNOWLEDGMENTS

Now that our year-long desserts party has come to an end, the editors of *Gourmet* Books would like to thank all those who added their personal touch to *Gourmet's Sweets*.

Everyone in *Gourmet*'s test kitchens was involved. New recipes were developed by Alexis Touchet (Chocolate), Lori Walther (Icy), Liz Vought (Fruit), Katy Massam (Anytime), Shelley Wiseman (Homey), and Alix Palley (Bites). *Gourmet* alums also created new recipes: Leslie Pendleton (the two dessert menus and Holidays), Amy Mastrangelo (Showstoppers—including our profiteroles cover recipe), and Peggy Anderson (Berries and Lighter). Zanne Stewart and Kemp Minifie's creative input is evident throughout.

The collaboration of photographer Romulo Yanes and stylist Susan Victoria resulted in an outstanding jacket and two beautiful party photographs. New sweets were styled by Alexis Touchet (jacket) and Katy Massam, Shelley Wiseman, and Alix Palley (dessert parties). Marjorie Webb and Nancy Purdum prop-styled all other photographs.

On the editorial side, Hobby McKenney, Jane Daniels, and Kathleen Duffy Freud offered invaluable assistance, and Anne Wright, John Kern, Aaron Murray, and Jason Snyder made all production stages flow seamlessly. Finally, we thank Joel Avirom, our designer, for capturing on paper the true delight and whimsy of sweets.

RECIPE KEY

- Read each recipe through before beginning to cook.

- Measure baking pans and skillets across the top, not across the bottom.

- Measure liquids in glass or clear plastic liquid-measuring cups.

- Measure dry ingredients in nesting dry-measuring cups (usually made of metal or plastic) that can be leveled off with a straightedge such as a knife.

- Measure flour by spooning (not scooping) it into a dry-measuring cup and leveling off with a straightedge without tapping or shaking cup.

- Do not sift flour unless specified in recipe. When sifted flour is called for, sift the flour before measuring it. (Although many brands of packaged flour say "presifted" on the label, disregard this.)

- "Large" eggs are labeled as such. Do not substitute extra-large or jumbo.

CONTENTS

INTRODUCTION

— · —

Desserts are one of life's true pleasures, and, despite all the calorie-counting that goes on these days, I'm happy to report that they are still very much in fashion. Everyone in the food-magazine industry knows that putting a chocolate dessert on the cover boosts sales, and restaurateurs are the first to acknowledge that a creative pastry chef draws enthusiastic customers. So let's admit it—most of us gleefully splurge at least once in awhile.

The fine art of splurging is what *Gourmet's Sweets* is all about. This volume opens with two fabulous all-dessert parties: One, designed for a hot summer's day in the garden, offers icy refreshers along with peach, mango, and blackberry temptations; the other, for an elegant winter's eve, delights with Champagne, creamy cakes, and buttery confections. The recipes in both menus can be made almost completely ahead of time—so, once you add the finishing touches, you, too, can enjoy the feast.

The ten chapters that follow capture the whimsical nature of desserts—each provides a variety of sweets to fulfill a particular craving or need. For example, when you feel like something comforting, delve into our "homey" chapter, with its soothing pies, puddings, and crisps; if you're looking for an easy-to-handle sweet for a party or an outing, try our "bites" chapter, packed with cookies, brownies, and other small treats. "Showstoppers" offers towering cakes, including an exquisite wedding cake, eye-catching pastries, and on and on.

Much of life is about balance. Lately, as I jog around the reservoir in Central Park, I find myself thinking about how I will reward myself—and *Gourmet's Sweets* comes to mind. Will I try the peanut butter cookies, the peach "pizza," or the banana chiffon pie? It's a difficult, yet thoroughly enjoyable, exercise.

GAIL ZWEIGENTHAL
EDITOR-IN-CHIEF

A

GARDEN DESSERT PARTY

A CHAMPAGNE DESSERT

Bittersweet Chocolate Soufflé ∙ Chocolate Hazelnut Torte
Bittersweet Chocolate Mousse in Phyllo with Raspberry Sauce
Chocolate Cherry Bread Pudding
Fallen Chocolate Rum Cakes on Napoleon Crisps
Turtle Brownies ∙ Sambuca Brownies ∙ Cappuccino Brownies
Caramel Chocolate Puddings
White Chocolate Blackberry Mousses
Milk Chocolate Pots de Crème
Chocolate Orange Marbled Cheesecake
Chocolate-Glazed Chocolate Cake ∙ Chocolate Cream Pie
Chocolate Cake with Pecan Coconut Filling
Chocolate Bourbon Tart

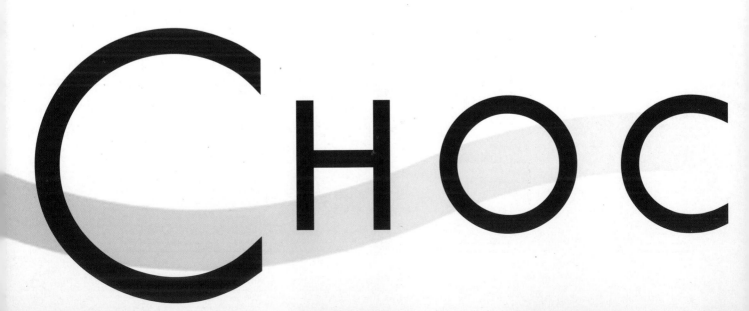

CHOC

OLATE

Chocolate—smooth, slightly bitter, and aromatic—is one of the world's great luxuries. The best dark chocolates have a high percentage of cocoa solids, ideally around 60%, and when used for baking, really make a difference. European brands like Lindt and Callebaut guarantee marvelous flavor (Lindt, which we used for testing these recipes, is generally available at supermarkets, and Callebaut can be bought in bulk at specialty food shops). When chocolate is the central, undiluted flavor, the more expensive Valrhona brand is incomparable. The quality of white and milk chocolates can vary tremendously—look for Callebaut or Lindt. Callebaut and Valrhona chocolate can be ordered by mail from New York Cake and Baking Distributors, tel. (800) 942-2539.

BITTERSWEET CHOCOLATE SOUFFLÉ

⅓ cup granulated sugar plus additional for coating soufflé dish

6 ounces fine-quality bittersweet chocolate

3 tablespoons all-purpose flour

3 large egg yolks plus 6 large egg whites

1½ cups milk

2 teaspoons vanilla

¼ teaspoon salt

GARNISH: confectioners' sugar

ACCOMPANIMENT: sweetened whipped cream

Preheat oven to 375° F. Butter a 6-cup soufflé dish and coat with additional granulated sugar, knocking out excess sugar. Butter and sugar a 6-inch-wide doubled piece of foil or wax paper long enough to fit around dish. Fit prepared dish with collar extending 2 inches above rim.

Finely chop chocolate. In a bowl whisk together flour and 1 tablespoon granulated sugar. In a small bowl whisk together yolks and ¼ cup milk and add to flour mixture, whisking until smooth.

In a heavy saucepan bring remaining 1¼ cups milk just to a boil and whisk into yolk mixture in a slow stream. Transfer mixture to pan and cook over moderate heat, whisking, until it just comes to a boil. Cook mixture at a bare simmer, whisking constantly, until very thick, about 2 minutes. Remove pan from heat and whisk in chocolate and vanilla until custard is smooth. Transfer custard to a large bowl.

In another bowl with an electric mixer beat whites with salt until they just hold soft peaks. Beat in remaining granulated sugar in a slow stream, beating until meringue just holds stiff peaks. Stir one fourth of meringue into custard to lighten and fold in remaining meringue gently but thoroughly. Spoon mixture into soufflé dish. *Soufflé may be prepared up to this point 1 hour ahead and chilled, covered with a paper towel and plastic wrap. Do not let paper towel touch surface of soufflé. Put cold soufflé in preheated oven.* Bake soufflé in middle of oven 30 to 35 minutes, or until firm and set in center.

Carefully remove collar from soufflé dish and sift confectioners' sugar over soufflé. Serve soufflé immediately with whipped cream. SERVES 8.

Photo on page 15

CHOCOLATE HAZELNUT TORTE

For Torte

- 6 ounces fine-quality bittersweet chocolate (not unsweetened)
- 1 cup hazelnuts (about 4 ounces)
- 2/3 cup plus 3 tablespoons sugar
- 1 stick (1/2 cup) unsalted butter, softened
- 5 large eggs, separated
- 1 teaspoon vanilla
- 3/4 teaspoon salt

For Glaze

- 6 ounces fine-quality bittersweet chocolate (not unsweetened)
- 1/2 cup heavy cream

GARNISH: finely chopped toasted hazelnuts

ACCOMPANIMENT: whipped cream or vanilla ice cream

Preheat oven to 375° F. Butter an 8½-inch springform pan and line bottom with round of wax paper. Butter wax paper and flour baking pan, knocking out excess flour.

Make Torte: Chop chocolate. In a metal bowl set over a saucepan of barely simmering water melt chocolate, stirring until smooth, and cool.

Spread hazelnuts in a shallow baking pan and toast in middle of oven until they begin to turn pale golden, 7 to 10 minutes. Wrap nuts in a kitchen towel and rub to remove any loose skins (do not worry about skins that do not come off). Cool nuts completely. Transfer nuts to a food processor and finely grind with 3 tablespoons sugar.

In a large bowl with an electric mixer beat together butter and remaining 2/3 cup sugar until light and fluffy. Add yolks 1 at a time, beating well after each addition, and beat in vanilla, salt, and melted chocolate. Beat in hazelnut mixture until combined well.

In another large bowl with cleaned beaters beat whites with a pinch salt until they just hold stiff peaks. Whisk about one fourth whites into chocolate mixture to lighten and fold in remaining whites gently but thoroughly. Spread batter evenly in springform pan and bake in middle of oven 45 to 55 minutes, or until a tester comes out with crumbs adhering. Cool torte completely in pan on a rack and remove side of pan. Invert torte onto a plate and discard wax paper.

Make Glaze: Chop chocolate and put in a small metal bowl. In a small saucepan bring cream to a boil and pour over chocolate. Stir glaze just until completely smooth and let stand until slightly thickened, about 20 minutes.

Spread glaze evenly over top and side of torte. With a small icing spatula or butter knife make parallel lines through glaze across top to create a design. Garnish top and bottom edges of torte with chopped toasted hazelnuts. *Let torte stand until glaze is set, about 2 hours. Torte may be made 1 day ahead and kept loosely covered at cool room temperature.*

Serve torte with whipped cream or ice cream. SERVES 8.

Photo below

BITTERSWEET CHOCOLATE MOUSSE IN PHYLLO

— · —

two 17- by 12-inch *phyllo* sheets

For Sauce
- a 10-ounce package frozen raspberries in light syrup
- 2 tablespoons granulated sugar
- 1 tablespoon *eau-de-vie de framboise* or raspberry liqueur

For Mousse
- 3 ounces fine-quality bittersweet chocolate (not unsweetened)
- 2 tablespoons granulated sugar
- 1 tablespoon cornstarch
- ½ cup water
- 1 large egg
- 1 tablespoon *eau-de-vie de framboise* or raspberry liqueur
- ¼ cup well-chilled heavy cream

3 tablespoons well-chilled heavy cream
confectioners' sugar for dusting shells
unsweetened cocoa powder for dusting shells
chocolate curls (procedure on page 19)

Preheat oven to 350° F.

Stack *phyllo* sheets and cut out three 6-inch squares (6 total), discarding scraps. Stack *phyllo* squares between 2 sheets plastic wrap and then cover with a damp kitchen towel. Line each of two ½-cup muffin cups with 1 *phyllo* square, pressing gently into bottom, with edges overhanging top of cup. Repeat with remaining squares in same 2 cups, overlapping corners in different directions. (Do not reposition *phyllo* once in cup or it may tear.)

Bake *phyllo* shells in middle of oven until edges are golden brown, 5 to 10 minutes. Carefully remove *phyllo* shells from cups and transfer to a rack to cool completely. *Phyllo shells may be made 1 day ahead and kept in an airtight container at room temperature.*

Make Sauce: In a saucepan simmer raspberries and sugar, stirring occasionally, 10 minutes and stir in liqueur. In a blender purée mixture (use caution when blending hot liquids) and pour through a sieve into a heatproof bowl, scraping with a spatula. *Chill sauce, covered, at least 30 minutes and up to 2 days.*

Make Mousse: Chop chocolate. In a small saucepan whisk together sugar and cornstarch and add water and egg, whisking until smooth. Bring mixture to a boil over moderate heat, whisking, and simmer, whisking vigorously, 1 minute. Remove pan from heat and add chocolate and liqueur, stirring until chocolate is melted. Transfer chocolate mixture to a metal bowl and set in a larger bowl of ice and cold water. Beat chocolate mixture until cold and lightened in color. In another bowl with cleaned beaters beat cream until it just holds stiff peaks and fold into chocolate mixture gently but thoroughly. *Chill chocolate mousse, covered, at least 30 minutes and up to 2 days.*

Assemble Dessert: In a bowl whisk cream until it just begins to thicken. Pour some raspberry sauce onto 2 dessert plates and dot with thickened cream. Pull point of a skewer or wooden pick through cream to form hearts. With a sieve dust *phyllo* shells with confectioners' sugar and cocoa powder. Arrange *phyllo* shells on top of sauce and spoon about ⅓ cup mousse into each shell (do not overfill). Top mousse with chocolate curls. **SERVES 2.**

Photo opposite

To Make Chocolate Curls

fine-quality bittersweet chocolate
(not unsweetened)

Chop chocolate and in a double boiler or small metal bowl set over a saucepan of barely simmering water melt chocolate, stirring until smooth. With a metal spatula spread melted chocolate on a baking sheet (not non-stick) as thinly and evenly as possible. Cool chocolate until firm to the touch but not hard. (Alternatively, chill melted chocolate on sheet; if it becomes too hard let it soften slightly at room temperature.) With a pastry scraper or metal spatula held at an angle scrape chocolate slowly from sheet, letting it curl. Carefully transfer curls as formed to a plate lined with wax paper. *Chocolate curls may be made 1 day ahead and chilled, loosely covered.* ONE OUNCE CHOCOLATE YIELDS ENOUGH CHOCOLATE CURLS TO GARNISH 4 SERVINGS.

CHOCOLATE CHERRY BREAD PUDDING

a 1-pound loaf brioche or challah
9 ounces fine-quality bittersweet chocolate (not unsweetened)
1 cup dried tart cherries* (about 4 ounces)
1½ cups heavy cream
1¼ cups milk
¾ cup sugar
4 large eggs
1 teaspoon vanilla
¼ teaspoon salt
2 tablespoons unsalted butter

available at specialty foods shops and some super-markets and by mail order from American Spoon Foods, tel. (888) 735-6700

Into a large baking pan tear brioche or challah into bite-size pieces. *Dry bread, uncovered, at room temperature 12 hours. (Alternatively, dry bread in a 250° F. oven 1 hour.)*

Butter a 2- to 3-quart shallow baking dish.

Chop chocolate and transfer ½ cup to a bowl with cherries. Transfer remaining chocolate to a large bowl. In a saucepan bring cream just to a boil and pour over chocolate. Let chocolate stand 1 minute and whisk until smooth. Whisk in milk, sugar, eggs, vanilla, and salt until combined well. Add dried bread and fold until coated well. Spoon half of bread mixture into baking dish, spreading evenly, and sprinkle evenly with chocolate and cherries. Top cherry mixture with remaining bread mixture. Cut butter into bits and dot pudding with butter. *Chill pudding, covered, at least 1 hour and up to 1 day.*

Preheat oven to 350° F.

Bake pudding in middle of oven until slightly puffed and golden, about 40 minutes. Serve pudding warm or at room temperature. SERVES 8 TO 10.

FALLEN CHOCOLATE RUM CAKES ON NAPOLEON CRISPS

— · —

For Napoleon Crisps

3 tablespoons unsalted butter

4 gingersnaps

⅓ cup sugar

¼ cup unsweetened cocoa powder

three 17- by 12-inch *phyllo* sheets

For Cakes

2 tablespoons sugar

1 tablespoon unsweetened cocoa powder

12 ounces fine-quality bittersweet chocolate (not unsweetened)

½ stick (¼ cup) unsalted butter

¼ cup dark rum

6 large egg yolks

5 large egg whites

ACCOMPANIMENT: sweetened whipped cream

Make Crisps: Preheat oven to 350° F.

Melt butter and cool slightly. In a food processor finely grind gingersnaps with sugar and cocoa powder. Stack *phyllo* sheets between 2 overlapping sheets plastic wrap and then cover with a damp kitchen towel. Put 1 *phyllo* sheet on a piece of parchment paper and brush lightly with some butter. Sprinkle sheet evenly with half of cocoa sugar. Top cocoa sugar with a second *phyllo* sheet and brush lightly with some butter. Sprinkle sheet with remaining cocoa sugar and top with remaining *phyllo* sheet, pressing layers together gently. Brush top lightly with butter. Slide a baking sheet under parchment and chill *phyllo* 10 minutes.

Transfer *phyllo* with parchment to a cutting board. Using the bottom of a 1-cup ramekin as a guide cut out 6 rounds with a sharp knife, cutting through parchment. Cut scraps into pieces and transfer rounds and scraps (on parchment) to a large baking sheet. Cover rounds and scraps directly with another parchment sheet and bake in lower third of oven 12 to 15 minutes, or until golden. Cool crisps and scraps on baking sheet on a rack. *Cocoa crisps and scraps may be made 1 week ahead and kept in an airtight container at room temperature.* Remove parchment paper from crisps and scraps.

Make Cakes: Preheat oven to 375° F.

In a small bowl stir together sugar and cocoa powder. Butter six 1-cup ramekins and coat insides with cocoa sugar, knocking out excess cocoa sugar.

Chop chocolate and in a metal bowl set over a saucepan of barely simmering water melt chocolate and butter with rum, whisking until smooth. Remove bowl from heat and cool chocolate mixture 5 minutes. Whisk in yolks 1 at a time.

In a bowl with an electric mixer beat whites with a pinch salt until they just hold stiff peaks. Whisk about one fourth whites into chocolate mixture to lighten and fold in remaining whites gently but thoroughly. Divide batter among ramekins and bake cakes in middle of oven 12 minutes. Cool cakes in ramekins on a rack 3 minutes (cakes will deflate).

Run a thin knife around edge of each ramekin. Arrange a crisp on top of a cake and invert crisp and cake onto a plate. Arrange crisps on remaining cakes and invert in same manner. Top each cake with a dollop of whipped cream. Coarsely crumble some *phyllo* scraps and sprinkle over cream. Serve cakes warm. **SERVES 6.**

TURTLE BROWNIES

For Brownie Layer
- 4 ounces semisweet chocolate
- 1 ounce unsweetened chocolate
- 1 stick (½ cup) unsalted butter
- 1 cup packed brown sugar
- 1 teaspoon vanilla
- 2 large eggs
- ¾ cup plus 2 tablespoons all-purpose flour
- ¼ teaspoon baking powder
- ½ teaspoon salt

For Caramel-Pecan Layer
- ¾ cup granulated sugar
- ⅓ cup light corn syrup
- 3 tablespoons water
- ⅓ cup heavy cream
- 1 teaspoon vanilla
- 1½ cups pecans (about 6 ounces)
- GARNISH: 1 ounce semisweet chocolate

Make Brownie Layer: Preheat oven to 350° F. and butter and flour a 9-inch square baking pan, knocking out excess flour.

Chop chocolates and cut butter into pieces. In a 1½-quart heavy saucepan melt chocolates and butter over low heat, stirring until smooth, and remove pan from heat. Cool mixture to lukewarm and stir in brown sugar and vanilla. Add eggs 1 at a time, beating well with a wooden spoon until mixture is glossy and smooth. Into a bowl sift together flour, baking powder, and salt and add to chocolate mixture, beating just until combined well.

Spread batter evenly in baking pan and bake in middle of oven 30 to 35 minutes, or until a tester comes out clean. Cool brownie layer completely in pan on a rack.

Make Caramel-Pecan Layer: In a 3-quart heavy saucepan bring granulated sugar, corn syrup, water, and a pinch salt to a boil over moderate heat, stirring until sugar is dissolved, and boil, without stirring, until it turns a golden caramel. Remove pan from heat and carefully add cream and vanilla (mixture will bubble up and steam). Stir in pecans and quickly pour mixture over brownie layer, spreading evenly.

Cool brownies completely in pan on a rack.

Make Garnish: In a metal bowl set over a saucepan of barely simmering water melt chocolate, stirring until smooth, and remove bowl from heat. Transfer melted chocolate to a small heavy-duty plastic bag and squeeze chocolate to 1 corner. Snip a small hole in corner of bag and pipe chocolate decoratively over brownies.

Chill brownies, loosely covered, until caramel is firm, at least 4 hours.

Cut chilled brownies into 16 squares and remove from pan while still cold. Bring brownies to room temperature before serving. *Brownies keep, covered and chilled in one layer, 5 days.* **MAKES 16 BROWNIES.**

Photo below

SAMBUCA BROWNIES

2 ounces unsweetened chocolate

1 stick (½ cup) unsalted butter

½ cup pine nuts

2 large eggs

1 cup sugar

4 tablespoons Sambuca

¾ cup plus 1 tablespoon all-purpose flour

½ teaspoon salt

¼ teaspoon baking powder

Preheat oven to 350° F. Butter and flour an 8-inch square baking pan, knocking out excess flour.

Chop chocolate and cut butter into pieces. Toast pine nuts until golden. In a double boiler or a metal bowl set over a saucepan of barely simmering water melt chocolate and butter, stirring until smooth, and remove top of double boiler or bowl from heat. Cool mixture to room temperature.

In a large bowl with an electric mixer beat together eggs and sugar until thickened and pale and beat in chocolate mixture and Sambuca. Into a bowl sift together flour, salt, and baking powder and beat into chocolate mixture just until combined.

Spread batter evenly in baking pan and sprinkle evenly with pine nuts. Bake brownies in middle of oven 30 to 35 minutes, or until a tester comes out with crumbs adhering. Cool brownies completely in pan on a rack and cut into 16 squares. *Brownies keep, layered between sheets of wax paper in an airtight container at cool room temperature, 5 days.* MAKES 16 BROWNIES.

Photo on page 21

CAPPUCCINO BROWNIES

For Brownie Layer

8 ounces fine-quality bittersweet chocolate (not unsweetened)

1 cup walnuts

1½ sticks (¾ cup) unsalted butter

2 tablespoons instant espresso powder*

1 tablespoon boiling water

1½ cups granulated sugar

2 teaspoons vanilla

4 large eggs

1 cup all-purpose flour

½ teaspoon salt

For Cream Cheese Frosting

8 ounces cream cheese, softened

¾ stick (6 tablespoons) unsalted butter, softened

1½ cups confectioners' sugar

1 teaspoon vanilla

1 teaspoon cinnamon

For Glaze

6 ounces fine-quality bittersweet chocolate (not unsweetened)

1½ tablespoons instant espresso powder*

1 tablespoon boiling water

2 tablespoons unsalted butter

½ cup heavy cream

available at specialty foods shops, some supermarkets, and by mail order from Adriana's Caravan, tel. (800) 316-0820

Make Brownie Layer: Preheat oven to 350° F. Butter and flour a 13- by 9-inch baking pan.

Chop chocolate and walnuts and cut butter into pieces. In a cup dissolve espresso powder in boiling water. In a metal bowl set over a saucepan of barely simmering water melt chocolate and butter with espresso mixture, stirring until smooth. Remove bowl from heat and cool mixture to lukewarm. Stir in sugar and vanilla. Stir in eggs 1 at a time, stirring well after each addition, and stir in flour and salt until just combined. Stir in walnuts. Pour batter into baking pan and smooth top. Bake brownie layer in middle of oven 22 to 25 minutes, or until a tester comes out with crumbs adhering. Cool brownie layer completely in pan on a rack.

Make Frosting: In a bowl with an electric mixer beat cream cheese and butter until light and fluffy. Sift confectioners' sugar over mixture and add vanilla and cinnamon, beating until combined well.

Spread frosting evenly over brownie layer. *Chill brownies 1 hour, or until frosting is firm.*

Make Glaze: Chop chocolate. In a cup dissolve espresso powder in boiling water. In a metal bowl set over a saucepan of barely simmering water melt chocolate and butter with cream and espresso mixture, stirring until glaze is smooth. Remove bowl from heat and cool glaze to room temperature.

Spread glaze carefully over frosting layer. *Chill brownies, covered, at least 3 hours.*

Cut chilled brownies with a sharp knife and serve chilled or at room temperature. *Brownies keep, covered and chilled, 3 days.* **MAKES ABOUT 24 BROWNIES.**

Photo opposite

CARAMEL CHOCOLATE PUDDINGS

8 ounces fine-quality bittersweet chocolate (not unsweetened)
¼ cup unsweetened cocoa powder
3½ tablespoons cornstarch
1 cup sugar
3 whole large eggs
2 large egg yolks
4 cups milk
2 teaspoons vanilla

ACCOMPANIMENT: lightly sweetened whipped cream

Finely chop chocolate. In a bowl whisk together cocoa powder, cornstarch, ¼ cup sugar, and a pinch salt and whisk in whole eggs, yolks, and ¾ cup milk until combined well.

In a dry 2½- to 3-quart heavy saucepan cook remaining ¾ cup sugar over moderate heat, stirring with a fork, until melted. Cook caramel, without stirring, swirling pan, until deep golden. Remove pan from heat and carefully add remaining 3¼ cups milk (caramel will bubble and steam). Return pan to heat and cook caramel mixture over moderate heat, stirring occasionally, until caramel is dissolved.

Bring caramel mixture just to a boil. Whisk about half of mixture in a slow stream into cocoa mixture and whisk mixture into caramel mixture remaining in pan. Cook custard over moderate heat, whisking, until thickened, 3 to 4 minutes. Cook custard at a bare simmer, whisking, 1 minute. Remove pan from heat and add chocolate and vanilla, whisking until smooth. Cool pudding slightly and pour into 6 goblets. *Chill puddings, surfaces covered with plastic wrap, at least 2 hours and up to 2 days.*

Serve each pudding with a dollop of whipped cream. **SERVES 6.**

WHITE CHOCOLATE BLACKBERRY MOUSSES

For Blackberry Purée

    2 cups fresh or thawed frozen blackberries

    3 tablespoons light corn syrup

    1 teaspoon cold water

    ½ teaspoon cornstarch

    1 tablespoon dark rum

For Mousse

    6 ounces fine-quality white chocolate

    ¼ cup sugar

    2½ tablespoons cornstarch

    3 large eggs

    1½ cups milk

    ⅛ teaspoon salt

    1½ cups well-chilled heavy cream

Make Purée: In a food processor or blender purée blackberries with corn syrup. Pour purée through a fine sieve into a heavy saucepan, pressing hard on solids, and simmer, stirring occasionally, until reduced to about ½ cup, about 10 minutes. In a small cup stir water into cornstarch and stir into purée with rum. Simmer purée, stirring, 1 minute, or until thickened, and cool completely.

Make Mousse: Chop white chocolate. In a 2½- to 3-quart heavy saucepan whisk together sugar and cornstarch and whisk in eggs, milk, and salt until combined well. Bring custard to a boil over moderate heat, whisking, and simmer, whisking vigorously, 1 minute. Remove pan from heat. Add chocolate and stir custard until chocolate is melted. Transfer custard to a metal bowl and set in a larger bowl of ice and cold water. With a hand-held mixer beat custard until cold and slightly thickened. In another bowl with cleaned beaters beat cream until it just holds stiff peaks and fold into custard gently but thoroughly.

Spoon about ¼ cup mousse into a stemmed glass and drizzle 1 teaspoon blackberry purée around edge of glass. Repeat layering with mousse and purée twice, drizzling top with ½ teaspoon purée. Using a wooden skewer, decoratively swirl purée into mousse. Make 5 more mousses in same manner. *Chill mousses, covered with plastic wrap, at least 1 hour and up to 1 day.* SERVES 6.

MILK CHOCOLATE POTS DE CRÈME

    6 ounces fine-quality milk chocolate

    4 large egg yolks

    1 tablespoon sugar

    ½ teaspoon freshly grated nutmeg

    2 cups heavy cream

    ½ teaspoon vanilla

    unsweetened cocoa powder for dusting custards

Preheat oven to 325° F.

Finely chop chocolate. In a bowl whisk yolks, sugar, nutmeg, and a pinch salt until pale yellow, about 2 minutes. In a heavy saucepan bring cream just to a boil and whisk into yolk mixture in a slow stream. Add chocolate and vanilla and let stand 1 minute. Whisk custard just until smooth.

Arrange four 6-ounce ramekins or *pots de crème* (small earthenware cups with lids) in a large baking pan and divide custard among them. Skim froth. Pour enough boiling water into pan to reach halfway up sides of ramekins and cover pan with foil or *pots de crème* with lids. Bake custards in middle of oven until a knife inserted in center comes out clean, 25 to 30 minutes. Transfer ramekins to a rack and cool completely. *Chill custards, covered, until cold, at least 2 hours, and up to 1 day.* Lightly dust custards with cocoa powder before serving. SERVES 4.

CHOCOLATE ORANGE MARBLED CHEESECAKE

For Crust
    ½ stick (¼ cup) unsalted butter
    32 chocolate wafers

For Filling
    3 ounces fine-quality bittersweet chocolate
      (not unsweetened)
    1 navel orange
    2 pounds cream cheese, softened
    1½ cups sugar
    ⅓ cup sour cream
    ¼ cup all-purpose flour
    1 teaspoon vanilla
    ½ teaspoon salt
    4 large eggs
    1 tablespoon Grand Marnier
    ¼ cup unsweetened cocoa powder
      (not Dutch-process)

For Glaze
    6 ounces fine-quality bittersweet chocolate
      (not unsweetened)
    ⅔ cup heavy cream
    2 tablespoons Grand Marnier
    1 tablespoon unsalted butter

Make Crust: Butter a 9-inch springform pan. Wrap bottom and outside of pan with a large piece of heavy-duty foil, making sure foil reaches at least 2 inches up side, to waterproof.

Melt butter and cool slightly. In a food processor finely grind chocolate wafers. Add butter and pulse until combined well. Press crumb mixture evenly onto bottom of pan.

Preheat oven to 350° F.

Make Filling: Chop chocolate and in a metal bowl set over a saucepan of barely simmering water melt chocolate, stirring until smooth. Remove bowl from heat and cool chocolate. With a vegetable peeler remove zest from orange and mince enough to measure 1 tablespoon.

In a bowl with an electric mixer beat cream cheese until light and fluffy and gradually beat in sugar until combined well. Beat in sour cream, flour, vanilla, and salt until combined and beat in eggs 1 at a time, until just combined. Transfer about 2 cups filling to a bowl and beat in chocolate, zest, Grand Marnier, and cocoa powder. Pour half of plain filling onto crust and drop chocolate filling by large spoonfuls onto it. Pour remaining plain filling over chocolate filling.

Put springform pan in a roasting pan. Put roasting pan in middle of oven and with a measuring cup slowly add enough water to reach 1½ inches up side of springform pan, being careful not to let any water inside foil.

Bake cake 1½ hours. (Top of cake will be golden-brown and dry to the touch. Cake will continue to set as it cools and chills.) Transfer pan to a rack. *Cool cheesecake 2½ hours.*

Make Glaze: Finely chop chocolate. In a heavy saucepan bring cream, Grand Marnier, and butter just to a boil over moderately high heat. Stir in chocolate and simmer glaze, stirring occasionally, 7 minutes, or until thickened. Cool glaze, stirring occasionally, 5 minutes and pour over top of cheesecake. *Chill cheesecake, loosely covered, at least 6 hours and up to 2 days.*

Remove side of pan and serve cheesecake chilled. **SERVES 10 TO 12.**

CHOCOLATE-GLAZED CHOCOLATE CAKE

- - · - -

2 sticks (1 cup) unsalted butter
2 cups all-purpose flour
¾ teaspoon baking soda
¼ teaspoon baking powder
½ teaspoon salt
1¼ cups packed dark brown sugar
½ cup granulated sugar
1 cup fresh brewed coffee
¾ cup unsweetened cocoa powder
   (not Dutch-process)
3 large eggs
½ cup sour cream
1 teaspoon vanilla
½ cup apricot jam
6 ounces fine-quality bittersweet chocolate
   (not unsweetened)
½ cup heavy cream

Preheat oven to 350° F. Butter and flour a 10-inch bundt pan, knocking out excess flour.

Melt butter. Into a large bowl sift together flour, baking soda, baking powder, and salt and stir in sugars. In another bowl whisk coffee into cocoa powder until smooth and whisk in butter, eggs, sour cream, and vanilla until combined. Whisk cocoa mixture into flour mixture until combined. Pour batter into bundt pan and bake in middle of oven about 40 minutes, or until a tester comes out clean. Cool cake in pan on a rack 15 minutes and turn out onto rack to cool completely.

In a small heavy saucepan boil jam, stirring occasionally, 2 minutes. Pour jam through a fine sieve into a bowl, pressing hard on solids. Brush warm jam all over cake, including center tube. *Let cake stand 1 hour.*

Finely chop chocolate. In a heavy saucepan bring cream just to a boil and remove pan from heat. Add chocolate to cream and stir until smooth. With cake on rack set over a baking pan (to catch drips) pour warm glaze over top of cake and with an offset spatula spread glaze evenly over top, side, and inner tube of cake. Let cake stand until glaze is set, about 30 minutes, and transfer to a plate. *Cake may be made 2 days ahead and chilled, covered. Bring cake to room temperature before serving.* SERVES 12.

CHOCOLATE CREAM PIE

- - · - -

For Crust
   ¾ stick (6 tablespoons) unsalted butter
   about 45 vanilla wafers
   ⅓ cup sugar

For Filling
   5 ounces fine-quality bittersweet chocolate
      (not unsweetened)
   4 ounces unsweetened chocolate
   3 tablespoons unsalted butter
   1 cup sugar
   ½ cup cornstarch
   ¾ teaspoon salt
   6 large egg yolks
   4½ cups milk
   1½ teaspoons vanilla

   GARNISH: sweetened whipped cream and grated
      bittersweet chocolate

Make Crust: Preheat oven to 350° F.

Melt butter and cool slightly. In a food processor finely grind enough vanilla wafers to measure 2 cups crumbs. In a bowl stir together crumbs, butter, and sugar and press evenly onto bottom and up side of a 10-inch (1½-quart) pie plate. Bake crust in middle of oven until crisp, 15 to 20 minutes, and cool on a rack.

Make Filling: Chop chocolates. Cut butter into bits and soften. In a metal bowl set over a pan of barely simmering water melt chocolates, stirring until smooth, and remove bowl from heat. In a 3-quart heavy saucepan whisk together sugar, cornstarch, salt, and yolks until combined well and add milk in a stream, whisking. Bring milk mixture to a boil over moderate heat, whisking, and simmer, whisking, until thick, about 1 minute. Using a rubber spatula force custard through a fine sieve into a bowl and whisk in melted chocolate, butter, and vanilla until smooth. Cover surface of filling with plastic wrap and cool completely.

Pour filling into crumb crust. *Chill pie, surface covered with plastic wrap, at least 6 hours and up to 24 hours.*

Spoon whipped cream decoratively onto pie and sprinkle with grated chocolate. **SERVES 8.**

Photo below

CHOCOLATE CAKE
WITH PECAN
COCONUT FILLING

For Cake Layers

3 ounces fine-quality bittersweet chocolate (not unsweetened)

¼ cup water

2 cups all-purpose flour

½ cup unsweetened cocoa powder

1 teaspoon baking soda

½ teaspoon salt

1½ sticks (¾ cup) unsalted butter, softened

⅔ cup packed light brown sugar

⅔ cup granulated sugar

2 whole large eggs

1 teaspoon vanilla

1 cup well-shaken buttermilk

For Filling

1 cup pecans

1 cup heavy cream

1 cup granulated sugar

1 stick (½ cup) unsalted butter

3 large egg yolks

1 teaspoon vanilla

1⅓ cups sweetened flaked coconut

For Frosting

4 ounces fine-quality bittersweet chocolate (not unsweetened)

1 cup heavy cream

Make Cake Layers: Preheat oven to 350° F. Butter two 9-inch round cake pans and line bottoms with rounds of wax paper. Butter paper and dust pans with flour, knocking out excess flour.

Chop chocolate and in a small metal bowl set over a pan of barely simmering water melt chocolate with ¼ cup water, stirring occasionally until smooth. Remove metal bowl from heat and cool chocolate. Into a bowl sift together flour, cocoa powder, baking soda, and salt. In a large bowl with an electric mixer beat together butter and sugars until light and fluffy. Add eggs 1 at a time, beating well after each addition, and beat in chocolate and vanilla. Beat in flour mixture alternately with buttermilk, beginning and ending with flour mixture and beating well after each addition.

Divide batter between pans, smoothing tops, and bake in middle of oven until a tester comes out clean, 30 to 35 minutes. Cool cake layers in pans on racks 10 minutes. Run a knife around edge of each pan and invert layers onto racks. Carefully remove wax paper and cool layers completely. *Cake layers may be made 2 days ahead and kept, wrapped in plastic wrap, at cool room temperature.*

Make Filling: Finely chop pecans and lightly toast. In a heavy saucepan cook cream, sugar, and butter over moderately low heat, stirring, until sugar is dissolved. In a bowl whisk yolks. Whisk about ½ cup cream mixture into yolks and whisk yolk mixture into cream mixture remaining in pan. Cook custard over moderately low heat, whisking, until thickened, 6 to 8 minutes. (Do not boil custard.) Stir in vanilla, pecans, and coconut and cool, stirring occasionally. *Filling may be made 2 days ahead and chilled, covered. Let filling stand at room temperature until soft enough to spread.*

Make Frosting: Finely chop chocolate and put in a metal bowl. In a small saucepan bring cream just to a boil and pour over chocolate. Let chocolate mixture stand 1 minute and whisk until smooth. *Chill chocolate mixture until cold, 1 hour.* With an electric mixer beat frosting until it just holds soft peaks. (Do not overbeat frosting or it will become grainy.)

Assemble Cake: With a long serrated knife halve each cake layer horizontally. On a cake stand arrange 1 cake layer, cut side up, and spread with 1 cup filling. Top filling with second layer, cut side down, and spread top with 1 cup filling. Top filling with third layer, cut side up, and spread with remaining 1 cup filling. Top filling with remaining layer, cut side down.

Spread frosting over side and top of cake. *Cake may be assembled 1 day ahead and chilled, loosely covered. Bring cake to room temperature before serving.* SERVES 10 TO 12.

CHOCOLATE BOURBON TART

For Crust
   1 stick (½ cup) unsalted butter
   eleven 5- by 2½-inch graham crackers
   ½ cup walnuts
   ¼ cup granulated sugar

For Filling
   1 pound fine-quality bittersweet chocolate
      (not unsweetened)
   1 whole large egg
   1 large egg yolk
   2 cups heavy cream
   ¼ cup bourbon

For Bourbon Cream
   1 cup well-chilled heavy cream
   2 tablespoons confectioners' sugar
   1 tablespoon bourbon

Make Crust: Preheat oven to 375° F.

In a small saucepan melt butter and cool slightly. In a food processor finely grind graham crackers and walnuts with sugar. Add butter and pulse until combined well. Press crumb mixture evenly onto bottom and up side of a 10-inch fluted tart pan with a removable rim. Bake crust in middle of oven 6 minutes, or until golden around edge, and cool completely on a rack.

Make Filling: Finely chop chocolate. In a bowl whisk together whole egg and yolk with a pinch salt. In a 2½- to 3-quart heavy saucepan bring cream just to a boil and whisk about half into eggs. Stir egg mixture into remaining cream and cook over moderate heat, whisking until custard is slightly thickened, about 1 minute, and an instant-read thermometer registers 160° F. Remove pan from heat and add chocolate and bourbon. Let filling stand 1 minute and stir until smooth.

Pour filling into crust and cool. *Chill tart, covered, until firm, at least 2 hours, and up to 1 day.*

Make Bourbon Cream: In a large bowl with an electric mixer beat cream with sugar until it just holds soft peaks. Add bourbon and beat until cream just holds stiff peaks.

Serve chocolate tart, chilled, with bourbon cream. SERVES 10.

Frangipane Tart with Strawberries and Raspberries
Huckleberry Cobbler
Gingered Brioche Summer Pudding with Sour Cream Mascarpone
Cranberry Pear Hazelnut Financier ▪ Fresh Berry Gratins
"Mirrored" Blueberry Mousse Pie with Gingersnap Crust
Raspberry and Fig Phyllo Tart ▪ Blueberry Lemon Pastries
Strawberry Rhubarb Fool ▪ Blackberry Upside-Down Cake
Strawberries with Molasses Sour Cream Sauce
Cranberry Orange Bread Pudding ▪ Raspberry Mango Trifle
Blackberry Curd Roulade ▪ Raspberry Mango Trifle
Raspberry Surprise Cupcakes
Fresh Berries with Vanilla Custard Sauce
Almond Rice Pudding with Raspberry Drizzle
Berry Tartlets ▪ Blackberry and Apricot Compote

BERRI

Berries, served with a splash of cream or a scoop of ice cream, are sublime. So, why an entire chapter on berries? As you know, these little gems are packed with bursts of pure, intense flavor and they make some of our favorite desserts. You may not realize, however, that combining different berries, or pairing a berry with another kind of fruit, brings spectacular results. For optimum freshness, try to buy berries at farm stands and farmers markets. (That is, unless you can pick your own wild berries, which are by far the most flavorful.) Look for smaller, plump, fully-colored berries; avoid those that have whitish spots (mold) as well as those in stained baskets (signals overripe or crushed berries). Berries are quite perishable and should be consumed quickly; just before using gently rinse them in a bowl filled with water, then drain in a colander.

FRANGIPANE TART WITH STRAWBERRIES AND RASPBERRIES

pastry dough (page 33)
¾ cup blanched almonds
¾ stick (6 tablespoons) unsalted butter, softened
½ cup sugar
1 large egg
1 teaspoon almond extract
1 tablespoon Disaronno Amaretto or other almond-flavored liqueur
1 tablespoon all-purpose flour
¼ cup strawberry or raspberry jam
2 cups strawberries
2 cups picked-over raspberries

Preheat oven to 375° F.

On a lightly floured surface roll out dough into a rectangle about ⅛ inch thick and fit into an 11- by 8-inch rectangular tart pan with a removable fluted rim. (Alternatively, roll out dough into a round and fit into a 10- or 11-inch round tart pan.) Chill shell while making *frangipane*.

In a food processor finely grind almonds. In a small bowl beat together butter and sugar and beat in almonds, egg, almond extract, liqueur, and flour until combined well. Spread *frangipane* evenly onto bottom of shell and bake in middle of oven 20 to 25 minutes, or until shell is pale golden. (If *frangipane* begins to turn too brown, loosely cover with foil.) Cool tart in pan on a rack.

In a small saucepan melt jam, stirring, and pour through a fine sieve into a heatproof bowl, pressing hard on solids. Keep jam warm. Trim strawberries and cut lengthwise into ⅛-inch-thick slices. Decoratively arrange strawberry slices, overlapping them, with raspberries in rows on *frangipane* and gently brush with jam. *Tart may be made 6 hours ahead and kept loosely covered at cool room temperature.* **SERVES 6 TO 8.**

Photo on page 31

PASTRY DOUGH

The amount of water necessary to make pastry dough is likely to change slightly from time to time, depending on variables such as humidity and the moisture content of butter and flour. This recipe may be doubled if necessary. If doubled, form dough into 2 disks and wrap separately in plastic wrap.

> ¾ stick (6 tablespoons) cold unsalted butter
> 1¼ cups all-purpose flour
> 2 tablespoons cold vegetable shortening
> ¼ teaspoon salt
> 2 to 4 tablespoons ice water

To Blend by Hand: Cut butter into ½-inch cubes. In a bowl with fingertips or a pastry blender blend together flour, butter, shortening, and salt until most of mixture resembles coarse meal with remainder in small (pea-size) lumps. Drizzle 2 tablespoons ice water evenly over mixture and gently stir with a fork until incorporated. Test mixture by gently squeezing a small handful: When it has proper texture it should hold together without crumbling apart. If necessary, add more water, 1 tablespoon at a time, stirring until incorporated and testing mixture, to give mixture proper texture. (Do not overwork or add too much water; pastry will be tough.)

To Blend in a Food Processor: Cut butter into pieces. In a food processor pulse together flour, butter, shortening, and salt until most of mixture resembles coarse meal with remainder in small (roughly pea-size) lumps. Add 2 tablespoons ice water and pulse 2 or 3 times, or just until incorporated. Test mixture by gently squeezing a small handful: When it has proper texture it should hold together without crumbling apart. If necessary, add more water, 1 tablespoon at a time, pulsing 2 or 3 times after each addition until incorporated and testing mixture, to give mixture proper texture. (Do not overprocess or add too much water; pastry will be tough.)

To Form Dough after Blending by Either Method: Turn mixture out onto a work surface and divide into 4 portions. With heel of hand smear each portion once in a forward motion to help distribute fat. Gather dough together and form it, rotating it on work surface, into a disk. *Chill dough, wrapped in plastic wrap, until firm, at least 1 hour, and up to 1 day.* MAKES ENOUGH DOUGH FOR A SINGLE-CRUST 9-INCH PIE OR AN 11-INCH TART.

HUCKLEBERRY COBBLER

> 5 cups picked-over huckleberries or blueberries
> 1 cup plus 6 tablespoons sugar
> 2 tablespoons fresh lemon juice
> 1 tablespoon finely grated fresh lemon zest
> 1 tablespoon cornstarch
> 1½ cups all-purpose flour
> 1½ teaspoons baking powder
> ½ teaspoon cinnamon
> ½ teaspoon salt
> 9 tablespoons cold unsalted butter
> 1½ teaspoons vanilla
> ¾ cup half-and-half

Preheat oven to 375° F. and butter a 2-quart baking dish or a 9-inch square baking pan.

In a bowl toss together berries, 1 cup sugar, lemon juice, zest, and cornstarch until combined well and transfer to baking dish or pan, spreading evenly. Into a bowl sift together flour, baking powder, cinnamon, and salt. Cut butter into pieces and in a food processor pulse with flour mixture and remaining 6 tablespoons sugar until mixture resembles coarse meal. Add vanilla and half-and-half and pulse until a dough just forms. Spoon dough in mounds over berry mixture and bake in middle of oven until topping is golden and cooked through, about 40 minutes. SERVES 4 TO 6.

GINGERED BRIOCHE SUMMER PUDDING

4 firm-ripe nectarines (about 1¾ pounds)

4 firm-ripe plums (about 1½ pounds)

¾ cup water

1 cup sugar

5 teaspoons finely grated peeled fresh gingerroot, or to taste

3 cups picked-over blueberries

2 teaspoons fresh lemon juice

half a 1-pound loaf brioche or challah

ACCOMPANIMENT: sour cream *mascarpone* (recipe follows)

Halve nectarines and plums lengthwise and pit. Cut nectarines and plums into ½-inch wedges. In a large saucepan bring water, sugar, and gingerroot to a boil, stirring until sugar is dissolved. Stir in cut fruit and blueberries and simmer gently, covered, stirring occasionally, until blueberries just begin to burst, about 5 minutes. Remove pan from heat and stir in lemon juice. Transfer fruit mixture to a shallow baking dish to cool as quickly as possible. Transfer 1½ cups cooled fruit mixture to a bowl and reserve, covered and chilled.

Preheat oven to 400° F.

Cut bread into four to eight ½-inch-thick slices (depending on shape of loaf). On a baking sheet arrange slices in one layer and toast in middle of oven, turning them if necessary, until golden brown on both sides. Transfer toast to a rack to cool.

In an 8-inch square glass baking dish set inside a larger shallow baking dish arrange half of toast slices, slightly overlapping if necessary and trimming to fit, and top with half of unchilled fruit mixture. Layer remaining slices and unchilled fruit mixture in same manner and cover surface of pudding with plastic wrap. Put another 8-inch square glass or metal baking dish on top of plastic wrap and weight

pudding evenly with about 6 pounds of weight (such as cans of food). *Chill pudding at least 8 hours and up to 1 day.*

Just before serving, remove weights, baking dish, and plastic wrap from pudding, reserving juice that has spilled over into larger baking dish, and cut pudding into 6 portions. Transfer pudding with a spatula to plates and spoon reserved juices and chilled fruit mixture on top and around them.

Serve pudding with sour cream *mascarpone*. SERVES 6.

Photo opposite

SOUR CREAM MASCARPONE

½ cup sour cream

½ cup *mascarpone* cheese

2 tablespoons confectioners' sugar, or to taste

In a bowl whisk together all ingredients until combined well. *Mixture may be made 1 day ahead and chilled, covered.* MAKES ABOUT 1 CUP.

CRANBERRY PEAR HAZELNUT FINANCIER

- - -

1 cup hazelnuts (about ¼ pound)

1 firm-ripe medium pear

1 cup picked-over fresh or frozen cranberries

1 cup granulated sugar

⅔ cup all-purpose flour

¾ teaspoon salt

1 stick (½ cup) unsalted butter

6 large egg whites

1½ teaspoons vanilla

confectioners' sugar for sprinkling cake

ACCOMPANIMENT: whipped cream or vanilla
    ice cream

Preheat oven to 350° F. Butter and flour a 9- by 2-inch round cake pan.

Spread hazelnuts in a shallow baking pan and toast in middle of oven until they begin to turn pale golden, 7 to 10 minutes. Wrap hazelnuts in a kitchen towel and rub to remove any loose skins (do not worry about skins that do not come off). Cool nuts completely.

Increase temperature to 400° F.

Peel pear and core. Coarsely chop pear and in a bowl toss with cranberries and ¼ cup granulated sugar. In a food processor finely grind nuts with remaining ¾ cup granulated sugar, flour, and salt.

Melt butter and cool. In a bowl with an electric mixer beat whites with a pinch salt until they just hold stiff peaks and fold in nut mixture gently but thoroughly. Fold in melted butter and vanilla (batter will deflate) and spread batter evenly in cake pan. Arrange fruit mixture evenly over batter and bake in middle of oven 40 to 45 minutes, or until a tester comes out clean.

Cool cake in pan on a rack 5 minutes and invert onto a plate. Cool cake, fruit side up, on rack until ready to serve. *Cake may be made 6 hours ahead and kept loosely covered at room temperature.*

Sprinkle cake with confectioners' sugar and serve warm or at room temperature with whipped cream or ice cream. SERVES 6 TO 8.

FRESH BERRY GRATINS

- - -

½ cup sour cream

2 ounces cream cheese, softened

¼ cup packed light brown sugar

4 cups assorted picked-over berries such as raspberries, blackberries, strawberries, and/or blueberries

3 tablespoons finely crushed *amaretti** (Italian almond macaroons)

available at specialty foods shops and some supermarkets

In a bowl with an electric mixer beat together sour cream, cream cheese, and brown sugar until smooth. *Topping may be made 1 day ahead and chilled, covered.*

If using strawberries, halve if large. Divide all berries among 6 shallow ¾-cup ramekins (about 5 inches wide and 1 inch deep). Spread topping evenly over berries in each ramekin and sprinkle each with 1½ teaspoons *amaretti* crumbs.

Preheat broiler.

Arrange ramekins in a shallow baking pan and broil gratins 2 to 3 inches from heat 2 minutes, or until bubbling and golden. SERVES 6.

"MIRRORED" BLUEBERRY MOUSSE PIE WITH GINGERSNAP CRUST

For Crust
3 tablespoons unsalted butter
thirty-six 1½-inch gingersnap cookies
  (about 5 ounces)
2 tablespoons sugar

For Filling
1½ cups plain yogurt
3 cups picked-over blueberries
  (about 1 pound)
½ cup sugar
1 tablespoon fresh lemon juice
1 tablespoon *crème de cassis*
1 envelope unflavored gelatin
  (about 1 tablespoon)
¼ cup milk
1 cup well-chilled heavy cream

For Topping
½ cup black-currant jelly
¼ cup *crème de cassis*
2 tablespoons water
2 teaspoons unflavored gelatin
  (from 1 envelope)

Make Crust: Preheat oven to 350° F.

Melt butter and cool slightly. In a food processor finely grind cookies with sugar. Add butter and pulse until combined well. Press crumb mixture evenly into bottom of a 9-inch non-stick springform pan. Bake crust in middle of oven 10 to 15 minutes, or until crisp and golden, and cool completely in pan on a rack.

Make Filling: In a large sieve lined with a paper towel and set over a bowl, drain yogurt 30 minutes and discard liquid. While yogurt is draining, in a heavy saucepan stir together blueberries, sugar, and lemon juice and bring to a simmer over moderately high heat, stirring frequently and mashing berries with back of a wooden spoon. Reduce heat to moderately low and continue to cook mixture, stirring and mashing berries, until slightly thickened, about 5 minutes. Remove pan from heat and stir in *crème de cassis*. Transfer mixture to a bowl. Set bowl in a larger bowl of ice and cold water and cool mixture, stirring frequently, until cold. Remove bowl from ice water and add yogurt, stirring until combined.

In a small saucepan sprinkle gelatin over milk and let stand 1 minute to soften gelatin. Heat milk mixture over low heat, stirring occasionally, until gelatin is dissolved and stir into blueberry yogurt mixture. In a bowl with an electric mixer beat cream until it just holds stiff peaks. Whisk about one third cream into blueberry-yogurt mixture to lighten and fold in remaining cream gently but thoroughly. Pour filling into crust, spreading evenly. *Chill pie, loosely covered with plastic wrap, until set, at least 4 hours, and up to 1 day.*

Make Topping: In a small saucepan melt jelly over low heat, whisking until smooth, and remove pan from heat. Stir in *crème de cassis* and water. Sprinkle gelatin over jelly mixture and let stand 1 minute to soften gelatin. Heat jelly mixture over low heat, stirring, until gelatin is dissolved and remove pan from heat. Cool mixture, stirring constantly, until barely warm. Spoon topping over pie, tilting pan to spread it evenly over surface. *Chill pie 1 hour, or until topping is set.* Run a thin knife around side of pan and carefully remove side. SERVES 8 TO 10.

RASPBERRY AND FIG PHYLLO TART

1 pound firm-ripe fresh figs (preferably small)

2 tablespoons Armagnac

¼ cup plus 3 tablespoons sugar

2 tablespoons fresh lemon juice

2 tablespoons honey

1 cup picked-over raspberries

6 tablespoons sliced almonds (about 2 ounces)

½ stick (¼ cup) unsalted butter

ten 17- by 12-inch *phyllo* sheets

ACCOMPANIMENT: *crème fraîche* or sour cream

Quarter figs lengthwise. In a heavy saucepan cook figs, Armagnac, ¼ cup sugar, lemon juice, and honey over moderately low heat, stirring gently, until sugar and honey are dissolved, about 3 minutes. Gently stir in raspberries. Transfer mixture to a bowl and cool, stirring occasionally.

Preheat oven to 350° F.

Lightly toast almonds and cool. In a food processor finely grind 3 tablespoons almonds with remaining 3 tablespoons sugar and transfer to a small bowl. Melt butter. Brush bottom and side of a 10-inch tart pan with removable rim with some melted butter.

Trim stack of *phyllo* into 15- by 12-inch rectangles and cover stack with 2 overlapping sheets of plastic wrap and then a damp kitchen towel. Keeping remaining *phyllo* covered, arrange 1 *phyllo* sheet in pan, letting edges overhang evenly. Brush *phyllo* with some butter and sprinkle with 1½ teaspoons ground almond mixture. Gently fold in edges of *phyllo* and brush edges with some butter. Continue to layer remaining 9 *phyllo* sheets in same manner, brushing with butter and sprinkling with almond mixture, and arranging sheets so folded corners overlap to form an even edge.

In a fine sieve set over a small saucepan drain fruit mixture, reserving juices. Arrange fruit mixture evenly in *phyllo* shell and bake in middle of oven 45 minutes, or until crust is golden brown. Cool tart in pan on a rack.

While tart is cooling, simmer reserved juices until thickened and reduced to about 3 tablespoons and brush over fruit. Sprinkle tart with remaining 3 tablespoons sliced almonds. *Tart may be made 6 hours ahead and kept loosely covered at room temperature.*

Serve tart with *crème fraîche* or sour cream. SERVES 8.

BLUEBERRY LEMON PASTRIES

1½ cups picked-over blueberries
¼ cup plus 3 tablespoons sugar
3 tablespoons fresh lemon juice
6 ounces cream cheese, softened
1 teaspoon finely grated fresh lemon zest
2 puff pastry sheets (from one 17¼-ounce package frozen puff pastry sheets), thawed
1 large egg

In a heavy saucepan cook 1 cup blueberries, ¼ cup sugar, and 2 tablespoons lemon juice over moderately low heat, stirring frequently, until blueberries are burst, about 5 minutes. Remove pan from heat and stir in remaining ½ cup blueberries. Transfer mixture to a heatproof bowl and cool. In a bowl beat together cream cheese, remaining 3 tablespoons sugar, remaining tablespoon lemon juice, and zest until smooth. *Blueberry and cream cheese mixtures may be made 1 day ahead and chilled separately, covered.*

On a lightly floured surface roll out 1 puff pastry sheet into a 10½-inch square (about ⅛ inch thick). Cut square into nine 3½-inch squares and transfer to an ungreased baking sheet. Chill squares, covered with plastic wrap. Make more squares with second pastry sheet and chill in same manner.

Preheat oven to 375° F.

In a bowl beat egg and brush each square with some of it. Fold in corners of each square so that they meet in middle of square, pressing them down gently with a fingertip. Brush pastries with some remaining egg. Spoon 1 rounded teaspoon cream cheese mixture in center of each pastry and top with 1 rounded teaspoon blueberry mixture. Bake pastries in batches in middle of oven 20 minutes, or until golden, transferring to racks to cool slightly. **MAKES 18 SMALL PASTRIES.**

STRAWBERRY RHUBARB FOOL

1½ cups plain yogurt
4 cups strawberries (about 1 pound)
½ pound rhubarb (about 2 thick stalks)
¾ cup packed light brown sugar
2 tablespoons fresh lemon juice
½ cup well-chilled heavy cream
2 tablespoons granulated sugar

GARNISH: fresh strawberries

In a large sieve lined with a paper towel and set over a bowl, drain yogurt 30 minutes and discard liquid. While yogurt is draining, slice enough strawberries to measure 3 cups and enough rhubarb to measure 2 cups. In a heavy saucepan cook fruit, brown sugar, and lemon juice at a bare simmer, stirring occasionally, until rhubarb is very soft, about 15 minutes and transfer to a bowl. Drain mixture in a sieve set over saucepan, pressing gently on solids, (there should be about ¾ cup juices) and return cooked fruit to bowl. Set bowl in a larger bowl of ice and cold water and cool cooked fruit, stirring occasionally. Simmer juices in pan until thickened and reduced to about ¼ cup and stir into cooked fruit.

In another bowl with an electric mixer beat cream with granulated sugar until cream just holds soft peaks. In a large bowl stir together drained yogurt and cooled fruit mixture and fold in whipped cream gently but thoroughly. *Chill fool, covered, until very cold, at least 2 hours, and up to 1 day.*

Spoon fool into 8 goblets and serve chilled, garnished with strawberries. **SERVES 8.**

BLACKBERRY UPSIDE-DOWN CAKE

— · —

For Topping

3 tablespoons unsalted butter

⅓ cup packed light brown sugar

3 cups picked-over blackberries

For Batter

1¾ cups cake flour (not self-rising)

1½ teaspoons baking powder

¼ teaspoon salt

½ teaspoon ground ginger

¼ teaspoon cinnamon

1¼ sticks (10 tablespoons) unsalted butter, softened

1 cup packed light brown sugar

1 teaspoon vanilla

1 teaspoon finely grated fresh lemon zest

3 large eggs

½ cup half-and-half

ACCOMPANIMENT: sweetened whipped cream

Preheat oven to 375° F.

Make Topping: In a well-seasoned 10½-inch cast-iron skillet melt butter over moderate heat until foam subsides. Reduce heat to low. Sprinkle brown sugar evenly in skillet and heat, undisturbed, 3 minutes (not all brown sugar will be melted). Remove skillet from heat and arrange blackberries in an even layer in skillet.

Make Batter: Into a bowl sift together flour, baking powder, salt, and spices. In a bowl with an electric mixer beat together butter and brown sugar until light and fluffy and beat in vanilla and zest. Add eggs 1 at a time, beating well after each addition. With mixer on low speed, add flour mixture and half-and-half alternately in batches, beginning and ending with flour mixture, and beating until just combined.

Spoon batter over topping in skillet, spreading evenly (do not disturb topping), and bake in middle of oven 30 minutes, or until golden brown and springy to the touch. Cool cake in skillet on a rack 10 minutes. Run a thin knife around edge of skillet. Invert a plate over skillet and invert cake onto plate (keeping plate and skillet firmly pressed together). Carefully lift skillet off cake and replace any fruit that is stuck to bottom of skillet if necessary.

Serve cake warm or at room temperature with whipped cream. SERVES 8.

STRAWBERRIES WITH MOLASSES SOUR CREAM SAUCE

— · — ◒

2 cups strawberries

½ cup sour cream

½ teaspoon sugar

⅛ teaspoon vanilla

2 tablespoons unsulfured molasses

ACCOMPANIMENT IF DESIRED: chocolate crackle cookies (page 149)

Trim strawberries and halve if large. In a small bowl whisk together sour cream, sugar, vanilla, and 1 tablespoon molasses until smooth. Divide strawberries between 2 bowls and top with sour cream sauce. Drizzle remaining tablespoon molasses over servings. SERVES 2.

Photo opposite

CRANBERRY ORANGE BREAD PUDDING

— ■ —

a 12-ounce bag picked-over fresh or thawed
frozen cranberries (about 3 cups)

1 cup packed light brown sugar

2½ tablespoons finely grated fresh orange zest
(from about 3 navel oranges)

½ cup fresh orange juice

a 1-pound loaf brioche or challah

4 whole large eggs

3 large egg yolks

1 cup plus 3 tablespoons granulated sugar

3 cups milk

2 tablespoons Grand Marnier or other
orange-flavored liqueur

2 teaspoons vanilla

¼ teaspoon salt

⅛ teaspoon freshly grated nutmeg

2 tablespoons cold unsalted butter

Preheat oven to 350° F. and butter a 9-inch square
baking pan.

In a heavy saucepan simmer 2 cups cranberries,
brown sugar, 1 tablespoon zest, and orange juice,
uncovered, stirring occasionally, 10 minutes, or until
cranberries are burst and mixture is thickened.
*Mixture may be made 2 days ahead and chilled
in an airtight container.* Transfer mixture to baking
pan, spreading evenly.

Cut bread into 1½-inch cubes and arrange in
one layer over cranberry mixture, pressing to fit. In
a large bowl whisk together whole eggs, yolks, 1
cup granulated sugar, milk, liqueur, remaining 1½
tablespoons zest, vanilla, salt, and nutmeg until
combined well. Pour egg mixture, about one third at
a time, evenly over bread, letting each addition be
absorbed before adding next. *Pudding may be
prepared up to this point 1 day ahead and
chilled, covered. Bring pudding to room temperature before proceeding.*

In a food processor pulse remaining 1 cup cranberries, remaining 3 tablespoons granulated sugar,
and butter until coarsely chopped. Sprinkle mixture
evenly over pudding.

Put baking pan in a roasting pan. Add enough
hot water to larger pan to reach halfway up side of
baking pan and bake pudding in middle of oven 45
minutes, or until puffed, golden, and set. Transfer
pudding to a rack to cool. Serve pudding warm or
at room temperature. SERVES 8.

BLACKBERRY CURD
ROULADE

For Cake

½ cup cake flour (not self-rising)
¼ teaspoon salt
4 whole large eggs
½ cup granulated sugar
1 teaspoon vanilla

For Blackberry Curd

1½ cups picked-over blackberries
½ cup granulated sugar
3 tablespoons unsalted butter
2 tablespoons cornstarch
2 large egg yolks

For Blackberry Cream

½ cup well-chilled heavy cream
1 tablespoon granulated sugar
⅓ cup picked-over blackberries

confectioners' sugar for dusting towel

Make Cake: Preheat oven to 350° F. Line bottom and sides of a 15½- by 10½- by 1-inch jelly-roll pan with foil. Butter foil and dust with flour, knocking out excess flour.

Into a bowl sift together flour and salt. In a bowl with an electric mixer beat together eggs, granulated sugar, and vanilla until thick, pale, and mixture forms a ribbon when beaters are lifted. Fold flour into egg mixture gently but thoroughly. Spread batter evenly in pan and bake in middle of oven 10 minutes, or until golden and springy to the touch. Cool cake in pan on a rack. *Cake may be made 3 days ahead and kept in pan, wrapped well in plastic wrap, at cool room temperature.*

Make Blackberry Curd: In a food processor purée blackberries and pour through a fine sieve into a 3-quart heavy saucepan, pressing hard on solids. Stir in granulated sugar, butter, cornstarch, and yolks and simmer, stirring constantly, 3 minutes, or until thickened. Transfer curd to a bowl and cool. *Curd may be made 1 day ahead and chilled, covered.*

Make Blackberry Cream: In a small bowl with cleaned beaters beat cream with granulated sugar until it just holds stiff peaks. Quarter blackberries and fold into cream gently but thoroughly.

Put a kitchen towel on a work surface and generously dust with confectioners' sugar. Invert cake onto towel and gently peel off foil. Spread curd evenly on cake and top with blackberry cream. Beginning with a short side and using towel as a guide, roll up *roulade* jelly-roll fashion and transfer to a platter, seam side down. *Roulade may be made 6 hours ahead and chilled, loosely covered.* SERVES 10.

Photo on page 11

RASPBERRY
MANGO TRIFLE

For Custard

- 1 vanilla bean
- 2½ cups milk
- 6 large egg yolks
- ½ cup granulated sugar
- 1 tablespoon cornstarch
- 1 tablespoon dark rum

For Raspberry Sauce

- 4 cups fresh or thawed frozen unsweetened raspberries (about 1 pound)
- ½ cup granulated sugar
- 1 tablespoon fresh lemon juice
- 1 tablespoon *eau-de-vie de framboise* or raspberry liqueur

- 2 firm-ripe large mangoes
- a 12-ounce store-bought angel food cake
- 2 cups picked-over fresh raspberries
- 1⅓ cups well-chilled heavy cream
- 2 tablespoons confectioners' sugar

Make Custard: Have ready a large bowl of ice and cold water. Split vanilla bean lengthwise. In a heavy saucepan bring milk just to a boil with vanilla bean and remove pan from heat. Scrape seeds from bean with tip of a knife into hot milk. In a bowl whisk together yolks, granulated sugar, and cornstarch, and add hot milk in a slow stream, whisking. Transfer custard to saucepan and boil, whisking, 1 minute, or until thick and smooth. Pour custard through a fine sieve into a metal bowl and stir in rum. Set bowl in ice water and cool custard, stirring occasionally.

Make Raspberry Sauce: Have ready a large bowl of ice and cold water. In a saucepan simmer berries with sugar and lemon juice, stirring occasionally, 10 minutes and stir in liqueur. In a blender purée mixture (use caution when blending hot liquids) and pour through cleaned sieve into a heatproof bowl, pressing hard on solids. Set bowl in ice water and cool sauce, stirring occasionally.

Assemble Trifle: Peel mangoes and pit. Cut flesh into ½-inch cubes. Cut cake into twenty-four ¾-inch-thick wedges and arrange 6 wedges, cut sides down, in one layer in a 4-quart straight-sided glass bowl. Spoon about half of custard evenly over cake wedges and sprinkle about ½ cup each raspberries and mango pieces over custard. Arrange 6 more cake wedges in one layer on top of fruit and spoon about half of raspberry sauce over cake. Sprinkle about ½ cup each raspberries and mango pieces over raspberry sauce. Make 2 more layers in same manner, beginning with cake wedges and ending with fruit. *Chill trifle, covered with plastic wrap, until cold, at least 4 hours, and up to 1 day.*

In a bowl with an electric mixer beat cream with confectioners' sugar until it just holds stiff peaks and spoon over trifle. **SERVES 8 TO 10.**

Photo above

RASPBERRY SURPRISE CUPCAKES

— · —

For Cupcakes

    1 cup cake flour (not self-rising)
    1 teaspoon baking powder
    ¼ teaspoon salt
    ¾ stick (6 tablespoons) unsalted butter,
      softened
    ½ cup granulated sugar
    1 teaspoon vanilla
    1 teaspoon finely grated fresh lemon zest
    2 large eggs
    ⅓ cup heavy cream
    18 raspberries

For Icing

    1¾ cups confectioners' sugar
    2 tablespoons unsalted butter, softened
    1 tablespoon finely grated fresh lemon zest
    3 tablespoons fresh lemon juice
    GARNISH: 9 raspberries

Make Cupcakes: Preheat oven to 350° F. and line nine ½-cup muffin cups with paper liners.

Into a bowl sift together flour, baking powder, and salt. In a bowl with an electric mixer beat together butter and granulated sugar until light and fluffy and beat in vanilla and zest. Add eggs 1 at a time, beating well after each addition. Add flour mixture and cream alternately in batches, beginning and ending with flour mixture and beating until just combined. Spoon batter into lined cups, filling them half full. Gently press 2 raspberries into batter in each cup and spoon remaining batter over raspberries (each cup should be about two thirds full), smoothing tops. Bake cupcakes in middle of oven 15 minutes, or until pale golden, and turn out onto a rack to cool.

Make Icing: Into a bowl sift confectioners' sugar. Add remaining ingredients and with an electric mixer beat icing until smooth.

Spread icing over cupcakes with a small spatula and garnish with raspberries. **MAKES 9 CUPCAKES.**

FRESH BERRIES WITH VANILLA CUSTARD SAUCE

— · — ⊕ +

    ½ vanilla bean
    2 cups half-and-half
    2 large eggs
    ½ cup sugar
    4 cups picked-over fresh berries

Have ready a large bowl of ice and cold water. Split vanilla bean lengthwise. In a heavy saucepan bring half-and-half with vanilla bean just to a boil and remove pan from heat. In a bowl whisk together eggs and sugar until combined well and add half-and-half mixture in a slow stream, whisking. Return mixture to saucepan and cook over moderately low heat, stirring constantly with a wooden spoon, until thickened and an instant-read thermometer registers 170° F. (do not boil). Pour custard through a fine sieve into a metal bowl. Set bowl in ice water and cool sauce, stirring occasionally. *Chill sauce, covered, until cold, at least 1 hour, and up to 2 days.*

Divide sauce among 4 bowls and top each with 1 cup berries. **SERVES 4.**

ALMOND RICE PUDDING WITH RASPBERRY DRIZZLE

— · —

4 cups milk

⅔ cup plus 3 tablespoons sugar

¼ teaspoon almond extract

2 tablespoons unsalted butter

1 cup Arborio or other short-grain rice

1 cup water

1½ cups picked-over raspberries (about 6 ounces)

¼ cup red-currant jelly

1 tablespoon fresh lemon juice

½ cup well-chilled heavy cream

2 tablespoons sliced almonds

In a large saucepan heat milk, ⅔ cup sugar, and almond extract over moderate heat, stirring occasionally, until sugar is dissolved and keep warm over low heat. In a 3-quart heavy saucepan melt butter over low heat. Stir in rice and cook, stirring with a wooden spoon, until rice is coated with butter, about 1 minute. Add water and cook over moderate heat, stirring constantly, until just absorbed. Stir in 1 cup warm milk mixture and cook, stirring constantly and keeping at a bare simmer throughout, until just absorbed. Continue simmering and adding milk mixture, about 1 cup at a time, stirring constantly and letting each addition be almost absorbed before adding next, until rice is tender and creamy-looking, about 30 minutes. Transfer rice mixture to a large bowl and cool to room temperature.

While rice mixture is cooling, in a saucepan simmer raspberries, jelly, remaining 3 tablespoons sugar, and lemon juice, stirring, until berries fall apart and mixture is thickened, about 5 minutes. Force mixture through a fine sieve into a bowl, pressing hard on solids, and cool.

In another bowl with an electric mixer beat cream until it holds stiff peaks and fold into cooled rice mixture. Spoon about half of pudding into a 1½-quart glass bowl, spreading evenly, and drizzle with about half of raspberry sauce. Spoon remaining pudding over sauce and drizzle with remaining sauce. *Chill pudding, covered, until cold, at least 2 hours, and up to 1 day.*

Lightly toast almonds and sprinkle over pudding. Serve rice pudding chilled or at room temperature. **SERVES 6 TO 8.**

BERRY TARTLETS

— · —

2 sticks (1 cup) unsalted butter, softened

¾ cup sugar

1 large egg yolk

2 teaspoons vanilla

1 teaspoon finely grated fresh orange zest

½ teaspoon salt

2½ cups flour

about 5 cups mixed berries such as raspberries, blueberries, or blackberries

1 cup red-currant jelly

Preheat oven to 400° F. and butter thirty 2½-inch tartlet cups. (If you do not have 30 tartlet cups, butter as many cups as you have and bake the shells in batches.)

In a bowl with an electric mixer beat together butter and sugar until light and fluffy and beat in yolk, vanilla, zest, and salt. Add flour and beat just until a dough forms. Form dough into 30 walnut-size balls and press into bottoms and up sides of cups. Arrange cups on 2 baking sheets.

Bake shells in upper and lower thirds of oven, switching position of sheets halfway through baking, until golden, about 10 minutes total, and transfer sheets to racks to cool. Carefully remove shells from cups and cool completely on racks. *Shells keep, layered between sheets of wax paper in airtight containers at room temperature, 1 day; or frozen, 2 months. If frozen, bring shells to room temperature before proceeding.*

Put each kind of berry into a separate bowl. In a small saucepan bring jelly to a boil, stirring until melted. Divide hot jelly among bowls of berries and toss to coat. Spoon coated berries into shells, mounding them slightly, and combining different berries if desired. *Tartlets may be made 8 hours ahead and kept loosely covered at room temperature.* **MAKES THIRTY 2½-INCH TARTLETS.**

Photo on page 10

BLACKBERRY AND APRICOT COMPOTE

2 firm-ripe apricots
¼ cup water
¼ cup sugar
¼ teaspoon finely grated fresh lime zest
1 cup dry white wine
1 cup picked-over blackberries

ACCOMPANIMENT IF DESIRED: almond macaroons (page 154)

Halve apricots lengthwise and pit. Cut each apricot half into 4 wedges and transfer to a heatproof bowl.

In a small saucepan bring water and sugar to a boil over moderate heat, stirring until sugar is dissolved. Stir in zest and wine and simmer 5 minutes. Pour syrup over apricots and stir in blackberries. *Chill compote 20 minutes.*

Serve compote with macaroons. **SERVES 2.**

Photo left

Old-Fashioned Cherry Vanilla Pie

Baked Pears on Sugared Puff Pastry with Caramel Sauce

Peach and Strawberry Longcake

Strawberry Rhubarb Éclairs

Passion-Fruit Panna Cottas with Tropical Fruit Salsa

Melon Mélange with Honey Ginger Syrup

Apple Walnut Upside-Down Cake with Calvados Caramel Sauce

Peaches and Cherries with Almond Syrup

Peach Cobbler with Ginger Biscuit Topping

Spiced Caramel Oranges ▪ Apple Blackberry Pie

Sliced Baked Apples ▪ Plum and Hazelnut Crostata

Pear Galette with Amaretti Crumble

Prunes in Wine and Armagnac

Banana and Rum Spiced Crêpes

Plum Shortcakes ▪ Honey Vanilla Poached Apricots

Spiced Shortcakes with Minted Peaches

Lime Mousse Tart ▪ Blood Orange and Coconut Tart

FRUIT

Fruits have an array of tastes (smooth, subtle, sweet, or tangy) and offer plenty of options for the cook. Here we focus on seasonal common fruits (and a few exotic ones), transforming them into uncommonly good sweets without a lot of fuss. Sometimes, a clever presentation makes all the difference: We guarantee an "Ahh" from your guests as you present our Sliced Baked Apples (the apples are cut, restacked before baking, and given a cinnamon-stick stem) or our Old-Fashioned Cherry Vanilla Pie (with a lovely wide lattice crust). At other times, unique fruit pairings tingle the taste buds—be sure to try our Apple Blackberry Pie and Peach and Strawberry Longcake. Always choose firm-ripe fruits when making desserts; overripe ones can be used for sauces.

OLD-FASHIONED CHERRY VANILLA PIE

— • —

6 cups fresh or frozen pitted tart cherries
  (about 3½ pints fresh, picked over)

1 cup plus 3 tablespoons sugar

¼ cup quick-cooking tapioca

½ teaspoon salt

½ teaspoon cinnamon

2 tablespoons vanilla

2 recipes pastry dough (page 33)

ACCOMPANIMENT: vanilla ice cream

Pit fresh cherries, if using. In a small bowl stir together 1 cup plus 2 tablespoons sugar, tapioca, salt, and cinnamon. In a large heavy skillet cook fresh or frozen cherries over moderately high heat, stirring, until slightly softened, about 2 minutes. With a slotted spoon transfer cherries to a heatproof bowl. Add sugar mixture to cherry juices in skillet and simmer, stirring, until thickened, about 3 minutes. Stir cherry sauce and vanilla into cherries and cool.

Line lower rack in oven with foil and preheat oven to 400° F.

On a lightly floured surface with a floured rolling pin roll out 1 piece dough into an 11-inch round (about ⅛ inch thick) and fit into a 9-inch (1-quart) pie plate, leaving a ¾-inch overhang. Pour filling into shell and chill, loosely covered with plastic wrap.

On floured surface roll out remaining dough into an 11-inch round (about ⅛ inch thick) and with a sharp knife or fluted pastry wheel cut into 1-inch-wide strips. Working on a sheet of wax paper set on a baking sheet, weave pastry strips in a close lattice pattern (see photo). *Chill or freeze lattice on wax paper on a flat surface 20 minutes, or until firm.* Brush edge of filled shell with cold water and slide lattice off wax paper and onto pie. Let lattice stand 10 minutes to soften. Trim edges flush with rim of pie plate and crimp decoratively. Gently brush lattice top with cold water and sprinkle with remaining tablespoon sugar.

Bake pie in middle of oven 45 minutes, or until pastry is golden and filling just begins to bubble, and transfer to a rack to cool slightly.

Serve pie warm with ice cream. **SERVES 8.**

Photo on page 49

BAKED PEARS ON SUGARED PUFF PASTRY WITH CARAMEL SAUCE

For Pastry Bases

- ¼ cup granulated sugar
- 1 puff pastry sheet (from a 17¼-ounce package frozen puff pastry), thawed

For Pears and Sauce

- 2 large firm-ripe Bartlett pears (about 1 pound total)
- 2 tablespoons unsalted butter
- ½ cup granulated sugar
- 1 tablespoon fresh lemon juice
- ½ cup heavy cream
- 1 tablespoon *poire William* (French pear brandy), or to taste

confectioners' sugar for dusting pastry bases

Preheat oven to 375° F.

Make Pastry Bases: Lightly butter a heavy baking sheet.

Sprinkle a work surface with granulated sugar and roll out puff pastry about ⅛ inch thick, turning over once to coat both sides with sugar. Cut out 4 rectangles, each about 4½ by 3½ inches, and transfer to baking sheet, reserving scraps for another use. Prick pastry all over with a fork and chill on baking sheet in freezer until well chilled, about 15 minutes.

Lightly butter bottom of another heavy baking sheet and put directly on top of pastry rectangles to weight them while baking. Bake pastry (between 2 baking sheets) in middle of oven 25 to 35 minutes, or until golden brown, and transfer to a rack to cool. *Pastry bases may be made 1 day ahead and kept in an airtight container at room temperature.*

Make Pears and Sauce: Lightly butter a baking dish just large enough to hold 4 pear halves in one layer.

Cut butter into bits. Peel, halve, and core pears. Arrange pear halves, cut sides up, in baking dish. Divide butter among pear cavities and sprinkle ¼ cup granulated sugar over pears. Drizzle lemon juice over pears and bake in middle of oven 15 minutes. Remove baking dish from oven and turn pears over. Baste pears with cooking juices and return to oven. Bake pears until tender, about 15 minutes more. Transfer pears to a plate and keep warm.

Transfer cooking juices to a small heavy saucepan. Add remaining ¼ cup granulated sugar and boil, swirling pan, until mixture is a deep golden caramel. Slowly add cream (caramel will bubble up) and simmer sauce, whisking, until slightly thickened, about 5 minutes. Stir in *poire William.*

Dust each pastry base with confectioners' sugar and top with a pear half. Serve baked pears with caramel sauce. **SERVES 4.**

Photo below

PEACH AND STRAWBERRY LONGCAKE

For Longcake

1 large egg
¾ cup milk
¼ teaspoon lemon extract
2 cups all-purpose flour
¼ cup packed brown sugar
1 tablespoon baking powder
5 tablespoons cold unsalted butter
1 tablespoon granulated sugar

For Filling and Topping

4 peaches (about 1 pound)
½ cup granulated sugar
2 cups strawberries
¼ cup chopped almonds
1 kiwifruit

ACCOMPANIMENT: fresh peach ice cream
(page 73)

Make Longcake: Preheat oven to 400° F. and butter a baking sheet.

In a small bowl whisk together egg, milk, and lemon extract. In a bowl stir together flour, brown sugar, and baking powder. Cut 4 tablespoons butter into bits and with a pastry blender or your fingertips blend into flour mixture until mixture resembles meal. Add egg mixture and stir with a fork until a dough just forms. Gather dough into a ball.

On a floured surface knead dough gently 10 times. Roll or pat out dough into a 15- by 6-inch oval. Carefully transfer oval to baking sheet and sprinkle top with granulated sugar. Cut remaining tablespoon butter into bits and dot oval with it. Bake longcake in middle of oven 20 to 25 minutes, or until golden. Transfer cake to a rack and cool.

Make Filling and Topping: Have ready a bowl of ice and cold water. In a large saucepan of boiling water blanch peaches 1 minute and transfer to ice water to stop cooking. Drain peaches and peel them. Thinly slice peaches and in a bowl toss with ¼ cup sugar. Trim strawberries and thinly slice. In a bowl toss strawberries with remaining ¼ cup sugar and transfer half of strawberry mixture to a small bowl. Mash remaining strawberry mixture with a fork. *Let fruit mixtures stand, covered, at room temperature 30 minutes.*

While fruit mixtures are standing, lightly toast almonds and peel kiwifruit. Halve kiwifruit lengthwise and thinly slice crosswise.

Assemble Cake: With a long serrated knife halve cake horizontally and transfer bottom layer to a platter. Spread mashed strawberry mixture onto bottom layer and arrange one layer of peaches on top. Arrange top layer of cake on top of peaches, pressing it gently. Add sliced strawberry mixture and kiwifruit to remaining peaches, tossing gently, and spoon over cake.

Sprinkle fruit with almonds and serve cake with ice cream. SERVES 8.

Photo opposite

STRAWBERRY RHUBARB ÉCLAIRS

— · —

For Éclairs

1 stick (½ cup) unsalted butter
1 cup water
½ teaspoon salt
1 cup all-purpose flour
4 large eggs

For Fruit Mixture

1¾ pounds fresh or frozen rhubarb
¾ cup granulated sugar
2 tablespoons cornstarch
¼ cup water
1 tablespoon fresh lemon juice
1½ cups strawberries

For Cheese Filling

1½ cups *mascarpone* or whipped cream cheese
½ cup confectioners' sugar
½ teaspoon vanilla

Make Éclairs: Preheat oven to 400° F. and butter 2 baking sheets.

Cut butter into bits. In a heavy saucepan bring water and butter to a boil with salt over high heat. Reduce heat to moderate. Add flour all at once and cook, beating with a wooden spoon, until mixture pulls away from side of pan, forming a ball. Remove pan from heat and add eggs 1 at a time, beating well after each addition until batter is smooth and satiny. Cool batter slightly.

Spoon batter into a large pastry bag fitted with a ½-inch star-shaped tip and pipe six 5-inch strips on each baking sheet, leaving 2 inches between strips. Bake éclairs in upper and lower thirds of oven, switching position of sheets halfway through baking, 40 minutes total, or until golden. Turn oven off and leave éclairs in oven 5 minutes more. Transfer éclairs to racks and cool completely. *Éclairs*

may be prepared up to this point 1 day ahead and kept in an airtight container at room temperature. If éclairs soften, reheat on a baking sheet in a 375° F. oven 5 minutes, or until crisp, and cool on a rack.

Make Fruit Mixture: If using fresh rhubarb, trim and cut enough stalks crosswise into ¾-inch pieces to measure 3 cups, reserving remainder for another use. If using frozen rhubarb, measure 3 cups unthawed pieces. In a 3-quart saucepan whisk together granulated sugar and cornstarch and add rhubarb, water, and lemon juice. Bring mixture to a simmer over moderate heat, stirring frequently, and simmer until rhubarb is tender and sauce is thick and clear, about 3 minutes. Transfer rhubarb mixture to a metal bowl and set in a larger bowl of ice and cold water. Cool mixture completely, stirring occasionally with a rubber spatula. Trim strawberries and cut into ½-inch pieces. Stir strawberries into cool rhubarb mixture.

Make Cheese Filling: In a bowl whisk together cheese, confectioners' sugar, and vanilla until smooth and transfer to cleaned pastry bag fitted with a ¼-inch plain tip.

Assemble Éclairs: With a serrated knife cut a lengthwise slit down center of each éclair, cutting almost but not all the way through. Pipe cheese filling into éclairs and spoon fruit mixture over filling. Serve éclairs immediately. **SERVES 12.**

PASSION-FRUIT PANNA COTTAS WITH TROPICAL FRUIT SALSA

—·—

For Panna Cottas

1 cup confectioners' sugar

¼ teaspoon salt

2¼ cups heavy cream (¾ cup well-chilled)

1½ cups passion-fruit purée* such as Goya brand, thawed if frozen

1 tablespoon plus ¼ teaspoon unflavored gelatin (less than 2 envelopes)

1 teaspoon fresh lemon juice

For Salsa

½ papaya

½ mango

¼ pineapple

1 kiwifruit

1 tablespoon fresh lime juice

1 tablespoon granulated sugar

available at Latino markets and some supermarkets and by mail order from Marché aux Délices, tel. (888) 547-5471

Make Panna Cottas: In a saucepan stir together confectioners' sugar, salt, 1½ cups cream, and ½ cup passion-fruit purée. Sprinkle gelatin over mixture and let stand 1 minute to soften gelatin. Bring gelatin mixture and lemon juice to a boil over moderate heat, stirring, and cool slightly. Pour mixture into a metal bowl and set in a larger bowl of ice and cold water. Cool mixture, stirring occasionally with a rubber spatula, until thick but not completely set (mixture should mound slightly when dropped from a spoon), about 20 minutes.

In a bowl with an electric mixer beat remaining ¾ cup well-chilled cream until it just holds stiff peaks and fold in remaining cup fruit purée. Gently fold whipped cream mixture into gelatin mixture until smooth and spoon into six ¾-cup molds. *Chill panna cottas, covered, until firm, at least 4 hours, and up to 2 days.*

Make Salsa: Peel all fruits and cut into ¼-inch dice, discarding seeds from papaya and core from pineapple. In a bowl toss fruit with lime juice and sugar and macerate 15 minutes. *Salsa may be made 1 day ahead and chilled, covered.*

Fill a bowl halfway with warm water. To unmold *panna cottas*, loosen edges of *panna cottas* and dip molds into water. Dry each mold and invert onto a plate. Spoon salsa around *panna cottas*. SERVES 6.

MELON MÉLANGE WITH HONEY GINGER SYRUP

—·— +

¼ cup fresh orange juice

¼ cup fresh lime juice

3 tablespoons honey

1 tablespoon finely chopped crystallized ginger

2 teaspoons finely grated fresh orange zest

1 firm-ripe honeydew melon (about 4½ pounds)

1 firm-ripe cantaloupe (about 3 pounds)

a 3-pound piece watermelon

1 tablespoon finely chopped fresh mint leaves

In a small saucepan simmer juices, honey, ginger, and zest, stirring, until slightly thickened and reduced to about ⅓ cup. Cool syrup.

Halve melons and discard seeds. With a large (¾-inch) melon baller scoop enough balls of melon into a large bowl to measure about 8 cups. Add honey ginger syrup and mint and toss until combined well. *Chill melon mélange, covered, until cold, about 2 hours, and up to 1 day.* SERVES 6 TO 8.

APPLE WALNUT UPSIDE-DOWN CAKE

For Topping

3 to 3½ Golden Delicious apples (about 1½ pounds)

1½ sticks (¾ cup) unsalted butter

⅔ cup sugar

½ cup coarsely chopped walnuts

For Cake Batter

½ Golden Delicious apple

1½ cups all-purpose flour

1½ teaspoons baking powder

¾ teaspoon salt

½ teaspoon cinnamon

1 stick (½ cup) unsalted butter, softened

⅔ cup sugar

1 teaspoon vanilla

2 tablespoons minced peeled fresh gingerroot

2 large eggs

½ cup sour cream

ACCOMPANIMENTS

Calvados caramel sauce (recipe follows)

whipped cream

Make Topping: Peel, core, and quarter apples.

In a well-seasoned 10¼- by 2-inch cast-iron skillet or a 10- by 2-inch non-stick skillet melt butter over moderately low heat just until melted (butter should not separate). Stir in sugar until combined well. Arrange apple quarters decoratively, rounded sides down, in skillet and sprinkle walnuts evenly in between apples. Cook mixture, undisturbed, 25 to 35 minutes, or until apples are tender in centers and sugar is a golden caramel.

Preheat oven to 375° F.

Make Cake Batter While Topping is Cooking: Peel apple and finely chop. In a bowl whisk together flour, baking powder, salt, and cinnamon. In another bowl with an electric mixer beat together butter and sugar until light and fluffy. Beat in vanilla and gingerroot and add eggs 1 at a time, beating well after each addition. Beat in sour cream and with mixer on low speed beat in flour mixture gradually until just combined. Fold chopped apple into batter.

Remove skillet from heat and spoon batter over topping. Leaving a ¼-inch border of cooked apples uncovered, with a metal spatula spread batter evenly, being careful not to disturb topping. If using a non-stick skillet with a plastic handle, wrap handle in a double thickness of foil. Put skillet in a shallow baking pan and bake cake in middle of oven 25 to 35 minutes, or until a tester comes out with crumbs adhering and cake is golden brown. Cool cake in skillet on a rack 10 minutes. Run a thin knife around edge of skillet and carefully invert cake onto a plate.

Serve cake warm or at room temperature with caramel sauce and whipped cream. **SERVES 8.**

Photo opposite

CALVADOS CARAMEL SAUCE

1½ cups sugar

½ cup water

3 tablespoons Calvados or other apple brandy

2 tablespoons unsalted butter

In a dry 2-quart heavy saucepan cook sugar over moderate heat, stirring with a fork, until melted and cook without stirring, swirling pan, until a golden caramel. Remove pan from heat and carefully add water and brandy down side of pan (caramel will bubble and steam). Return pan to heat and simmer, stirring, until caramel is dissolved. Stir in butter. *Sauce may be made 3 days ahead and chilled, covered. Reheat sauce to warm before serving.* **MAKES ABOUT 1¼ CUPS.**

PEACHES AND CHERRIES WITH ALMOND SYRUP

— · —

½ cup whole blanched almonds
½ cup sliced almonds
1 cup water
⅓ cup sugar
3 tablespoons Disaronno Amaretto
1 teaspoon fresh lemon juice
⅛ teaspoon salt
6 ripe peaches or nectarines
1 pound sweet cherries (about 6 cups)

Preheat oven to 350° F.

Keeping whole and sliced almonds separate, spread nuts evenly on baking sheet and toast 7 minutes, or until fragrant. Cool almonds completely.

In a small saucepan simmer water and sugar, stirring until sugar is dissolved, 5 minutes. In a blender finely grind whole almonds with hot syrup, about 1 minute (use caution when blending hot liquids), and cool slightly. Pour almond mixture through a fine sieve into a small bowl, pressing hard on solids, and stir in Amaretto, lemon juice, and salt. *Chill almond syrup, covered, until cold, at least 1 hour, and up to 2 days.*

Peel peaches or nectarines and cut into thin wedges. Pit cherries. In a large bowl gently toss fruit with syrup and ¼ cup sliced almonds until combined.

Serve fruit topped with remaining ¼ cup sliced almonds. **SERVES 6**.

PEACH COBBLER WITH GINGER BISCUIT TOPPING

— · —

3 pounds peaches (about 8 medium)
½ cup granulated sugar
¼ cup packed brown sugar
2 tablespoons all-purpose flour
1 tablespoon fresh lemon juice

For Topping

1½ cups all-purpose flour
¼ cup plus 2 tablespoons sugar
2 teaspoons baking powder
¼ teaspoon baking soda
1½ teaspoons ground ginger
¾ teaspoon cinnamon
½ teaspoon salt
⅓ cup vegetable shortening
⅓ cup milk
1 large egg
2 tablespoons unsulfured molasses

ACCOMPANIMENT: vanilla ice cream

Preheat oven to 400° F.

Peel peaches and cut into ¾-inch wedges. In a 3-quart saucepan bring peaches, sugars, flour, and lemon juice to a simmer, stirring occasionally, and simmer 15 minutes.

Make Topping: Into a bowl sift together flour, sugar, baking powder, baking soda, spices, and salt. With a pastry blender blend in shortening until mixture resembles sand. In a cup with a fork beat together milk, egg, and molasses until combined well and stir into flour mixture until just combined.

Pour peach mixture into a shallow 2-quart baking dish and immediately spoon topping evenly over hot peach mixture. Bake cobbler in middle of oven 20 minutes, or until peach mixture is bubbling and topping is cooked through. **SERVES 6**.

SPICED CARAMEL
ORANGES

½ cup sugar
1 cup water
two 3-inch cinnamon sticks
¾ teaspoon whole allspice
3 tablespoons dark rum
6 navel oranges

In a dry heavy saucepan cook sugar over moderate heat, stirring with a fork, until melted. Cook caramel, without stirring, swirling pan, until a golden caramel.

Remove pan from heat and carefully add water down side of pan (caramel will bubble and steam). Stir in spices. Return pan to heat and simmer sauce, stirring occasionally, until caramel is dissolved. Remove pan from heat and carefully add rum. Simmer sauce 5 minutes more.

With a sharp knife cut peel and pith from oranges and cut oranges crosswise into ¼-inch thick slices. Transfer slices to a large bowl and pour caramel sauce over them. *Macerate oranges, covered and chilled, at least 2 hours and up to 1 day. Bring caramel oranges to room temperature before serving.* **SERVES 6.**

Photo below

APPLE BLACKBERRY PIE

- - -

For Filling

¾ cup granulated sugar

¼ cup packed light brown sugar

¼ cup cornstarch

½ teaspoon cinnamon

2 pounds Golden Delicious apples
  (about 4 large)

1 cup picked-over blackberries

1 tablespoon fresh lemon juice

2 recipes pastry dough (page 33)

½ stick (¼ cup) unsalted butter

Preheat oven to 375° F.

Make Filling: In a large bowl stir together sugars, cornstarch, and cinnamon. Peel, quarter, and core apples. Cut apples into ½-inch wedges and add with blackberries and lemon juice to sugar mixture, tossing until combined well.

On a lightly floured surface with a floured rolling pin roll out 1 piece dough into a 12-inch round (about ⅛ inch thick) and fit into a 9-inch (1-quart) pie plate. Trim edge of dough. Transfer filling to shell. Cut butter into ½-inch pieces and scatter over filling.

On floured surface roll out remaining dough into a 12-inch round (about ⅛ inch thick). With a pastry brush dipped in water, moisten edge of shell. Gently fold dough round into quarters and unfold over filling. Trim top crust, leaving a ½-inch overhang and fold under bottom crust, pressing edge gently to seal. With a paring knife, beginning in center of pie, cut a loose spiral in top crust cutting to 1 inch from edge, to form a steam vent.

Bake pie in middle of oven 1 hour and 10 minutes, or until filling is bubbling and pastry is deep golden, and transfer to a rack to cool slightly. Serve pie warm or at room temperature. *Pie may be made 1 day ahead and kept, loosely covered, at room temperature.* SERVES 8.

SLICED BAKED APPLES

- - -

4 McIntosh apples of same size

3 tablespoons fresh lemon juice

½ stick (¼ cup) unsalted butter

¼ cup packed light brown sugar

2 tablespoons light rum

four 3-inch cinnamon sticks

GARNISH: apple or mint leaves

Preheat oven to 450° F.

Peel and core apples. Cut apples crosswise into ¼-inch-thick rings, stacking each apple into its original shape in a pie plate. Brush apples with lemon juice. Cut butter into bits and fill core cavities with some of butter, brown sugar, and rum. Sprinkle apples with remaining butter, brown sugar, and rum and bake in middle of oven, basting frequently with pan juices, 25 minutes.

Reduce temperature to 350° F.

Insert cinnamon sticks in cavities and bake apples, basting frequently, 20 minutes more, or until tender and well-browned and juices are thick and syrupy.

With a slotted spatula carefully transfer apples to 4 plates, keeping them intact, and spoon syrup over them.

Serves apples warm, garnished with apple or mint leaves. SERVES 4.

Photo above

PLUM AND HAZELNUT CROSTATA

— ※ —

For Pastry Dough
⅓ cup toasted hazelnuts
⅓ cup sugar
1 stick (½ cup) cold unsalted butter
1⅓ cups all-purpose flour
½ teaspoon salt
1 large egg
3 tablespoons ice water

For Filling
¼ cup toasted hazelnuts
2 tablespoons cornstarch
1 large egg white
⅓ cup plus 2 tablespoons sugar
1 pound plums

Make Pastry Dough: In a food processor finely grind nuts with sugar. Cut butter into ½-inch pieces. In a bowl with a pastry blender or with your fingertips blend nut mixture, butter, flour, and salt until most of mixture resembles coarse meal with remainder in small (roughly pea-size) lumps. In a cup with a fork stir together egg and ice water until combined well. Drizzle 2 tablespoons egg mixture evenly over hazelnut mixture and stir with a fork until incorporated. Test dough for proper texture by gently squeezing a small handful: It should hold together without crumbling apart. If necessary, add more egg mixture, 1 tablespoon at a time, stirring until incorporated, and test mixture again. (Do not overwork dough or pastry will be tough.) Gather dough together and form into a disk. *Chill dough, wrapped in plastic wrap, until firm, at least 1 hour, and up to 1 day.*

On a work surface arrange two 15-inch-long sheets of plastic wrap, overlapping long sides by about 4 inches, and top with dough disk. Cover dough with 2 more overlapping pieces of plastic wrap and roll out dough into a 14-inch round. Remove top pieces

of plastic wrap and invert dough into a 12-inch tart pan with a removable fluted rim, easing to fit (do not trim edge). Chill shell, covered with plastic wrap, while preparing filling.

Preheat oven to 375° F.

Make Filling: In a food processor finely grind nuts and in a small bowl stir together with 1 tablespoon cornstarch. In another bowl with an electric mixer beat white until it holds soft peaks and gradually beat in ⅓ cup sugar, beating until meringue just holds stiff peaks. With a rubber spatula gently fold nut mixture into meringue.

Halve and pit plums and cut into ½-inch wedges. In a bowl toss plums with remaining 2 tablespoons sugar and tablespoon cornstarch.

Remove plastic wrap from shell and trim edge, leaving a ¼-inch overhang. Spoon meringue into shell, spreading evenly, and arrange plums on meringue. Fold dough edge toward center of *crostata* over filling, forming a 1½-inch border. Bake *crostata* in middle of oven 45 minutes, or until pastry is golden and meringue is pale golden. Cool *crostata* in pan on a rack. **SERVES 8.**

PEAR GALETTE WITH AMARETTI CRUMBLE

— ·· —

For Crumble

½ cup crushed *amaretti** (Italian almond macaroons)

¼ cup all-purpose flour

2 tablespoons packed light brown sugar

½ stick (¼ cup) butter, softened

1 puff pastry sheet (from a 17¼-ounce package frozen puff pastry), thawed

1 tablespoon milk

½ cup granulated sugar

1 tablespoon cornstarch

1½ pounds firm-ripe pears, preferably Bosc

2 tablespoons cold unsalted butter

1 tablespoon fresh lemon juice

2 tablespoons sliced almonds

available at specialty foods shops and some supermarkets

Preheat oven to 375° F.

Make Crumble: In a bowl stir together all crumble ingredients until combined well.

On a lightly floured surface with a lightly floured rolling pin roll out pastry into a 12-inch square. With a small knife cut a ½-inch strip from each side of square, reserving strips. Transfer pastry square to a baking sheet and brush edges of square with milk. Arrange reserved strips of pastry on milk to form a border, overlapping strips at corners and trimming overhang. Bake pastry in middle of oven 15 minutes, or until puffed and pale golden.

While pastry is baking, in a bowl whisk together sugar and cornstarch. Peel and core pears and cut lengthwise into ½-inch wedges. Cut butter into bits and add to sugar mixture with pears and lemon juice, tossing gently until combined.

With back of a spoon press down puff pastry inside border and spoon pear mixture into pastry shell. Sprinkle pear mixture with crumble and sliced almonds. Bake *galette* in middle of oven 15 minutes, or until pear mixture is bubbling and pastry is golden brown. Serve *galette* warm or at room temperature. **SERVES 6.**

PRUNES IN WINE AND ARMAGNAC

— · — ⊕+

2 cups dry red wine

¾ cup sugar

two 12-ounce boxes pitted prunes

1 cup Armagnac

ACCOMPANIMENT: vanilla ice cream and/or semolina cookies (page 150)

In a saucepan bring wine and sugar to a boil, stirring until sugar is dissolved, and boil 1 minute. Add prunes and Armagnac and simmer, covered, 15 minutes. Cool mixture, covered, 15 minutes and spoon into a very clean 1½-quart ceramic or glass container. Cool mixture completely, covered. *Prunes keep, covered and chilled, 1 month.*

Serve prunes with ice cream or cookies. **SERVES 6 TO 8.**

BANANA AND RUM SPICED CRÊPES

— ◆ —

For Crêpes

¾ stick (6 tablespoons) unsalted butter
1¼ cups milk
1 cup all-purpose flour
3 large eggs
¼ teaspoon salt
¼ teaspoon cinnamon
⅛ teaspoon ground allspice

For Filling

1¼ pounds firm-ripe red or yellow bananas
2 tablespoons unsalted butter
⅓ cup sugar
⅓ cup apple juice
2 tablespoons dark rum
1 tablespoon fresh lemon juice
3 whole cloves

Make Crêpes: Melt ½ stick butter. In a bowl whisk together melted butter, milk, flour, eggs, salt, cinnamon, and allspice until combined well. *Chill crêpe batter, covered, 1 hour.*

Melt remaining 2 tablespoons butter. Heat a 7½-inch crêpe pan over moderate heat until hot and brush with butter. Add a scant 2 tablespoons batter to pan, swirling to coat bottom evenly. Cook crêpe until underside is pale golden and holes appear on top, about 30 seconds. Turn crêpe over and cook until underside is golden, 15 to 30 seconds. Slide crêpe onto a kitchen towel to cool. Make more crêpes in same manner, brushing pan with butter for each crêpe and stacking cooled crêpes between sheets of wax paper on a plate. *Crêpes may be made 2 days ahead and chilled, stacked between sheets of wax paper and wrapped well in plastic wrap.*

Preheat oven to 250° F.

Make Filling: Diagonally cut bananas crosswise into ¾-inch-thick slices. In a skillet heat butter over moderate heat until foam subsides. Add bananas and cook, turning occasionally, until golden. Add remaining filling ingredients, gently stirring until combined well, and simmer until bananas are tender, about 2 minutes. With a slotted spoon transfer bananas to a bowl and simmer sauce until slightly thickened, about 2 minutes more. Return bananas to sauce and keep filling warm over very low heat.

Wrap stacked crêpes well in foil and heat in oven until warm, 5 to 15 minutes. Discard cloves from filling. With a slotted spoon put 3 or 4 banana slices on a crêpe and fold crêpe into quarters. Fill and fold remaining crêpes in same manner, arranging 2 crêpes on each of 6 plates. Pour warm sauce over crêpes. **SERVES 6.**

PLUM SHORTCAKES

— · —

For Plum Mixture

- 10 medium purple plums
- ½ cup sugar
- 2 teaspoons fresh lemon juice

For Shortcakes

- 2 cups all-purpose flour
- 1 tablespoon baking powder
- 3 tablespoons sugar
- ½ teaspoon salt
- 1¼ cups heavy cream
- milk for brushing rounds

ACCOMPANIMENT: whipped cream

Make Plum Mixture: Pit plums and cut into ½-inch pieces. In a saucepan bring plums, sugar, and lemon juice to a boil and simmer, covered, 10 to 15 minutes, or until plums are tender but still hold their shape. Transfer plum mixture to a bowl and cool. *Plum mixture may be made 1 day ahead and chilled, covered. Bring mixture to room temperature before serving.*

Make Shortcakes: Preheat oven to 425° F.

Into a bowl sift together flour, baking powder, sugar, and salt and stir in cream with a fork until a dough just forms. Gather dough into a ball and on a floured surface knead gently 6 times. Roll or pat out dough ½ inch thick. With a 3-inch round cutter dipped in flour cut out as many rounds as possible and transfer rounds to an ungreased baking sheet. Gather scraps and reroll dough. Cut out more rounds to make 6 rounds in all. Brush tops of rounds with milk and bake shortcakes in middle of oven 15 minutes, or until pale golden. Transfer shortcakes to a rack and cool. *Shortcakes may be made 4 hours ahead and kept in an airtight container at room temperature.*

Halve shortcakes horizontally with a serrated knife and serve with plum mixture and whipped cream. **SERVES 6.**

HONEY VANILLA POACHED APRICOTS

— · — ⊕+

- ½ vanilla bean
- 1 cup water
- 3 tablespoons honey
- 3 tablespoons sugar
- ¾ pound fresh apricots

Split vanilla bean half in half lengthwise. In a 1½-quart saucepan simmer water, honey, sugar, and vanilla bean, covered, 5 minutes. While syrup is simmering, halve apricots lengthwise and discard pits. Add apricots to syrup and simmer, covered, until apricots are tender but not falling apart, 2 to 5 minutes, depending on ripeness of fruit.

With a slotted spoon transfer apricots to a bowl. Boil syrup until reduced to about ½ cup and pour over apricots. *Chill apricot mixture 25 minutes, uncovered. Apricots may be made 1 day ahead and chilled, covered.* **SERVES 2.**

Photo opposite

SPICED SHORTCAKES WITH MINTED PEACHES

For Filling
   1 large firm-ripe peach
   1 tablespoon granulated sugar
   1 tablespoon finely chopped fresh mint leaves
   2 teaspoons fresh lemon juice

For Shortcakes
   ½ cup all-purpose flour
   2 tablespoons packed brown sugar
   1 teaspoon baking powder
   ¼ teaspoon cinnamon
   ⅓ cup plus 1 tablespoon heavy cream

For Whipped Cream
   ¼ cup well-chilled heavy cream
   1 teaspoon granulated sugar
   ¼ teaspoon vanilla

Make Filling: In a small saucepan of boiling water blanch peach 1 minute and drain. Peel and pit peach and thinly slice. In a small bowl toss peach with sugar, mint, and lemon juice.

Make Shortcakes: Preheat oven to 425° F. and lightly grease a baking sheet.

In a small bowl whisk together flour, brown sugar, baking powder, cinnamon, and a pinch salt. Stir in cream with a fork until a dough just forms. Turn dough out onto a lightly floured surface and with floured hands pat into a 6- by 3-inch rectangle. With a sharp knife trim edges and halve dough crosswise to form two 3-inch squares.

Arrange squares 2 inches apart on baking sheet and bake in middle of oven 12 to 15 minutes, or until golden. (Shortcake squares will spread more than they will rise.) Transfer shortcakes to a rack and cool 10 minutes.

Make Whipped Cream: In a bowl with an electric mixer beat cream with sugar until it just holds soft peaks and beat in vanilla.

Halve shortcakes horizontally with a serrated knife and serve with peach filling and whipped cream. **SERVES 2.**

LIME MOUSSE TART

For Crust
   1¼ cups graham cracker crumbs (about twelve 5- by 2½-inch crackers)
   5 tablespoons unsalted butter, softened
   ¼ cup sugar

For Mousse
   1 cup sugar
   ¼ cup cornstarch
   ¼ teaspoon salt
   2 cups milk
   1½ teaspoons unflavored gelatin (less than 1 envelope)
   3 large egg yolks
   3 tablespoons unsalted butter
   1 tablespoon finely grated fresh lime zest
   ½ cup fresh lime juice
   1 cup well-chilled heavy cream

Make Crust: Preheat oven to 325° F.

In a 9½-inch springform pan blend all crust ingredients with your fingertips until combined well and press evenly onto bottom and 1 inch up side of pan. Bake crust in middle of oven 10 minutes and transfer to a rack to cool.

Make Mousse: In a heavy saucepan whisk together sugar, cornstarch, and salt and gradually whisk in milk, whisking until mixture is smooth. Sprinkle gelatin over milk mixture and let stand 1 minute to soften gelatin.

In a small bowl whisk together yolks. Bring milk mixture to a boil over moderate heat, whisking constantly, and remove pan from heat. Gradually whisk about 1 cup milk mixture into yolks and whisk yolk mixture into remaining milk mixture. Simmer custard, whisking, 3 minutes (custard will be thick but pourable) and remove pan from heat. Whisk in butter, zest, and lime juice until combined and let custard stand 10 minutes to allow flavors to blend.

Pour custard through a fine sieve into a metal bowl, pressing custard with a rubber spatula if necessary, and set in a larger bowl of ice and cold water. Cool custard, stirring occasionally with a rubber spatula until thick but not completely set (custard should mound slightly when dropped from a spoon), about 20 minutes.

In a bowl with an electric mixer beat cream until it holds soft peaks. With a large rubber spatula gently fold whipped cream into custard and gently spoon mousse into crust. *Chill tart, uncovered, until set, about 4 hours. Tart keeps, covered and chilled, 3 days.* SERVES 8.

BLOOD ORANGE AND COCONUT TART

pastry dough (page 33)
3 cups sweetened flaked coconut
raw rice or dried beans for weighting shell
5 oranges (preferably navel and blood oranges)
½ stick (¼ cup) unsalted butter, softened
½ cup sugar
1 whole large egg
1 large egg yolk
1 teaspoon vanilla
1½ tablespoons all-purpose flour
⅛ teaspoon salt
½ cup orange marmalade

On a lightly floured surface with a floured rolling pin roll out dough into a 12-inch round. Fit dough into an 11-inch tart pan with a removable rim and trim overhang to ½ inch. Turn in overhang and press dough to side of pan. *Chill shell 30 minutes.*

Preheat oven to 325° F.

Spread 2 cups coconut in a shallow baking pan and toast in oven, stirring occasionally, 6 to 8 minutes, or until golden. Cool coconut in pan on a rack.

Increase temperature to 375° F.

Line shell with foil and fill with weights. Bake shell in middle of oven 15 minutes. Carefully remove foil and weights and bake shell 5 to 8 minutes more, or until pale golden. Cool shell on rack.

With a sharp knife cut peel and pith from oranges. Working over layers of paper towels, cut orange sections free from membranes, letting sections drop onto towels. Arrange sections in one layer and let drain.

In a bowl with an electric mixer beat together butter and sugar until combined well and beat in whole egg, yolk, and vanilla until smooth. Beat in flour, salt, toasted coconut, and remaining cup untoasted coconut and spread in shell. Arrange orange sections decoratively on filling. Bake tart in middle of oven 45 to 50 minutes, or until filling is set.

In a small heavy saucepan simmer marmalade 1 minute and with a rubber spatula force through a sieve into a small bowl. Brush tart evenly with marmalade and cool completely. *Tart may be made 1 day ahead and chilled, loosely covered.* SERVES 12.

Photo on page 13

Tropical Fruit Champagne Granita

Sangría Granita in Citrus Shells

Grapefruit and Campari Granita

Crème Fraîche Ice Cream ▪ Honey Ginger Ice Cream

Sour Cream Ice Cream ▪ Peanut Butter Brittle Ice Cream

Fresh Peach Ice Cream ▪ Cranberry Swirl Ice Cream Cake

Chocolate Mint Icebox Cake ▪ Orange Vanilla Bombes

Brandied Cherry Chocolate Chip Floats

Bourbon-Spiked Praline Ice-Cream Sodas

White Chocolate Toasted Almond Semifreddo

Banana Peanut Semifreddo ▪ Striped Sorbet Sandwiches

Watermelon Lime Sorbet ▪ Three Grape Sorbets

California Gingered Fruit Salsa Sundaes

Southern Peanut Butterscotch Sundaes

Butterscotch Sauce ▪ Peanut Butter Sauce

Melba Sauce ▪ Dark Chocolate Sauce

Raspberry Sauce ▪ Black Cherry and Port Sauce

ICY

cy treats are a sure sign of summer, but they provide pleasure at any time of year—especially when you make your own. As far as equipment is concerned, only a baking pan and your refrigerator freezer are required for our *granitas* and *semifreddos*, but you'll need an ice-cream maker for our homemade sorbets and ice creams (many inexpensive models, even electric ones, are widely available and easy to use). Our quicker desserts, however, call for store-bought ice cream: Try our Brandied Cherry Chocolate Chip Floats or Orange Vanilla Bombes; or just drizzle a classic topping, like Dark Chocolate Sauce, over your favorite flavor. We call for super-premium ice cream (like Häagen-Dazs) in some recipes, where its smooth richness makes a difference in texture.

TROPICAL FRUIT CHAMPAGNE GRANITA

½ cup sugar
½ cup water
1 pineapple
4 cups chilled passion-fruit nectar* or juice
¾ cup chilled Champagne
6 baby pineapples (optional)*

*available at specialty foods shops

In a saucepan bring sugar and water to a boil, stirring until sugar is dissolved, and cool syrup.

Peel pineapple and core. Cut pineapple into ½-inch chunks. In a blender or food processor purée 3 cups pineapple with ¼ cup plus 2 tablespoons syrup. Stir in passion-fruit nectar or juice and Champagne. Transfer mixture to a shallow metal baking pan. Freeze mixture, stirring and crushing lumps with a fork every hour, until mixture is firm but not frozen hard, about 3 to 4 hours. *Granita may be made 2 days ahead and frozen, covered.*

Just before serving, scrape *granita* with a fork to lighten texture. Horizontally halve baby pineapples and with a serrated knife hollow out enough of core and pineapple to hold about 1 cup *granita*. Serve *granita* in pineapples, mounding it, or in chilled goblets. **MAKES ABOUT 9 CUPS.**

Photo on page 69

SANGRÍA GRANITA IN CITRUS SHELLS

— ¤ —

2½ cups sugar

2 cups water

4 large navel oranges

6 large lemons

12 limes

a 750 ml bottle dry red wine such as
 Merlot or Beaujolais

In a saucepan bring sugar and water to a boil, stirring until sugar is dissolved, and simmer 3 minutes. Remove pan from heat and cool syrup at least 15 minutes.

While syrup is cooling, halve fruits lengthwise. Squeeze enough orange juice to measure 2 cups and enough lemon and lime juices to measure ⅔ cup each. Reserve citrus halves.

Stir citrus juices, wine, and a pinch salt into cooled syrup and transfer to a large shallow metal baking pan (about 13 by 9 inches). Freeze mixture, stirring and crushing lumps with a fork every hour, until mixture is firm but not frozen hard, about 3 to 4 hours. *Frozen granita may be made 2 days ahead and kept frozen in an airtight container.*

While *granita* is freezing, with a serrated spoon scrape flesh and any remaining pulp and membranes from about 20 reserved citrus halves (depending on size of halves) and discard remainder. Put citrus shells on a baking sheet in one layer. *Freeze citrus shells until frozen hard, about 3 hours. Frozen shells may be made 2 days ahead and kept frozen in heavy-duty sealable plastic bags.*

Just before serving, scrape *granita* with a fork to lighten texture and spoon into frozen citrus shells, mounding it slightly. MAKES ABOUT 20 GRANITA-FILLED SHELLS.

Photo on page 10

GRAPEFRUIT AND CAMPARI GRANITA

— ¤ —

1⅓ cups sugar

1 cup water

3 cups fresh pink grapefruit juice (from about 4 pink grapefruits), with some pulp

¼ cup Campari

GARNISH: four 3-inch-long pieces fresh grapefruit zest, removed with a vegetable peeler

In a saucepan bring sugar and water to a boil, stirring until sugar is dissolved, and cool syrup. Stir in grapefruit juice and Campari. Transfer mixture to a shallow metal baking pan. Freeze mixture, stirring and crushing lumps with a fork every hour, until mixture is firm but not frozen hard, 3 to 4 hours. *Granita may be made 2 days ahead and frozen, covered.*

Just before serving, scrape *granita* with a fork to lighten texture. Serve *granita* in chilled goblets, garnished with zest. MAKES ABOUT 7 CUPS.

Photo below

CRÈME FRAÎCHE ICE CREAM

— · —

1 pound *crème fraîche** (about 2 cups)
2 cups well-shaken buttermilk
⅓ cup fresh lemon juice
1¼ cups sugar

available at specialty foods shops and some supermarkets

In a blender blend together all ingredients, scraping down sides, until very smooth, about 2 minutes. Chill mixture until cold and freeze in an ice-cream maker. Transfer ice cream to an airtight container and put in freezer to harden. *Ice cream may be made 1 week ahead.* **MAKES ABOUT 1 QUART.**

HONEY GINGER ICE CREAM

— · —

a 6-inch piece fresh gingerroot
2 cups sweetened condensed milk
2 cups well-chilled heavy cream
3 tablespoons honey, or to taste

Peel gingerroot and finely chop enough to measure ¾ cup. In a small heavy saucepan simmer 1 cup condensed milk with gingerroot, stirring, 5 minutes. Pour mixture through a fine sieve into a bowl, pressing hard on solids, and stir in remaining cup condensed milk, cream, and honey. *Chill mixture, covered, until cold, about 1 hour.* Freeze cream mixture in an ice-cream maker. Transfer ice cream to an airtight container and put in freezer to harden. *Ice cream may be made 1 week ahead.* **MAKES ABOUT 1 QUART.**

SOUR CREAM ICE CREAM

— · —

1 vanilla bean
2 cups half-and-half
1 cup sugar
8 large egg yolks
2 cups (1 pint) sour cream

Split vanilla bean lengthwise. In a heavy saucepan stir together half-and-half, ¾ cup sugar, and vanilla bean and bring just to a boil. Remove pan from heat. In a bowl whisk together yolks and remaining ¼ cup sugar. Add hot half-and-half mixture in a stream, whisking, and transfer custard to pan. Cook custard over moderately low heat, stirring, until thickened and an instant-read thermometer registers 170° F.

Remove pan from heat. Scrape seeds from vanilla bean into custard and discard pod. Stir in sour cream until combined well and pour through a fine sieve into a bowl. *Chill custard until cold, about 1 hour.* Freeze custard in an ice-cream maker. Transfer ice cream to an airtight container and put in freezer to harden. *Ice cream may be made 1 week ahead.* **MAKES ABOUT 1 QUART.**

PEANUT BUTTER BRITTLE ICE CREAM

For Peanut Brittle

¾ cup sugar

1½ cups roasted unsalted peanuts
(about ½ pound)

2⅓ cups whole milk

2 cups (18 ounces) smooth peanut butter
(not natural-style)

⅔ cup sugar

1 tablespoon vanilla

ACCOMPANIMENT: dark chocolate sauce (page 81)

Make Peanut Brittle: Lightly oil a 12-inch sheet of heavy-duty foil. In a dry small heavy saucepan cook sugar over moderate heat, stirring with a fork, until melted. Cook caramel, without stirring, swirling pan, until golden. Add peanuts and a pinch salt, stirring until mixture is combined well (caramel will not completely coat nuts). Immediately transfer mixture to foil and cool completely, about 20 minutes. Peel off foil and break brittle into pieces. In a food processor pulse brittle until coarsely ground. *Brittle may be made 3 days ahead and kept in an airtight container at room temperature.*

In a deep heavy saucepan heat milk, peanut butter, and sugar over moderate heat, stirring constantly, just until smooth (do not let simmer), about 4 minutes. Stir in vanilla and cool to room temperature (do not chill). Freeze mixture in an ice-cream maker and transfer to an airtight container. Stir in 1½ cups brittle and put in freezer to harden. *Ice cream may be made 1 week ahead.*

Serve ice cream with dark chocolate sauce and sprinkle with remaining peanut brittle. MAKES ABOUT 1 QUART.

FRESH PEACH ICE CREAM

5 peaches (about 1¼ pounds)

1½ cups sugar

1½ cups milk

1½ cups heavy cream

1 teaspoon vanilla

Have ready a bowl of ice and cold water. In a kettle of boiling water blanch peaches 1 minute and transfer to ice water to stop cooking. Peel peaches and pit. Purée peaches in a food processor or blender.

In a large bowl stir together sugar, milk, and cream until sugar is dissolved and stir in peach purée and vanilla. Freeze mixture, in batches if necessary, in an ice-cream maker. Transfer ice cream to an airtight container and put in freezer to harden. *Ice cream may be made 1 week ahead.* MAKES ABOUT 1½ QUARTS.

Photo above

CRANBERRY SWIRL ICE-CREAM CAKE

— · —

28 chocolate wafers

½ stick (¼ cup) plus 1 tablespoon
  unsalted butter

1½ cups picked-over cranberries

½ cup light corn syrup

⅓ cup granulated sugar

⅓ cup water

1½ pints vanilla ice cream, softened

½ cup shelled natural pistachios

¼ teaspoon salt

1 cup well-chilled heavy cream

3 tablespoons confectioners' sugar

1 teaspoon vanilla

GARNISH: chocolate curls (page 19)
  or grated bittersweet chocolate

Lightly oil an 8-inch springform pan (about 2½ inches deep).

In a food processor finely grind wafers. Melt ½ stick butter. In a bowl with a fork stir together crumbs and melted butter until combined well and pat onto bottom and 1 inch up side of pan. *Freeze crust 30 minutes, or until firm.*

In a saucepan simmer cranberries, corn syrup, granulated sugar, and water, covered, 10 minutes, or until cranberries are burst. In a food processor or blender purée mixture and transfer to a small bowl. *Chill purée, covered, 1 hour, or until cold.* Stir purée until smooth.

Spread half of ice cream over crust and drizzle with all but ⅓ cup purée. Spread remaining ice cream over purée. Draw a knife through ice-cream mixture in loops to marble and smooth top. *Freeze mixture 30 minutes, or until firm.* Spread remaining ⅓ cup purée evenly over top and freeze cake 15 minutes more, or until purée is firm.

Chop pistachios and in a small skillet cook with salt in remaining tablespoon butter over moderate heat, stirring, 1 minute. Cool nuts. In a bowl with an electric mixer beat cream until it holds soft peaks. Add confectioners' sugar and vanilla and beat until cream holds stiff peaks. Fold in pistachios and spread evenly over cake. *Freeze cake, uncovered, 30 minutes, or until top is firm, then freeze cake, covered with plastic wrap and foil, at least 4 hours more and up to 5 days.*

Just before serving, wrap a warm damp kitchen towel around side of pan and remove side. Transfer cake to a plate and garnish with chocolate curls or grated chocolate. Using a knife dipped in hot water cut cake into wedges. SERVES 6 TO 8.

Photo opposite

CHOCOLATE MINT ICEBOX CAKE
⬤+

⅓ cup loosely packed fresh mint leaves
1 cup well-chilled heavy cream
3 tablespoons sugar
1 tablespoon unsweetened cocoa powder
one 9-ounce package chocolate wafers

GARNISH: fresh mint leaves

Finely chop mint. In a bowl with an electric mixer beat cream with mint, sugar, and cocoa powder until it holds soft peaks and spread about 1 mounded teaspoon on one side of each wafer. On a platter sandwich wafers together on their sides to form a log and cover top and sides with remaining cream mixture. *Chill cake, loosely covered with plastic wrap, at least 6 hours and up to 1 day.*

Diagonally cut cake into ¾-inch-thick slices and garnish with mint. SERVES 4 TO 6.

ORANGE VANILLA BOMBES
⬤+

one 6-ounce can frozen orange juice concentrate, slightly softened
1 pint plus 1 cup super-premium vanilla ice cream, softened
four 7-ounce disposable soft plastic cups
¾ cup Grand Marnier or other orange-flavored liqueur (optional)

In a bowl stir together concentrate and ice cream until combined well. Divide mixture among cups, tapping bottom of cups on counter to release any air pockets. (Alternatively, transfer mixture to an airtight container.) *Freeze cups, covered with plastic wrap, until mixture is frozen hard, about 2 hours. Bombes may be made up to 1 week ahead and kept frozen, covered.*

To unmold *bombes*, carefully tear rim of each cup and continue tearing to remove cup. Invert *bombes* onto each of 4 plates and drizzle with liqueur. MAKES 4 BOMBES OR ABOUT 1 QUART ICE CREAM.

BRANDIED CHERRY CHOCOLATE CHIP FLOATS

--- · --- ⊕+

a 16½-ounce can pitted Bing cherries in heavy syrup
3 tablespoons sugar
3 tablespoons brandy, or to taste
1½ pints chocolate chip ice cream
2 cups well-chilled seltzer or cherry soda

Drain cherries in a sieve set over a small saucepan and reserve cherries. Add sugar to syrup and simmer, stirring, until sugar is dissolved. Remove pan from heat and stir in reserved cherries and brandy. Cool brandied cherries. *Brandied cherries may be made 4 days ahead and chilled, covered.*

In each of 6 chilled tall glasses and using a small (1-ounce) ice-cream scoop or spoon, layer ice cream, brandied cherries, and syrup. Top off each glass with about ⅓ cup seltzer or cherry soda. **SERVES 6.**

BOURBON-SPIKED PRALINE ICE-CREAM SODAS

--- · ---

6 tablespoons sugar
¾ cup pecan halves (about 3 ounces)
2 pints vanilla ice cream, softened
3 cups well-chilled cream soda
1½ tablespoons bourbon, or to taste

Lightly oil a 12-inch sheet of heavy-duty foil. In a dry small heavy saucepan cook sugar over moderate heat, stirring with a fork, until melted. Cook caramel, without stirring, swirling pan, until golden.

Add pecans and a pinch salt, stirring until nuts are coated well. Immediately transfer mixture to foil and cool completely, about 20 minutes. Peel off foil and break praline into pieces. In a food processor finely grind praline. *Praline may be made 3 days ahead and kept in an airtight container at room temperature.*

In a large bowl stir ¾ cup praline into ice cream until just combined. *Freeze ice cream, covered, until firm, about 2 hours, and up to 1 week.*

Using a small (1-ounce) ice-cream scoop or spoon divide ice cream among 6 chilled tall glasses. Add ½ cup cream soda to each glass and top with bourbon. Sprinkle ice-cream sodas with remaining praline. **SERVES 6.**

WHITE CHOCOLATE TOASTED ALMOND SEMIFREDDO

--- · ---

a scant cup sliced almonds (about 3½ ounces)
¼ teaspoon salt
1 tablespoon unsalted butter
6 ounces fine-quality white chocolate such as Lindt
2 large eggs
⅓ cup sugar
1 teaspoon vanilla extract
¼ teaspoon almond extract
1½ cups well-chilled heavy cream

Line an 8½- by 4½- by 2½-inch metal loaf pan with plastic wrap, leaving a 2-inch overhang on ends, and chill in freezer.

Lightly toast almonds. In a skillet cook almonds with salt in butter over moderately low heat, stirring, until coated well, about 1 minute. Chill almonds until cold.

Chop chocolate and in a metal bowl set over a pan of hot but not simmering water melt it, stirring occasionally, until smooth. Remove bowl from heat and cool chocolate.

In another metal bowl with a hand-held electric mixer beat together eggs and sugar until combined. Set bowl over pan of simmering water and beat until thick and pale and an instant-read thermometer registers 140° F. Continue to beat mixture over simmering water 3 minutes (for egg safety) and remove from heat. Beat in chocolate and extracts.

In a bowl with cleaned beaters beat cream until it just holds stiff peaks and fold into egg mixture gently but thoroughly. Fold in almonds and pour mixture into loaf pan. *Freeze semifreddo, covered with plastic wrap, at least 8 hours and up to 2 days.*

Unmold *semifreddo* onto a platter, discarding plastic wrap. Cut *semifreddo* into thick slices and cut slices crosswise into thirds. **SERVES 6 TO 8.**

Photo on page 174

BANANA PEANUT SEMIFREDDO

1 cup roasted unsalted peanuts
3 large eggs
½ cup sugar
1 teaspoon vanilla
¼ teaspoon salt
5 ripe bananas
1½ cups well-chilled heavy cream

Line an 8½- by 4½- by 2½-inch metal loaf pan with plastic wrap, leaving a 2-inch overhang on ends, and chill in freezer.

In a food processor coarsely grind peanuts. In a metal bowl with a hand-held electric mixer beat together eggs and sugar until combined. Set bowl

over a pan of simmering water and beat mixture until thick and pale and an instant-read thermometer registers 140° F. Continue to beat mixture over simmering water 3 minutes (for egg safety) and remove from heat. Beat in vanilla and salt.

In a bowl coarsely mash bananas and fold into egg mixture with peanuts. In another bowl with cleaned beaters beat cream until it just holds stiff peaks and fold into banana mixture gently but thoroughly. Pour mixture into loaf pan. (There should be 1 cup excess mixture, which may be poured into a smaller pan.) *Freeze semifreddo, covered with plastic wrap, at least 8 hours and up to 5 days.*

Unmold *semifreddo* onto a platter, discarding plastic wrap, and cut into slices. **SERVES 6 TO 8.**

Photo below

STRIPED SORBET SANDWICHES

— · —

one 10¾-ounce store-bought frozen pound
 cake, thawed
2 tablespoons light rum or Grand Marnier
1½ cups strawberry sorbet, slightly softened
1½ cups mango sorbet, slightly softened

Line a baking sheet with overlapping sheets of
plastic wrap. With a long serrated knife trim ⅛ inch
crust off top of pound cake. Carefully cut cake horizontally into six ¼-inch-thick layers and arrange
2 layers 1 inch apart on sheet. Brush layers with
some rum or Grand Marnier and with a spatula
spread each evenly with ¾ cup strawberry sorbet.
Top each sorbet layer with another cake layer and
brush with remaining rum or Grand Marnier. Spread
each cake layer evenly with ¾ cup mango sorbet
and top with remaining cake layers, pressing stacks
gently. Fold plastic wrap over cake tops to enclose.
*Freeze cakes, wrapped well in plastic wrap,
until frozen, about 4 hours, and up to 1 week.*

Unmold cakes onto a cutting board, discarding
plastic wrap, and cut crosswise into ¾-inch-thick
slices. Arrange sandwiches on a chilled platter.
MAKES ABOUT 18 SANDWICHES.

Photo on page 11

WATERMELON LIME SORBET

— · —

a 4½-pound piece watermelon (about ¼
 of a large watermelon)
1 cup sugar
⅓ cup fresh lime juice

Cut watermelon into pieces and cut flesh from rind.
Coarsely chop flesh and discard seeds. In a blender
in batches purée enough watermelon to yield 5½
cups, transferring to a large bowl.

In a saucepan heat 1 cup purée with sugar over
moderate heat, stirring until sugar is dissolved, and
stir into remaining purée with lime juice. *Chill
mixture, covered, until cold, about 1 hour.* Freeze
mixture in an ice-cream maker. Transfer sorbet to
an airtight container and put in freezer to harden.
Sorbet may be made 3 days ahead. **MAKES ABOUT
1½ QUARTS.**

THREE GRAPE SORBETS

For Green Grape Sorbet

    2 cups chilled seedless green grapes
        (about ¾ pound)

    ¼ cup superfine granulated sugar

    1½ tablespoons fresh lemon juice

For Red Grape Sorbet

    2 cups chilled seedless red grapes
        (about ¾ pound)

    ¼ cup superfine granulated sugar

    1½ tablespoons fresh lemon juice

For Black Grape Sorbet

    2 cups chilled black grapes (about
        ¾ pound), halved and seeded

    ¼ cup superfine granulated sugar

    2 tablespoons fresh lemon juice

Make Sorbets: Making 1 grape sorbet at a time, in a blender purée sorbet ingredients until sugar is dissolved, about 3 minutes, and pour through a fine sieve into a bowl, pressing on solids. Discard solids and freeze each sorbet in an ice-cream maker. Transfer each sorbet as made to an airtight container and put in freezer to harden. *Sorbets may be made 1 week ahead.*

    With a soup spoon scoop sorbets, alternating flavors, into 4 fluted glasses. **MAKES ABOUT 1⅓ CUPS OF EACH SORBET.**

    Photo right

CALIFORNIA GINGERED FRUIT SALSA SUNDAES

½ cup picked-over raspberries

2 tablespoons sugar

1 firm-ripe small mango

6 large strawberries

½ pineapple

3 to 4 tablespoons minced crystallized ginger, or to taste

½ teaspoon balsamic vinegar

1 pint vanilla frozen yogurt

In a bowl coarsely crush raspberries with sugar and let stand 5 minutes. Finely dice mango and strawberries. Finely dice enough pineapple to measure ½ cup. Add diced fruit, crystallized ginger, and vinegar to raspberries, stirring to combine. Scoop frozen yogurt into 4 sundae dishes and top with salsa. **SERVES 4.**

Photo below

SOUTHERN PEANUT BUTTERSCOTCH SUNDAES

½ cup roasted salted peanuts

3 tablespoons Southern Comfort butterscotch sauce (recipe follows)

1 pint chocolate ice cream

Chop peanuts and reserve about 3 tablespoons for sprinkling. In a saucepan stir remaining peanuts and Southern Comfort into butterscotch sauce and cook over moderately low heat, stirring, until heated through.

Scoop ice cream into 4 sundae dishes and spoon sauce over it. Sprinkle sundaes with reserved peanuts. **SERVES 4.**

Photo below

BUTTERSCOTCH SAUCE

1 cup packed light brown sugar

¼ cup light corn syrup

½ stick (¼ cup) unsalted butter

½ cup heavy cream

1½ teaspoons vanilla

¼ teaspoon fresh lemon juice

In a small heavy saucepan cook brown sugar, corn syrup, butter, and a pinch salt over moderate heat, stirring until sugar is dissolved. Boil syrup, without stirring, until a candy thermometer registers 280° F., about 5 minutes. Remove pan from heat and stir in cream, vanilla, and lemon juice, stirring until smooth. (Sauce will thicken as it cools.) *Sauce keeps, covered and chilled, 1 week.* Serve sauce warm or at room temperature. **MAKES ABOUT 1⅓ CUPS.**

PEANUT BUTTER SAUCE ⊕

¼ cup packed light brown sugar
2 tablespoons light corn syrup
2 tablespoons unsalted butter
½ cup smooth peanut butter (not natural-style)
½ cup heavy cream
1½ teaspoons vanilla
hot water for thinning sauce

In a small heavy saucepan bring brown sugar, corn syrup, and butter to a boil, stirring until sugar is dissolved. Add peanut butter, whisking until smooth. Whisk in cream and vanilla and simmer 2 minutes. Whisk in hot water, 1 tablespoon at a time, to thin sauce to desired consistency. *Sauce keeps, covered and chilled, 1 week.* Serve sauce warm. MAKES ABOUT 1½ CUPS.

MELBA SAUCE ⊕+

2 cups fresh raspberries or two 10-ounce packages thawed frozen raspberries in light syrup (including syrup)
½ cup red-currant jelly
¼ cup sugar, or to taste
1 tablespoon *eau-de-vie de framboise* or raspberry liqueur (optional)

In a saucepan stir together raspberries, jelly, and sugar and bring to a boil over moderately high heat, stirring and crushing berries with back of a wooden spoon. Simmer mixture, stirring occasionally, 15 minutes, or until thickened. Force mixture through a fine sieve into a bowl, pressing hard on solids. Transfer sauce to cleaned pan and boil, stirring occasionally, 5 minutes, or until thickened to desired consistency. Stir in liqueur. *Chill sauce, covered, at least 2 hours and up to 1 week.* MAKES ABOUT 1⅓ CUPS.

DARK CHOCOLATE SAUCE ⊕

2 tablespoons unsalted butter
⅓ cup water or brewed coffee
½ cup packed dark brown sugar
½ cup unsweetened Dutch-process cocoa powder
⅛ teaspoon salt
½ teaspoon vanilla

Cut butter into pieces. In a heavy saucepan heat water or coffee with brown sugar over moderate heat, whisking, until sugar is dissolved. Add cocoa powder and salt, whisking until smooth. Add butter and vanilla, whisking until butter is melted. *Sauce keeps, covered and chilled, 1 week.* Serve sauce warm. MAKES ABOUT 1 CUP.

RASPBERRY SAUCE ⊕+

4 cups picked-over raspberries
¼ cup plus 2 tablespoons sugar, or to taste
1 teaspoon fresh lemon juice, or to taste

In a blender or food processor purée all ingredients. Force sauce through a fine sieve into a bowl, pressing hard on solids. *Chill sauce, covered, at least 1 hour and up to 1 day.* MAKES ABOUT 1¾ CUPS.

BLACK CHERRY AND PORT SAUCE ⊕+

one 12-ounce jar black-cherry preserves
2 tablespoons unsalted butter
¼ cup Tawny Port
1 tablespoon fresh lemon juice, or to taste

In a saucepan bring all ingredients to a boil, stirring, and simmer, stirring occasionally, 5 minutes. Cool sauce and purée in a blender. *Chill sauce, covered, until cold, at least 1 hour, and up to 1 week.* Serve sauce chilled or at room temperature. MAKES ABOUT 1½ CUPS.

Lemon Raspberry Wedding Cake

Sambuca Coffee Cream Cake

Pineapple Coconut Layer Cake

Espresso Crème Brûlée Napoleons

Berry Lemon Tart

Macadamia Rum Baked Alaska

Soft-Frozen Caramel Parfaits with Nut Brittle

Bittersweet Chocolate Torte with Armagnac Sabayon Cream

Spice Layer Cake with Mocha Buttercream and Toasted Pecans

Profiteroles with Burnt Orange Ice Cream and Hot Fudge Sauce

Lemon Rum Charlotte

Swedish Meringue Cake with Strawberries and Orange Filling

Chocolate Mousse and Raspberry Cream Dacquoise

Key Lime Mascarpone "Cannoli" with Mango Sauce

Marjolaine

Chocolate Raspberry Ganache Cake

Shows

TOPPERS

Showstoppers stand at the peak of the proverbial sweets pyramid. Visually, these finales are stunning; flavor-wise, they're sublime. Admittedly, they're ambitious, but longer recipes are arranged in steps, and make-ahead information is included whenever possible, allowing you to complete a dessert in stages. Be sure to take note of pans and other equipment you will need. Pan sizes can be a bit of an enigma: A brief look around our test kitchens showed us that markings are not always reliable. Measure pans across the top (not the bottom). Measuring flour accurately is also important (see our recipe key on page 5).

LEMON RASPBERRY WEDDING CAKE

—— · · ——

For Each Batch of Batter
(Note: 2 separate batches of batter are required; do not double)

2½ cups cake flour (not self-rising)

2½ teaspoons baking powder

1¼ teaspoons salt

1 stick (½ cup) plus 2 tablespoons unsalted butter, softened

1¼ cups sugar

3 large eggs

1½ teaspoons vanilla

1 cup milk

1½ tablespoons finely grated fresh lemon zest

For Syrup

1 large lemon

⅔ cup sugar

1 cup water

⅓ cup fresh lemon juice

2 tablespoons *eau-de-vie de framboise*

For Assembly

two 9-inch cardboard rounds*

two 7-inch cardboard rounds*

two 6-inch cardboard rounds,* trimmed to form 5-inch rounds

cake-decorating turntable* (optional)

lemon meringue buttercream (page 86)

about 5 cups picked-over raspberries

five 8-inch plastic straws

#66, #70, and #113 leaf tips*

DECORATION: crystallized edible flowers** and mint leaves

ACCOMPANIMENTS

crème fraîche ice cream (page 72)

additional raspberries

*available by mail order from New York Cake and Baking Distributors, tel. (800) 942-2539

**crystallized flowers and do-it-yourself kits available by mail order from Meadowsweets, tel. (888) 827-6477

Make First Batch of Batter: Preheat oven to 350° F. and butter a 10-inch round cake pan (at least 2 inches deep). Line bottom of pan with a round of wax paper. Butter paper and dust pan with flour, knocking out excess flour.

Into a bowl sift together flour, baking powder, and salt. In another bowl with an electric mixer beat together butter and sugar until light and fluffy and beat in eggs 1 at a time, beating well after each addition. Beat in vanilla. Add flour mixture and milk alternately in batches, beginning and ending with flour mixture and beating after each addition until just combined, and beat in zest (do not overmix).

Pour batter into pan and bake in middle of oven 35 to 40 minutes, or until a tester comes out clean. Cool cake in pan on a rack 5 minutes and invert onto rack. Peel off wax paper and cool cake completely.

Make Second Batch of Batter: Butter a 6-inch round cake pan and an 8-inch round cake pan (each at least 2 inches deep) and line with rounds of wax paper. Butter paper and dust pans with flour, knocking out excess flour. Make batter in same manner.

Pour 1¾ cups batter into 6-inch pan. Pour remaining batter into 8-inch pan. Bake 6-inch cake in middle of oven 30 to 35 minutes and 8-inch cake 35 to 40 minutes, or until a tester comes out clean. Cool cakes in pans on racks 5 minutes and invert onto racks. Peel off wax paper and cool cakes completely.

Cake layers may be made 2 weeks ahead and frozen, wrapped well in plastic wrap and foil. Defrost cake layers (without unwrapping) at room temperature.

Make Syrup: With a vegetable peeler remove zest from lemon in strips. In a small saucepan bring zest, sugar, and water to a boil, stirring until sugar is dissolved. Remove pan from heat and cool syrup completely. Discard zest and stir in lemon juice and *eau-de-vie. Syrup may be made 2 weeks ahead and chilled in an airtight container.*

Assemble Cake: With a long serrated knife horizontally halve each layer. Put each 10-inch layer, cut side up, on a 9-inch cardboard round. Put 8-inch layers similarly on 7-inch rounds and 6-inch layers on 5-inch rounds. Brush cut sides of all 6 layers generously with syrup, dividing it evenly among layers, and let layers stand 15 minutes to absorb syrup.

Spread about 1½ cups buttercream on top half of 10-inch layer and arrange enough raspberries, side by side and open ends down, in concentric circles to cover layer. Invert bottom half of 10-inch layer, cut side down, on top of berries and gently press layers together to form an even tier. (Discard top cardboard round.) Frost top and side smoothly

with some remaining buttercream and chill while assembling remaining 2 tiers.

Assemble and frost 8-inch tier in same manner (use about 1 cup buttercream between layers) and chill while assembling remaining tier. Assemble and frost 6-inch tier in same manner (use about ⅔ cup buttercream between layers). Chill frosted tiers until buttercream is firm.

Cut 3 straws in half and insert 1 straw piece all the way into center of 10-inch bottom tier. Trim straw level with top of tier and insert remaining 5 straw pieces in a circle about 1½ inches from center straw, trimming them. (Straws serve to support tiers.) Carefully put 8-inch middle tier (still on cardboard) in center of bottom tier. Cut remaining 2 straws in half and insert into middle tier, with 1 straw piece in center and remaining 3 straw pieces in a circle around it, trimming straws level with top of tier. Carefully put 6-inch top tier (still on cardboard) in center of middle tier.

Fill in any gaps between tiers with buttercream and transfer remaining buttercream to a pastry bag fitted with a small (#66) leaf tip. Pipe a decorative border around top edge of top tier. With a medium-sized (#70) leaf tip pipe border in same manner around bottom edges of top and middle tiers. With same tip pipe 5 evenly spaced ribbons from top to bottom of cake. (These ribbons will support cascades of crystallized flowers.)

Transfer cake to a cake stand or other serving plate and with a larger (#113) leaf tip pipe border around bottom edge of cake. With same tip pipe mound of buttercream on top of cake. (This mound will support crystallized flower arrangement.)

Arrange crystallized flowers and mint leaves decoratively on top and sides of cake. *Chill cake at least 6 hours and up to 1 day. Let cake stand at cool room temperature (buttercream is sensitive to warm temperatures) 2 to 4 hours before serving.*

Serve cake with *crème fraîche* ice cream and raspberries. **SERVES ABOUT 50 (INCLUDING TOP TIER).**

Photo on page 83

LEMON MERINGUE BUTTERCREAM

For Lemon Curd

5 large egg yolks
½ cup plus 2 tablespoons sugar
½ cup fresh lemon juice
½ stick (¼ cup) unsalted butter, softened

For Buttercream

10 sticks (5 cups) unsalted butter
2 cups sugar
⅔ cup water
8 large egg whites
¾ teaspoon cream of tartar
½ teaspoon salt
3 to 4 tablespoons *eau-de-vie de framboise*

Make Lemon Curd: In a small heavy saucepan whisk together yolks and sugar and whisk in lemon juice, butter, and a pinch salt. Cook mixture over moderately low heat, whisking, until it just reaches boiling point, 5 to 7 minutes (do not let boil). Pour curd through a fine sieve into a bowl and cool, its surface covered with plastic wrap. *Chill lemon curd, covered, at least 4 hours and up to 24.*

Make Buttercream: Cut butter into pieces and soften to cool room temperature. In a heavy saucepan bring sugar and water to a boil, stirring until sugar is dissolved. Boil syrup, without stirring, until a candy thermometer registers 248° F. While syrup is boiling, in a standing electric mixer beat whites with a pinch salt until foamy and beat in cream of tartar. Beat whites until they just hold stiff peaks and add hot syrup in a stream, beating. Beat mixture on medium speed until *completely* cool, 15 to 20 minutes. Beat in butter 1 piece at a time, and beat until thick and smooth. (Buttercream will at first appear very thin but as more butter is beaten in, it will thicken.) Beat in lemon curd and salt, beating until smooth, and drizzle in *eau-de-vie* 1 tablespoon at a time, beating. *Buttercream may be made 4 days ahead and chilled in an airtight container or 2 weeks ahead and frozen in an airtight container. Let buttercream come completely to room temperature (this may take several hours if frozen) and beat before using.* **MAKES ABOUT 12 CUPS.**

SAMBUCA COFFEE
CREAM CAKE

— · —

For Cake Layers

1 cup whole blanched almonds
½ cup all-purpose flour
½ teaspoon salt
¾ stick (6 tablespoons) unsalted butter
4 large egg whites
1 cup sugar
1 teaspoon vanilla

For Creams

1 teaspoon unflavored gelatin
2 tablespoons water
2 tablespoons instant espresso powder*
2 cups well-chilled heavy cream
¼ cup plus 1 tablespoon sugar
1 teaspoon vanilla

2½ tablespoons Sambuca

available at specialty foods shops, some supermarkets, and by mail order from Adriana's Caravan, tel. (800) 316-0820

Make Cake Layers: Preheat oven to 375° F. and butter a 15½- by 10½- by 1-inch jelly-roll pan. Line bottom of pan with parchment paper and butter parchment. Dust pan with flour, knocking out excess flour.

In a baking pan toast almonds in oven until pale golden, about 7 minutes, and cool completely. In a food processor finely grind toasted almonds. Transfer almonds to a bowl and stir in flour and salt, breaking up any lumps. Melt butter and cool.

In a large bowl with an electric mixer beat whites until they hold soft peaks. Gradually beat in sugar and vanilla and beat whites until very thick and glossy, about 5 minutes. Fold in almond mixture gently but thoroughly and fold in butter until just combined.

Spread batter evenly in jelly-roll pan and bake in middle of oven 15 to 20 minutes, or until pale golden. Slide cake on parchment onto a rack and cool. Invert cake onto a work surface and carefully peel off parchment. Cut cake lengthwise into 3 equal pieces. *Cake layers may be made 1 day ahead and kept, wrapped in plastic wrap, at room temperature.*

Make Creams: In a small saucepan sprinkle gelatin over water and let stand 1 minute to soften gelatin. Heat mixture over low heat, stirring, until gelatin is melted and mixture is clear and cool to room temperature (gelatin must be cool but still liquid to blend with cream).

In a small bowl whisk together espresso powder, ¼ cup cream, and 1 tablespoon sugar until espresso powder is dissolved. In a large bowl with cleaned beaters beat remaining 1¾ cups cream with remaining ¼ cup sugar and vanilla until it begins to thicken. Beat in gelatin mixture in a stream and beat until cream just holds stiff peaks (do not overbeat). Transfer ½ cup cream mixture to a pastry bag fitted with a small plain tip and chill. Whisk coffee mixture into remaining cream mixture until it holds stiff peaks.

Assemble Cake: Arrange 1 cake layer on a platter and sprinkle with one third Sambuca. Spread cake layer with one fourth coffee cream mixture. Repeat layering twice and with a long metal spatula frost sides of cake with remaining coffee cream. Pipe plain cream mixture decoratively over top of cake. *Chill cake, uncovered, until frosting is firm, about 1 hour. Cake may be made 1 day ahead and chilled, loosely covered with plastic wrap.* SERVES 14 TO 16.

Photo on page 13

PINEAPPLE COCONUT LAYER CAKE

— · —

For Cake Layers

2⅓ cups cake flour (not self-rising)

2½ teaspoons baking powder

½ teaspoon salt

1 cup milk

1½ teaspoons vanilla

5 large eggs

2 sticks (1 cup) unsalted butter, softened

1½ cups sugar

For Filling

a 28-ounce can crushed pineapple in
    unsweetened juice

1 tablespoon cornstarch

a rounded ¼ cup sugar

2⅔ cups sweetened flaked coconut
    (a 7-ounce bag)

For Seven-minute Frosting

2 large egg whites

1½ cups sugar

½ cup water

1 tablespoon light corn syrup

1 teaspoon vanilla

Preheat oven to 350° F. Butter two 9- by 2-inch round cake pans and line bottoms with rounds of wax paper or parchment paper. Butter paper and dust pans with flour, knocking out excess flour.

Make Cake Layers: Into a bowl sift together flour, baking powder, and salt. In a glass measuring cup stir together milk and vanilla. In a bowl lightly beat eggs. In another bowl with an electric mixer on medium speed beat butter 1 minute and add sugar in a steady stream, beating until light and fluffy, about 4 minutes, scraping down side of bowl occasionally.

Beat in eggs a little at a time, beating well after each addition, until pale and fluffy. Stir in flour mixture in 4 batches alternately with milk mixture, beginning and ending with flour mixture and stirring after each addition until batter is smooth.

Divide batter between pans, smoothing tops, and bake in middle of oven until a tester inserted in center comes out clean, about 30 minutes. Cool cake layers in pans on racks 10 minutes. Run a thin knife around edge of each pan and invert layers onto racks. Peel off wax paper and cool layers completely. *Cake layers may be made 5 days ahead and frozen, wrapped in plastic wrap and foil. Thaw cake layers in refrigerator 1 day before proceeding with recipe.*

Make Filling: In a heavy saucepan stir together pineapple, cornstarch, and sugar until cornstarch is dissolved. Bring mixture to a boil, stirring constantly, and simmer, stirring, 3 minutes. Cool filling completely. *Filling may be made 3 days ahead and chilled, covered.*

Assemble Cake: With a long serrated knife horizontally halve each cake layer. On a cake plate stack cake layers, spreading filling between them.

Toast coconut until golden and cool.

Make Frosting: In top of a double boiler or in a large metal bowl with a hand-held electric mixer beat together all frosting ingredients except vanilla until combined. Set mixture over a pan of boiling water and beat on high speed until it holds stiff, glossy peaks, about 7 minutes. (Depending on mixer and weather this may take longer than 7 minutes.) Remove top of double boiler or bowl from heat and beat in vanilla. Continue to beat frosting until cooled and spreadable.

Spread cake with frosting and coat with coconut.
SERVES 12.

Photo opposite

ESPRESSO CRÈME BRÛLÉE NAPOLEONS

For Custard

1 vanilla bean
1½ cups heavy cream
1 cup whole milk
⅔ cup granulated sugar
2 tablespoons instant espresso powder*
8 large egg yolks

For Phyllo Squares

½ cup pecans
¼ cup granulated sugar
5 tablespoons unsalted butter
eight 18- by 14-inch *phyllo* sheets
1½ tablespoons confectioners' sugar

ACCOMPANIMENT: Kahlúa caramel sauce (recipe follows)

available at specialty foods shops, some supermarkets, and by mail order from Adriana's Caravan, tel. (800) 316-0820

Make Custard: Preheat oven to 300° F. Set a 13- by 9-inch baking dish in a larger baking pan.

Split vanilla bean lengthwise. In a saucepan bring cream, milk, sugar, espresso powder, and vanilla bean just to a boil, whisking until espresso powder is dissolved, and remove pan from heat. *Let mixture stand, covered, 30 minutes.* Scrape seeds from vanilla bean into mixture. In a small bowl lightly beat yolks and whisk into cream mixture.

Pour custard through a fine sieve into baking dish and add enough hot water to baking pan to reach halfway up sides of dish. Bake custard in middle of oven 30 to 35 minutes, or until center is set. Transfer baking dish to a rack and cool custard. *Custard may be made 2 days ahead and chilled, covered.*

Make Phyllo Squares: Preheat oven to 350° F.

In a baking pan toast pecans until fragrant, 5 to 10 minutes, and cool completely. In a food processor finely grind pecans with sugar. Melt butter. Trim stack of *phyllo* sheets to 12 by 9 inches and cover with 2 overlapping sheets plastic wrap and then a damp kitchen towel.

On a work surface generously brush 1 *phyllo* sheet with some melted butter and sprinkle evenly with about 1½ tablespoons pecan mixture. Top coated *phyllo* sheet with 3 more sheets, brushing and sprinkling each in same manner, and cut coated stack of *phyllo* into twelve 3-inch squares. Arrange squares, nut sides up, on a baking sheet and cover with a sheet of parchment (to lightly weight squares). Bake squares in middle of oven 8 to 10 minutes, or until golden brown and crisp, and transfer to a rack to cool. Make 12 more squares in same manner.

Preheat broiler.

Arrange baked squares very close together on 2 baking sheets. Sift half of confectioners' sugar evenly over 1 sheet of squares and broil 4 to 5 inches from heat just until sugar is caramelized, about 25 to 30 seconds (watch carefully). Transfer broiled *phyllo* squares to rack to cool. Sift remaining confectioners' sugar over remaining squares and broil in same manner. *Phyllo squares may be made 1 day ahead and kept in an airtight container at room temperature.*

Assemble Napoleons: Transfer custard to a bowl and whisk until smooth. On a plate top 1 phyllo square with a scant ¼ cup custard and arrange a second square on top, gently pressing to anchor. Top square with a scant ¼ cup custard and arrange a third square on top, gently pressing. Assemble 7 more napoleons in same manner.

Drizzle warm caramel sauce around napoleons.
SERVES 8.

KAHLÚA CARAMEL SAUCE ⊕

1 cup sugar
¼ cup water
¾ cup heavy cream
1½ tablespoons Kahlúa, or to taste

In a small heavy saucepan bring sugar and water to a boil, stirring until sugar is dissolved, and boil mixture without stirring, swirling pan occasionally, until a deep golden caramel. Remove pan from heat. Add cream (mixture will bubble up) and cook sauce over low heat, stirring, until smooth. Stir in Kahlúa and cool sauce slightly. *Sauce may be made 3 days ahead and cooled completely before being chilled in an airtight container. Reheat sauce over low heat, stirring.* MAKES ABOUT 1¼ CUPS.

BERRY LEMON TART

For Dough
1 stick (½ cup) cold unsalted butter
1 large egg yolk
2 tablespoons cold water
1¼ cups all-purpose flour
3 tablespoons sugar
¼ teaspoon salt

For Filling
¾ stick (6 tablespoons) unsalted butter
5 whole large eggs
1 cup plus 2 tablespoons sugar
⅔ cup fresh lemon juice
⅓ cup heavy cream
¼ teaspoon salt
1 tablespoon finely grated fresh lemon zest

pie weights or raw rice for weighting shell
1 large egg white
3 cups picked-over mixed fresh berries

ACCOMPANIMENT: sweetened whipped cream

Make Dough: Cut butter into ½-inch cubes and freeze. In a small bowl whisk together yolk and water. In a food processor pulse together flour, sugar, and salt. Add frozen butter and blend just until mixture resembles coarse meal. Add yolk mixture and pulse until mixture just forms a dough (do not overwork or pastry will be tough). Turn out dough onto a work surface. Form dough into a ball and flatten into a disk. *Chill dough, wrapped in plastic wrap, at least 2 hours and up to 1 day.*

Make Filling: Cut butter into pieces. In a heavy saucepan whisk together eggs, sugar, and lemon juice. Add cream, butter, and salt and cook over moderate heat, whisking, until it just reaches boiling point (do not boil). With a rubber spatula immediately force mixture through a fine sieve into a bowl. Whisk in zest and cool filling, its surface covered with wax paper. *Chill filling, covered, until cold, at least 3 hours, and up to 1 day.*

On a lightly floured surface roll out dough into a 12-inch round (about ⅛ inch thick). Fit dough into a 9½-inch tart pan with a removable fluted rim and trim overhang flush with pan. *Chill shell until firm, about 1 hour.*

Preheat oven to 400° F.

Line shell with foil and fill with pie weights or rice. Bake shell in middle of oven 10 minutes. Remove foil and weights carefully and bake shell until pale golden on bottom, 5 to 10 minutes more. Lightly beat egg white and brush bottom of shell lightly with it. Bake shell just until glaze is set, 1 to 2 minutes more. Cool shell in pan on a rack.

Reduce temperature to 325° F.

Spread filling evenly in shell and bake tart in middle of oven until filling is set, 30 to 35 minutes. Cool tart completely in pan on rack and remove rim. Transfer tart to a plate. *Tart may be made 1 day ahead and chilled, covered.*

Mound berries on tart. Serve tart chilled or at room temperature with whipped cream.

MACADAMIA RUM BAKED ALASKA

For Pound Cake
    2 cups cake flour (not self-rising)
    1 teaspoon baking powder
    ¼ teaspoon salt
    5 whole large eggs
    2 sticks (1 cup) unsalted butter, softened
    1¼ cups sugar
    1½ tablespoons dark rum

For Syrup
    ⅓ cup sugar
    ⅔ cup water
    3 tablespoons dark rum

For Ice-cream Mixture
    1 cup macadamia nuts
    1½ pints (3 cups) super-premium
        vanilla ice cream, softened

For Meringue
    12 large egg whites
    ½ teaspoon salt
    3 cups sugar

Make Pound Cake: Preheat oven to 325° F. Butter and flour a 9- by 5- by 3-inch loaf pan, knocking out excess flour.

Onto a sheet of wax paper sift together flour, baking powder, and salt. In a bowl lightly beat eggs. In a bowl with an electric mixer on medium speed beat butter 1 minute and beat in sugar in a steady stream, beating until light and fluffy. Add eggs a little at a time, beating well after each addition and scraping down side of bowl occasionally. Add rum, beating until mixture is pale and fluffy. Add flour mixture, about one third at a time, beating well after each addition, and beat until batter is smooth. Spoon batter into loaf pan, smoothing top, and bake in middle of oven until a tester comes out clean, about 1 hour and 10 minutes. Cool cake in pan on a rack 10 minutes. Invert cake onto rack and cool completely.

Make Syrup: In a small saucepan bring sugar and water to a boil, stirring until sugar is dissolved, about 2 minutes. Remove pan from heat and stir in rum. Cool syrup to room temperature.

Make Ice-cream Mixture: Preheat oven to 350° F.

Coarsely chop nuts. Toast nuts on a baking sheet in oven about 6 minutes, or until pale golden, and cool completely. In a metal bowl stir together ice cream and nuts and freeze until needed.

Assemble Cake: Line cleaned loaf pan with plastic wrap, leaving a 3-inch overhang on short sides. With a serrated knife horizontally halve cake and reserve bottom half for another use. Horizontally halve remaining cake and put bottom layer in loaf pan. Brush layer in pan and cut side of other layer with syrup. Working quickly, spread ice cream evenly over layer in pan and top with remaining layer, rounded side up. *Freeze cake, covered, until frozen hard, at least 6 hours, and up to 3 days.*

Make Meringue: Preheat oven to 450° F.

In large bowl of standing electric mixer stir together whites, salt, and sugar. Set bowl over a pan of simmering water and stir mixture just until sugar is dissolved. Remove bowl from heat and with mixer beat meringue until it holds stiff, glossy peaks.

Working quickly, remove cake from pan and arrange, flat side down, on an ovenproof shallow platter. With a rubber spatula spread cake evenly with a generous layer of meringue, covering it completely. Transfer remaining meringue to a pastry bag fitted with a large star tip and pipe it generously on and around dessert. Bake dessert in middle of oven 4 to 5 minutes, or until meringue is golden brown. Serve immediately. **SERVES 8.**

Photo opposite

SOFT-FROZEN CARAMEL PARFAITS WITH NUT BRITTLE

— · —

For Parfaits

½ vanilla bean

½ cup whole milk

1½ cups heavy cream (1 cup well-chilled)

1 cup sugar

3 tablespoons water

6 large egg yolks

six 7-ounce paper cups

For Brittle

½ cup almonds, hazelnuts, pecans, or walnuts

½ cup sugar

2 tablespoons strong brewed coffee

2 tablespoons light corn syrup

1 teaspoon baking soda

ACCOMPANIMENTS

whipped cream

raspberry sauce (page 81) or hot fudge
  sauce (page 99)

Make Parfaits: Split vanilla bean lengthwise. In a small saucepan bring milk, ½ cup cream, and vanilla bean just to a boil and remove pan from heat. *Let mixture stand, covered, 30 minutes.* Scrape seeds from vanilla bean into mixture.

In a heavy saucepan bring ¾ cup sugar and water to a boil, stirring until sugar is dissolved, and boil without stirring, swirling pan, until a deep golden caramel. Remove pan from heat. Carefully add cream mixture (mixture will bubble and steam) and whisk until smooth. Cook caramel mixture over low heat, whisking, until smooth.

In a metal bowl whisk together yolks, remaining ¼ cup sugar, and a pinch salt. Add hot caramel mixture in a stream, whisking, and transfer custard to saucepan. Cook custard over moderately low heat,

stirring, just until thickened and an instant-read thermometer registers 170° F. (do not boil). Pour custard through a fine sieve into a metal bowl and with an electric mixer beat until cool, mousse-like, and beaters leave distinct marks, about 10 minutes.

In another bowl with cleaned beaters beat remaining cup (chilled) cream until it just holds stiff peaks. Whisk about one fourth cream into caramel mixture to lighten and fold in remaining cream gently but thoroughly. Divide mixture among paper cups (they will be about three fourths full) and cover each cup with foil. *Freeze parfaits at least 12 hours and up to 2 days.*

Make Brittle: Preheat oven to 350° F.

In a baking pan toast nuts in oven until fragrant, 5 to 10 minutes. Cool nuts and chop coarse. In a small heavy saucepan bring sugar, coffee, and corn syrup to a boil, stirring until sugar is dissolved, and boil mixture until very thick and bubbly and a candy thermometer registers 310° F. (tilt saucepan to get accurate reading). Remove pan from heat and immediately stir in baking soda (mixture will foam and thicken). Working quickly, stir in nuts and pour mixture into baking pan. Cool brittle completely and transfer to a heavy-duty plastic bag. Coarsely crush brittle with a rolling pin. *Brittle keeps in an airtight container at room temperature 1 week.*

Assemble Parfaits: Carefully tear off each paper cup and invert frozen parfaits onto plates. Spoon whipped cream over parfaits and drizzle plates with sauce. Sprinkle parfaits with brittle. **SERVES 6.**

BITTERSWEET CHOCOLATE TORTE WITH ARMAGNAC SABAYON CREAM

12 ounces fine-quality bittersweet chocolate
(not unsweetened)
1¼ sticks (½ cup plus 2 tablespoons) unsalted
butter
¾ cup granulated sugar
1 teaspoon vanilla
¼ teaspoon salt
5 large eggs, separated
⅓ cup all-purpose flour
confectioners' sugar for dusting torte

ACCOMPANIMENT: Armagnac sabayon cream
(recipe follows)

Preheat oven to 350° F. Butter and flour a 9½-inch springform pan.

Chop chocolate and cut butter into pieces. In a metal bowl set over a saucepan of barely simmering water melt chocolate and butter, whisking until smooth. Remove bowl from heat and cool mixture to lukewarm. Whisk in granulated sugar, vanilla, and salt and add yolks 1 at a time, whisking well after each addition.

In a bowl with an electric mixer beat whites with a pinch salt until they just hold stiff peaks. Whisk flour into chocolate mixture until just combined and whisk in about one fourth whites to lighten. Fold in remaining whites gently but thoroughly and turn batter into baking pan, spreading evenly. Bake torte in middle of oven 30 to 35 minutes, or until a tester inserted about 1 inch from edge comes out with moist crumbs adhering. Cool torte in pan on a rack 10 minutes. Remove side of pan and cool torte completely. Invert torte onto rack and remove bottom of pan. Invert torte onto a plate. *Torte may be made 1 day ahead and kept, wrapped in plastic wrap, at room temperature.*

Dust torte with confectioners' sugar and serve with *sabayon* cream. **SERVES 10 TO 12.**

ARMAGNAC SABAYON CREAM

4 large egg yolks
¼ cup plus 2 tablespoons sugar
1¼ cups heavy cream (1 cup well-chilled)
¼ cup Armagnac

In a metal bowl whisk together yolks, sugar, ¼ cup cream, and Armagnac. Set bowl over a saucepan of simmering water and cook mixture, whisking constantly, until golden, very thick, and an instant-read thermometer registers 160° F. Remove bowl from heat and with a rubber spatula force *sabayon* through a fine sieve into another metal bowl. Set bowl in a larger bowl of ice and cold water and cool *sabayon*, gently stirring with rubber spatula, until cold. *Sabayon cream may be prepared up to this point 1 day ahead and chilled, covered.*

In a bowl with an electric mixer beat remaining cup (chilled) cream until it just holds stiff peaks and whisk about one fourth cream into *sabayon* to lighten. Fold in remaining cream gently but thoroughly. **MAKES ABOUT 2½ CUPS.**

SPICE LAYER CAKE WITH MOCHA BUTTERCREAM AND TOASTED PECANS

For Cake Layers

    2 cups all-purpose flour
    1 tablespoon cinnamon
    1½ teaspoons freshly grated nutmeg
    1½ teaspoons ground cloves
    ¾ teaspoon salt
    3 tablespoons unsweetened cocoa powder
       (not Dutch-process)
    1½ teaspoons baking soda
    1½ teaspoons baking powder
    2 sticks (1 cup) unsalted butter, softened
    1⅔ cups sugar
    4 large eggs
    1½ teaspoons vanilla
    1½ cups well-shaken buttermilk

    1½ cups pecans (about 6 ounces)
    mocha buttercream (recipe follows)

    GARNISH: pecan halves

Preheat oven to 350° F. Butter two 9- by 2-inch round cake pans and line bottoms with rounds of wax paper. Butter paper and dust pans with flour, knocking out excess flour.

Make Cake Layers: Into a bowl sift together flour, spices, salt, cocoa powder, baking soda, and baking powder. In a large bowl with an electric mixer beat together butter and sugar until light and fluffy. Beat in eggs 1 at a time, beating well after each addition, and beat in vanilla. Beat flour mixture into butter mixture in batches alternately with buttermilk, beginning and ending with flour mixture and beating after each addition until just combined.

Divide batter between pans, smoothing tops, and bake in middle of oven 30 to 35 minutes, or until

a tester comes out clean. Cool layers in pans on racks 5 minutes and invert onto racks to cool completely. *Cake layers may be made 1 day ahead and kept, wrapped well in plastic wrap or in airtight containers, at room temperature.*

In a shallow baking pan toast pecans in middle of oven until a shade darker, 7 to 10 minutes. Cool pecans and finely chop.

Assemble Cake: With a long serrated knife horizontally halve each cake layer. Put 1 cake layer on a plate, cut side up, and spread evenly with about ½ cup buttercream. Sprinkle ⅓ cup pecans evenly over buttercream and top with another cake layer, cut side down. Continue layering in same manner, making sure last layer is cut side down, and spread top and side of cake evenly with some remaining buttercream. Press remaining ½ cup chopped pecans decoratively onto side of cake. Transfer remaining buttercream to a pastry bag fitted with a large star tip and pipe rosettes evenly around top edge of cake. Garnish cake with pecan halves. **SERVES 12.**

Photo opposite

MOCHA BUTTERCREAM

    4 sticks (2 cups) unsalted butter
    2½ tablespoons instant espresso powder*
    3 ounces fine-quality bittersweet chocolate
       (not unsweetened)
    ½ cup water
    1 cup sugar
    4 large egg whites
    ¼ teaspoon cream of tartar
    ¼ teaspoon salt

    * *available at specialty foods shops, some supermarkets, and by mail order from Adriana's Caravan, tel. (800) 316-0820*

Cut butter into pieces and soften to cool room temperature. In a cup dissolve espresso powder in 1 tablespoon hot water. Chop chocolate and in a metal bowl set over a saucepan of barely simmering water melt it, stirring until smooth. Remove bowl from pan and cool chocolate.

In a 1½-quart heavy saucepan bring ½ cup water and sugar to a boil, stirring until sugar is dissolved. Boil syrup, without stirring, until a candy thermometer registers 248° F.

While syrup is boiling, in bowl of a standing electric mixer beat whites with a pinch salt until foamy and beat in cream of tartar. Beat whites until they just hold stiff peaks and add hot syrup in a stream, beating. Beat mixture on medium speed until *completely* cool, 5 to 10 minutes. Beat in butter, 1 piece at a time, until mixture is thick and smooth. (Buttercream will at first appear very thin but as more butter is beaten in, it will thicken.) Beat in espresso mixture, chocolate, and salt, beating until smooth. *Buttercream may be made 2 days ahead and chilled in an airtight container. Bring buttercream completely to room temperature and beat before frosting cake.* MAKES ABOUT 4½ CUPS.

PROFITEROLES WITH BURNT ORANGE ICE CREAM

For Ice Cream

1½ cups heavy cream

1½ cups whole milk

2 tablespoons finely grated fresh orange zest

1 cup sugar

½ cup strained fresh orange juice

6 large egg yolks

¼ teaspoon salt

½ teaspoon vanilla

For Profiteroles

¾ cup water

¾ stick (6 tablespoons) unsalted butter

¼ teaspoon salt

¾ cup all-purpose flour

3 whole large eggs

ACCOMPANIMENT: hot fudge sauce (recipe follows)

Make Ice Cream: In a saucepan bring cream, milk, and zest just to a boil and remove pan from heat. *Let mixture stand, covered, 30 minutes.*

In a heavy saucepan combine ¾ cup sugar and orange juice and bring to a boil, stirring until sugar is dissolved. Boil juice mixture without stirring, swirling pan occasionally, until a deep golden caramel and remove pan from heat. Carefully add about ½ cup cream mixture (mixture will bubble and steam) and whisk until smooth. Cook mixture over very low heat, whisking in remaining cream mixture ½ cup at a time, until hot.

In a metal bowl whisk together yolks, remaining ¼ cup sugar, and salt and add hot caramel mixture in a stream, whisking. Transfer custard to saucepan and cook over moderately low heat, stirring, until slightly thickened and an instant-read thermometer registers

170° F. (do not boil). Pour custard through a fine sieve into a bowl. Stir in vanilla and cool custard. *Chill custard, covered, at least 1 hour and up to 24.* Freeze custard in an ice-cream maker. Transfer ice cream to an airtight container and put in freezer to harden. *Ice cream may be made 2 days ahead.*

Make Profiteroles: Preheat oven to 400° F. and grease 2 large baking sheets.

In a small heavy saucepan bring water, butter, and salt to a boil over high heat, stirring until butter is melted. Reduce heat to moderate. Add flour all at once and cook, beating with a wooden spoon, until mixture pulls away from side of pan and forms a ball, about 30 seconds. Immediately transfer mixture to a bowl and with an electric mixer at high speed beat in eggs 1 at a time, beating well after each addition.

Transfer warm mixture to a large pastry bag fitted with a ½-inch plain tip and pipe 18 mounds with peaks (each mound about 1¼ inches in diameter) about 1 inch apart onto each baking sheet. Bake profiteroles in upper and lower thirds of oven, switching position of sheets halfway through baking, 20 to 25 minutes total, or until puffed and golden. Cool profiteroles on a rack. *Profiteroles may be made 1 day ahead and kept in an airtight container at room temperature. Reheat profiteroles on a baking sheet in a preheated 375° F. oven 5 minutes, or until crisp, and cool on a rack.*

Assemble Profiteroles: With a serrated knife horizontally halve each profiterole and sandwich a small scoop (about 1¼ inches) ice cream between halves. In each of 6 goblets or shallow bowls arrange 6 profiteroles and top with hot fudge sauce. SERVES 6.

Photo on front jacket

HOT FUDGE SAUCE

12 ounces fine-quality bittersweet chocolate
½ stick (¼ cup) unsalted butter
½ cup Dutch-process unsweetened cocoa powder
⅔ cup packed dark brown sugar
1 cup light corn syrup
1⅓ cups heavy cream
½ teaspoon salt
2 teaspoons vanilla

Chop chocolate and cut butter into pieces. In a heavy saucepan stir together cocoa powder, brown sugar, syrup, cream, salt, and half of chocolate and cook over moderate heat, stirring, until chocolate is melted. Cook mixture at a low boil, stirring occasionally, 5 minutes and remove pan from heat. Add remaining chocolate, butter, and vanilla and stir until smooth. Cool sauce slightly. *Sauce may be made 1 week ahead and cooled completely before being chilled in an airtight container. Reheat sauce over low heat, stirring.* MAKES ABOUT 4 CUPS.

LEMON RUM CHARLOTTE

For Candied Zest and Syrup
   1 lemon
   ¼ cup plus 3 tablespoons sugar
   1 cup water
   ⅓ cup dark rum or brandy

For Lemon Curd
   4 large egg yolks
   ⅓ cup sugar
   ½ cup fresh lemon juice
   3 tablespoons unsalted butter

   two 3-ounce packages spongecake ladyfingers (about 48)
   8 ounces *mascarpone* cheese
   1 cup well-chilled heavy cream

Make Candied Zest and Syrup: With a vegetable peeler remove zest from lemon in strips and cut into fine julienne strips. In a small saucepan cover zest with water and bring to a boil. Drain zest in a sieve and return to pan. Add ¼ cup sugar and ½ cup water and simmer zest, uncovered, stirring occasionally, 15 minutes, or until zest is translucent and liquid is syrupy. With a fork remove zest from syrup, letting excess syrup drip off, and transfer zest to a sheet of wax paper to cool. Reserve syrup in pan. In a bowl toss zest with remaining 3 tablespoons sugar, separating strips, until well coated. Transfer zest to another sheet of wax paper and arrange in one layer. *Dry candied zest 30 minutes.*

While zest is drying, stir rum or brandy and remaining ½ cup water into reserved syrup and boil, stirring, 5 minutes, or until reduced to about ⅔ cup. *Zest and syrup may be made 1 week ahead and chilled separately in airtight containers.*

Make Lemon Curd: In a saucepan whisk together yolks, sugar, lemon juice, and a pinch salt. Add butter and cook over moderate heat, whisking, until thickened and curd just begins to simmer. Transfer curd to a bowl and cool. *Chill curd, covered, until cold, at least 3 hours, and up to 3 days.*

Assemble Charlotte: Line bottom of an 8½-inch springform pan with a round of parchment paper.

Line side and bottom of pan with about three fourths ladyfingers, rounded sides out, and brush with about three fourths syrup.

In a bowl with an electric mixer beat together *mascarpone* and cream until mixture just holds stiff peaks (do not overbeat). Gently fold in lemon curd and pour half of lemon cream over ladyfingers in bottom of pan. Arrange remaining ladyfingers in one layer on top of lemon cream in pan and brush with remaining syrup. Pour remaining lemon cream over ladyfingers, smoothing top. *Chill charlotte, covered loosely, at least 2 hours and up to 1 day.*

Carefully remove side of pan and top charlotte with candied zest. SERVES 8.

SWEDISH MERINGUE CAKE

For Cake Layers

1½ cups cake flour (not self rising)
1½ teaspoons baking powder
¼ teaspoon salt
1½ sticks (¾ cup) unsalted butter, softened
1¾ cups granulated sugar
6 large eggs, separated
1 teaspoon vanilla
½ cup milk
½ cup sliced blanched almonds

For Orange Filling

½ cup granulated sugar
3 tablespoons cornstarch
1 teaspoon finely grated fresh orange zest
½ teaspoon finely grated fresh lemon zest
¾ cup fresh orange juice
2 tablespoons fresh lemon juice
2 large egg yolks

1½ pints picked-over strawberries
1 cup well-chilled heavy cream
2 tablespoons confectioners' sugar

Make Cake Layers: Preheat oven to 350° F. Butter three 9- by 2-inch round cake pans and line bottoms with rounds of wax paper. Butter paper and dust pans with flour, knocking out excess flour.

Into a bowl sift together flour, baking powder, and salt. In bowl of an electric mixer beat together butter and ¾ cup granulated sugar until light and fluffy. Add yolks 1 at a time, beating well after each addition, and beat in vanilla. Add flour mixture and milk alternately in batches, beginning and ending with flour mixture, and beating well after each addition. Divide batter among pans, spreading evenly and smoothing tops.

In an electric coffee/spice grinder finely grind almonds. In cleaned bowl of mixer with cleaned beaters beat whites with a pinch salt until they hold soft peaks. Gradually beat in remaining cup sugar and beat meringue until it just holds stiff peaks. Fold in almonds gently but thoroughly (do not beat in almonds). Spread meringue evenly over batter, smoothing it, and bake layers in middle of oven 30 to 35 minutes, or until a tester comes out clean. Cool layers in pans on racks. Run a thin knife around edges of each pan and invert layers onto racks. Peel off wax paper and cool layers completely. *Cake layers may be made 1 day ahead and kept wrapped in plastic wrap at room temperature.*

Make Filling: In a heavy saucepan whisk together granulated sugar, cornstarch, and a pinch salt. In a bowl whisk together zests, juices, and yolks and whisk into sugar mixture until combined well. Bring mixture to a boil, whisking, and boil gently, whisking, 2 minutes. Remove pan from heat and cool filling, whisking occasionally.

Assemble Cake: Reserve 11 strawberries for garnish. Trim remaining berries and finely chop. Arrange 1 cake layer, meringue side up, on a plate. Spread about half of filling over meringue and top with about half of chopped strawberries, spreading evenly. Arrange another layer, meringue side up, on strawberries and spread with remaining filling and chopped strawberries in same manner. Arrange remaining layer, meringue side up, on strawberries. *Cake may be assembled up to this point 6 hours ahead and chilled, covered with plastic wrap.*

In a bowl with an electric mixer beat cream until it holds soft peaks. Beat in confectioners' sugar and beat until cream just holds stiff peaks. Transfer whipped cream to a pastry bag fitted with a star tip and pipe a circle decoratively around top edge of cake. Pipe another circle 1 inch inside first circle and pipe a rosette in center. Pipe another circle around base of cake. Quarter 10 strawberries lengthwise and arrange decoratively inside concentric circles. Arrange remaining strawberry on rosette. **SERVES 12.**

Photo opposite

CHOCOLATE MOUSSE AND RASPBERRY CREAM DACQUOISE

— : —

For Meringues

1 cup hazelnuts

2 cups sugar

½ teaspoon salt

1 cup egg whites (about 8 large egg whites)

3 ounces fine-quality bittersweet chocolate (not unsweetened)

For Mousse

7 ounces fine-quality bittersweet chocolate (not unsweetened)

2 ounces unsweetened chocolate

3 tablespoons *eau-de-vie de framboise*

⅓ cup strong brewed coffee

1¼ cups sugar

½ cup water

4 large egg whites

¼ teaspoon cream of tartar

For Whipped Cream

1 tablespoon plus 2 teaspoons unflavored gelatin (less than 2 envelopes)

¼ cup *eau-de-vie de framboise*

2 tablespoons water

4 cups well-chilled heavy cream

¼ cup sugar

1½ teaspoons vanilla

2½ cups picked-over raspberries

GARNISH

3 ounces fine-quality bittersweet chocolate (not unsweetened)

about 1 cup picked-over raspberries

Make Meringues: Preheat oven to 375° F.

In a shallow baking pan toast hazelnuts in middle of oven until they begin to turn pale golden, 7 to 10 minutes. Wrap nuts in a kitchen towel and rub to remove any loose skins (do not worry about skins that do not come off). Cool nuts completely.

Reduce oven temperature to 250° F. and butter 3 baking sheets. Line baking sheets with parchment paper or foil and trace an 11-inch circle on each sheet of parchment or foil.

In a food processor finely grind hazelnuts with ½ cup sugar. Transfer nut mixture to a bowl and stir in ½ cup sugar and salt, stirring and fluffing until combined well. In a large bowl with an electric mixer beat whites with a pinch salt until they hold soft peaks. Gradually add remaining cup sugar, beating until whites hold stiff glossy peaks. Fold in hazelnut mixture gently but thoroughly and transfer to a pastry bag fitted with a ½-inch plain tip. Starting in middle of each parchment or foil circle, pipe a tight spiral to fill in circles. Bake meringues on 3 evenly spaced racks or in batches in oven, switching meringues from 1 rack to another every 20 minutes, for 1 hour total, or until firm when touched. Remove parchment or foil from baking sheets and cool meringues on it. Peel off parchment or foil carefully. *Meringues may be made up to this point 1 day ahead and kept wrapped well in plastic wrap at room temperature.*

Chop chocolate. In a metal bowl set over a pan of barely simmering water melt chocolate, stirring until smooth, and cool. Trim meringues to a uniform size if necessary with a serrated knife and reserve best meringue for top layer. Spread smooth side of 1 remaining meringue with melted chocolate (this will be middle layer) and reserve, chocolate side up. Put remaining meringue (this will be bottom layer) on a large flat cake platter.

Make Mousse: Chop chocolates. In a metal bowl set over pan of barely simmering water melt chocolates with *framboise* and coffee, whisking until smooth, and remove bowl from heat. Cool chocolate mixture. In a small heavy saucepan bring sugar and water to a boil, stirring until sugar is dissolved. Boil syrup, without stirring, until a candy thermometer registers 248° F.

While syrup is boiling, in bowl of a standing electric mixer beat whites with a pinch salt until foamy. Add cream of tartar and beat whites until they hold soft peaks. With mixer running, add hot syrup in a stream and beat on medium speed 15 to 20 minutes, or until completely cool. Whisk about 1 cup white mixture into chocolate mixture to lighten and fold chocolate mixture into remaining white mixture gently but thoroughly.

Mound mousse in middle of bottom meringue layer. Top mousse with chocolate-covered meringue layer, chocolate side up, and press layer down gently until mousse almost reaches edge. *Chill cake 1 hour, or until mousse is set.*

Make Whipped Cream: In a very small saucepan sprinkle gelatin over *framboise* and 2 tablespoons water and let stand 1 minute to soften gelatin. Heat mixture over low heat, stirring, until gelatin is dissolved and cool gelatin mixture as much as possible while still remaining liquid. In a chilled large bowl beat cream with sugar and vanilla until thick and beaters just begin to leave a mark. Add gelatin mixture in a stream, beating, and beat until cream just holds stiff peaks. (Do not overbeat.)

In a small bowl reserve about one fourth whipped cream and with a rubber spatula spread half of remaining whipped cream on top of chocolate-covered meringue layer. Arrange raspberries on top

and spread remaining half of whipped cream over them. Put reserved meringue on whipped cream, pressing down gently, and spread some reserved whipped cream on side of cake. Transfer remaining reserved whipped cream to a pastry bag fitted with a star tip and pipe decoratively on top and bottom edges of cake.

Garnish Cake: Chop chocolate. In a metal bowl set over a pan of barely simmering water melt chocolate, stirring until smooth and cool. Transfer melted chocolate to a small pastry bag fitted with a plain writing tip and pipe a spoke pattern on top of cake. Arrange raspberries around edge of cake and in center. *Chill cake at least 4 hours and up to 8.* SERVES 18.

Photo below

KEY LIME MASCARPONE "CANNOLI" WITH MANGO SAUCE

— · —

The key to successfully forming the following cannoli-shaped cookies is the temperature of the cookies: They should still be warm from the oven and pliable enough to roll around the cannoli forms but not so warm that they fall apart. If the cookies are too cool, they will harden. Finding just the right moment to shape the cookies may seem a bit tricky at first, but the rolling is actually quite easy after a practice batch. Therefore, this recipe provides enough dough for about 20 cookies, although only 12 are needed.

For "Cannoli" Shells

about twenty 6-inch squares parchment paper
¾ cup sweetened flaked coconut
5 tablespoons unsalted butter
2 tablespoons all-purpose flour
½ cup granulated sugar
2 tablespoons packed light brown sugar
1 tablespoon milk
four 3½- to 4-inch-long cannoli forms*
    (each about ⅝ inch in diameter)

For Filling

4 ounces cream cheese, softened
⅓ cup granulated sugar
2 teaspoons finely grated fresh lime zest
4 tablespoons bottled Key lime juice**
    or 5 tablespoons fresh lime juice
1 cup *mascarpone* cheese (about 8 ounces)

mango sauce (recipe follows)

ACCOMPANIMENTS
raspberries
sliced star fruit (sometimes called *carambola*)

*available by mail order from Bridge Kitchenware Corp., tel. (800) 274-3435, or (212) 838-1901

**available at specialty foods shops

Make "Cannoli" Shells: Preheat oven to 350° F. and lightly grease a heavy baking sheet. Arrange 4 parchment squares on baking sheet. (Oil or butter makes parchment squares stick to baking sheet).

Toast coconut and cool completely. Cut butter into pieces and soften. In a food processor finely grind coconut with flour. Add butter, sugars, and milk and blend until dough forms a ball, about 10 seconds. Spoon a well-rounded teaspoon of dough onto each of the 4 parchment squares and with slightly wet fingertips evenly pat into 2-inch rounds.

Bake cookies in middle of oven until very thin and golden brown, about 10 minutes. Immediately transfer cookies (on parchment) to a rack and let stand until just firm enough to hold their shape, 30 seconds. Working with 1 cookie at a time and using parchment as an aid, quickly roll cookie around a cannoli form to make a cylinder. (If cookies become too firm to roll, return them on parchment on baking sheet to oven 1 minute to soften.) Cool formed cookies on rack before removing cannoli forms. Make more cookies in same manner with remaining dough, baking and forming cookies in batches of 4 and allowing baking sheet to cool completely between each batch. *Cookies are very fragile. Cookies keep in one layer in an airtight container at room temperature 4 days.*

Make Filling: In a bowl with an electric mixer beat together cream cheese, sugar, zest, and juice until smooth and beat in *mascarpone*. *Chill filling, covered, until firm, at least 4 hours, and up to 1 day.*

Assemble Dessert: Whisk filling and transfer it to a pastry bag fitted with a ¼-inch plain or decorative tip. Carefully pipe filling into both ends of 12 cookies. Pour about ¼ cup mango sauce onto each of 6 dessert plates, tilting plate to distribute sauce evenly, and top with 2 "cannoli," raspberries, and star fruit slices. **SERVES 6.**

Photo below

MANGO SAUCE 🕐

3 ripe mangoes (each about ¾ pound)
2 tablespoons fresh lime juice, or to taste
1 tablespoon superfine granulated sugar, or to taste

Peel and cut flesh from mangoes, discarding pits. In a blender or food processor purée mango with remaining ingredients until smooth. Force purée through a fine sieve into a bowl. *Sauce may be made 2 days ahead and chilled, covered.* **MAKES ABOUT 1½ CUPS.**

MARJOLAINE

For Meringue Layers
1½ cups whole almonds (about 8 ounces)
1 cup sugar
3 tablespoons all-purpose flour
½ teaspoon salt
6 large egg whites

For Praline
⅓ cup whole almonds
⅓ cup sugar
2 tablespoons water

For Ganache
2 ounces fine-quality bittersweet chocolate (not unsweetened)
½ cup plus 2 tablespoons heavy cream (½ cup well-chilled)

For Whipped Cream
⅔ cup well-chilled heavy cream
1 tablespoon sugar

plain buttercream (recipe follows)
4 ounces fine-quality bittersweet chocolate (not unsweetened)

Make Meringue Layers: Preheat oven to 350° F. Lightly grease a 17¾- by 12¾- by 1-inch jelly-roll pan and line bottom and sides with parchment paper.

In a baking pan toast almonds until fragrant, about 10 minutes, and cool.

Reduce temperature to 325° F.

In a food processor finely grind toasted almonds with ½ cup sugar, flour, and ¼ teaspoon salt. In a bowl with an electric mixer beat whites with remaining ¼ teaspoon salt until they hold soft peaks. Beat in remaining ½ cup sugar in a slow stream and beat meringue until it holds stiff, glossy peaks. Fold in almond mixture gently but thoroughly and spread meringue evenly in jelly-roll pan. Bake meringue in middle of oven 25 to 30 minutes, or until golden and slightly springy to the touch, and cool in pan on a rack. Invert meringue onto a work surface and carefully peel off parchment paper. Trim edges of meringue and cut crosswise into 4 pieces, each about 10 by 4 inches.

Make Praline: Preheat oven to 350° F.

In a small baking pan toast almonds in oven until fragrant, about 10 minutes, and transfer to a small bowl to cool. Line baking pan with foil.

In a small heavy saucepan bring sugar and water to a boil, stirring until sugar is dissolved, and boil without stirring, swirling pan occasionally, until a golden caramel. Remove pan from heat and stir in almonds. Immediately pour mixture into baking pan and cool completely. Peel off foil and break praline into pieces. In a small food processor grind half of praline to a paste. Transfer paste to small bowl and reserve for buttercream. Transfer remaining praline to a heavy-duty sealable bag and coarsely crush with a rolling pin. Reserve crushed praline for coating sides of *marjolaine*.

Make Ganache: Chop chocolate. In a small metal bowl set over a saucepan of barely simmering water melt chocolate with 2 tablespoons cream, stirring until smooth. Remove bowl from heat and cool chocolate mixture completely. In a bowl with an electric mixer beat remaining ½ cup (chilled) cream until it holds soft peaks. Beat in chocolate mixture and beat until *ganache* just holds stiff peaks (do not overbeat). Chill *ganache*, covered.

Make Whipped Cream: In a large bowl with cleaned beaters beat cream with sugar until it holds stiff peaks. Chill cream, covered.

Flavor Buttercreams: In a bowl with cleaned beaters beat together ¾ cup plain buttercream and reserved praline paste until smooth and combined well.

Chop chocolate. In a metal bowl set over saucepan of barely simmering water melt chocolate, stirring until smooth. Remove bowl from heat and cool chocolate completely. In another bowl with cleaned beaters beat together remaining buttercream and melted chocolate until combined well.

Assemble Marjolaine: Arrange 1 piece meringue on a platter and spread evenly with *ganache*. Top *ganache* with second meringue layer and spread evenly with praline buttercream. Top praline buttercream with third meringue layer and spread evenly with whipped cream. Top whipped cream with fourth meringue layer and spread top and sides of *marjolaine* with chocolate buttercream. Press reserved crushed praline onto sides. *Chill marjolaine, uncovered, until chocolate buttercream is firm, about 1 hour; then cover marjolaine with plastic wrap and chill 1 day.*

Before slicing, let *marjolaine* stand at cool room temperature, uncovered, 1 to 1½ hours to allow buttercreams to soften. (Alternatively, slice chilled *marjolaine* and let slices stand at room temperature 20 to 30 minutes.) **SERVES 12.**

PLAIN BUTTERCREAM

2 sticks (1 cup) unsalted butter
¼ cup whole milk
4 large egg yolks
¼ cup plus 2 tablespoons sugar
½ teaspoon vanilla

Cut butter into pieces and soften to cool room temperature. In a small heavy saucepan bring milk just to a boil and remove pan from heat. In a small metal bowl whisk together yolks and sugar and whisk in hot milk in a stream. Transfer custard to pan and cook over moderately low heat, whisking, until it registers 160° F. on an instant-read thermometer (do not boil). With a rubber spatula force custard through a fine sieve into bowl of a standing electric mixer and beat until very thick, pale, and custard forms a ribbon when beater is lifted, 5 to 10 minutes. Beat in butter, a few pieces at a time, and beat buttercream until smooth. Beat in vanilla and a pinch salt. *Buttercream may be made 1 day ahead and chilled in an airtight container. Bring buttercream completely to room temperature and beat before using.* **MAKES ABOUT 2 CUPS.**

CHOCOLATE RASPBERRY GANACHE CAKE

For Génoise

⅓ cup sifted unsweetened Dutch-process cocoa powder such as Droste (sift before measuring)

⅓ cup all-purpose flour

⅓ cup cornstarch

a pinch baking soda

3 whole large eggs

3 large egg yolks

⅔ cup sugar

¼ teaspoon salt

For Syrup

⅓ cup water

⅓ cup sugar

⅓ cup raspberry liqueur such as Chambord

For Ganache

1 pound semisweet or bittersweet chocolate (not unsweetened)

1¼ cups heavy cream

2 tablespoons unsalted butter

2 tablespoons light corn syrup

½ cup seedless raspberry jam

For Glaze

8 ounces semisweet or bittersweet chocolate (not unsweetened)

1 cup heavy cream

GARNISH: raspberries

Make Génoise: Preheat oven to 350° F. Butter a 9- by 2-inch round cake pan and line bottom with a round of parchment paper or foil.

In a small bowl whisk together cocoa powder, flour, cornstarch, and baking soda.

In a metal bowl whisk together whole eggs, yolks, sugar, and salt until combined. Set bowl over a pan of simmering water and continue to whisk until mixture is just lukewarm. Remove bowl from

heat and with an electric mixer beat mixture on high speed until cool and doubled in volume.

Sift about one third cocoa mixture over egg mixture and fold in gently but thoroughly. Sift and fold in remaining cocoa mixture, about half at a time, in same manner. Pour batter into pan and smooth top. Bake *génoise* in middle of oven 30 minutes, or until firm to the touch and pulls away slightly from side of pan. Invert *génoise* onto a rack and immediately invert onto another rack to cool right side up. *Génoise may be kept chilled, wrapped in plastic wrap, 1 week or frozen 1 month. Thaw génoise before assembling cake.*

Make Syrup: In a small saucepan bring water and sugar to a boil over moderately low heat, stirring occasionally until sugar is dissolved. Cool syrup and stir in liqueur. *Syrup may be made 1 week ahead and chilled, covered.*

Make Ganache: Coarsely chop chocolate. In a saucepan bring cream, butter, and corn syrup to a boil over moderate heat and remove pan from heat. Add chocolate, swirling pan to submerge chocolate in hot mixture, and let stand 3 minutes. Whisk *ganache* until smooth and transfer to a bowl. *Chill ganache, covered, at least 2 hours and up to 3 days.*

Assemble Cake: Let *ganache* stand at room temperature until slightly softened and pliable but still cool. With a whisk or an electric mixer beat *ganache* just until light and fluffy.

Remove parchment paper from *génoise* and with a long serrated knife horizontally cut cake into 3 rounds.

Invert top layer of *génoise* onto a springform pan base or 9-inch cardboard round and brush with one third syrup. Spread layer with half of jam and spread one third *ganache* over jam. Top *ganache* with middle layer of *génoise* and repeat layering of syrup, jam, and *ganache*. Top with third layer of *génoise*, smooth side up, and brush with remaining syrup. Spread top and side of cake smoothly with remaining *ganache*. *Chill cake until ganache is set, about 30 minutes. Cake may be assembled ahead, wrapped in plastic wrap, and chilled 5 days, or frozen 1 month. Thaw cake before proceeding.*

Make Glaze: Coarsely chop chocolate. In a saucepan bring cream to a boil and remove pan from heat. Add chocolate, swirling pan to submerge chocolate in hot cream, and let stand 2 minutes. Whisk glaze until smooth and pour through a sieve into a bowl. Cool glaze to room temperature.

With cake on a rack set over a baking pan (to catch drips) pour glaze through sieve onto center of cake. Quickly spread glaze evenly over top and side of cake with a long, narrow metal spatula. Let cake stand until glaze is set, about 5 minutes.

Garnish cake with raspberries and keep at cool room temperature until ready to serve. SERVES 12.

Photo below

Apple Pie with Walnut Streusel
Cherry Cobbler ▪ Boston Cream Pie
Walnut Baklava Spirals
Pear and Star Anise Bread Pudding
Butterscotch Puddings
Orange Flans with Candied Zest
Hawaiian Tapioca with Caramelized Pineapple
Plum Crisp ▪ Banana Chiffon Pie
Black Walnut Pie ▪ Lemon Buttermilk Pie
Blueberry and Nectarine Buckle
Grasshopper Pie ▪ Banana Ginger Trifles
Lavender Crème Brûlées
Indian Pudding with Apples and Raisins
Gingerbread with Penuche Icing
Peach "Pizza" ▪ Czech Noodle and Apple Pudding
Cinnamon Raisin Rice Pudding

HOMEY

Homey recipes bring back delightful memories—of your grandma, or your best friend's mom, or maybe that nice neighbor who always had a dessert (like our Lemon Buttermilk Pie) cooling on her windowsill. Was creamy Butterscotch Pudding a favorite? Or was it Cherry Cobbler, bursting with juicy, fresh sour cherries? Good news: Both can be found here. Other cherished classics are enhanced by creative twists—our tapioca pudding has coconut milk and caramelized pineapple for tropical flavor; and a touch of lavender lends a hint of Provence to our *crème brûlées*.

APPLE PIE WITH WALNUT STREUSEL

For Pastry Dough

- 1½ cups all-purpose flour
- 2 tablespoons granulated sugar
- ¾ teaspoon salt
- 1 stick (½ cup) plus 2 tablespoons cold unsalted butter
- 4 to 6 tablespoons ice water

For Topping

- 2 tablespoons unsalted butter, softened
- 2 tablespoons packed brown sugar
- 2 tablespoons all-purpose flour
- ¼ cup chopped walnuts

For Filling

- 3 pounds Golden Delicious or Jonagold apples (about 6 medium)
- ½ cup packed brown sugar
- ¼ cup granulated sugar
- 2 tablespoons all-purpose flour
- 1 tablespoon fresh lemon juice
- ¾ teaspoon cinnamon

- 2 tablespoons milk
- 1 tablespoon granulated sugar

ACCOMPANIMENT: sour cream ice cream (page 72)

Make Dough: In a large bowl with a pastry blender or in a food processor blend or pulse together flour, sugar, salt, and butter until mixture resembles coarse meal with remainder in small (roughly pea-size) lumps. Add 2 tablespoons ice water and gently stir with a fork or pulse just until incorporated. Test mixture by gently squeezing a small handful: When it has proper texture it should hold together without crumbling apart. If necessary, add more water, 1 tablespoon at a time, stirring or pulsing until incorporated and testing mixture. (Do not overwork or add too much water; pastry will be tough.)

Turn mixture out onto a work surface and divide into 4 portions. With heel of hand smear each portion once in a forward motion to help distribute fat. Gather dough together and form it, rotating it on work surface, into a disk. *Chill dough, wrapped in plastic wrap, at least 30 minutes and up to 1 day.*

Make Topping: In a small bowl with your fingertips blend butter, brown sugar, and flour until smooth and blend in nuts. Chill topping, covered.

Make Filling: Peel and core apples. Cut apples into ½-inch wedges and in a bowl toss with remaining filling ingredients to coat.

Preheat oven to 350° F.

On a lightly floured surface roll out dough into a 15-inch round (about ⅛ inch thick) and fold into quarters. Unfold dough in a well-seasoned 10-inch cast-iron skillet or a 10-inch deep-dish (1½-quart) pie plate, easing to fit and letting dough hang over rim of skillet or pie plate. Spoon filling into shell and fold pastry overhang over filling, leaving center uncovered. Bake pie in middle of oven 1 hour (pie will not be completely cooked) and remove from oven.

Crumble topping over center of pie, breaking up any large chunks. Brush crust with milk and sprinkle with sugar. Bake pie in middle of oven 30 minutes more, or until crust is golden and filling is bubbling. Cool pie on a rack.

Serve pie warm or at room temperature with ice cream. **SERVES 8 TO 10.**

Photo on page 111

CHERRY COBBLER

For Cherry Filling

6 cups fresh or frozen pitted tart cherries
   (about 3½ pints fresh, picked over)

1 cup sugar

1½ tablespoons cornstarch

1 tablespoon Frangelico or Disaronno Amaretto

1 teaspoon vanilla

⅛ teaspoon ground allspice

For Biscuit Topping

5 tablespoons cold unsalted butter

1 cup all-purpose flour

2 tablespoons yellow cornmeal

2 tablespoons sugar

1½ teaspoons baking powder

½ teaspoon salt

½ cup milk

½ teaspoon vanilla

ACCOMPANIMENT: vanilla ice cream

Preheat oven to 375° F.

Make Filling: If using fresh cherries, pit them. In a large heavy saucepan whisk together sugar and cornstarch. Add fresh or frozen cherries, liqueur, vanilla, and allspice and bring mixture to a boil over moderate heat, stirring occasionally. Simmer filling, stirring, 2 minutes and transfer to a shallow 2-quart baking dish.

Make Topping: Cut butter into pieces. In a bowl with a pastry blender or in a food processor blend or pulse together flour, cornmeal, sugar, baking powder, salt, and butter until mixture resembles coarse meal. If using a food processor, transfer mixture to a bowl. Add milk and vanilla and stir until mixture forms a dough.

Drop topping by rounded tablespoons onto cherry filling (do not completely cover it) and bake in middle of oven 40 minutes, or until topping is golden and cooked through. Transfer cobbler to a rack to cool slightly.

Serve cobbler warm with ice cream. **SERVES 8.**

Photo below

BOSTON CREAM PIE

For Cake

1½ sticks (¾ cup) unsalted butter, softened
1¼ cups sugar
1 teaspoon vanilla
2 large eggs
2 cups cake flour (not self-rising)
2½ teaspoons baking powder
½ teaspoon salt
¾ cup milk

For Custard

3 tablespoons cornstarch
⅓ cup sugar
1 cup milk
3 large eggs
½ cup heavy cream
¼ teaspoon salt
1 vanilla bean
3 tablespoons unsalted butter

For Glaze

6 ounces fine-quality bittersweet chocolate
  (not unsweetened)
3 tablespoons water
2 tablespoons unsalted butter
1½ tablespoons light corn syrup
¼ teaspoon salt

GARNISH: seasonal fruit and blossoms (non-toxic)

Make Cake: Preheat oven to 350° F. Butter and flour a 9½-inch springform pan.

In a bowl with an electric mixer beat together butter, sugar, and vanilla until light and fluffy and beat in eggs 1 at a time, beating well after each addition. Into another bowl sift together flour, baking powder, and salt and beat mixture into butter mixture in batches alternately with milk, beginning and ending with flour mixture. Pour batter into pan and bake cake in middle of oven 50 to 55 minutes, or until a tester comes out clean. Cool cake in pan on a rack.

Make Custard: In a saucepan whisk together cornstarch, sugar, and milk and add eggs, cream, and salt, whisking until smooth. Split vanilla bean lengthwise and scrape seeds into cream mixture, reserving pod for another use. Bring custard to a boil over moderate heat, whisking constantly, and boil, whisking, 2 minutes. Remove pan from heat and whisk in butter. Cool custard completely, whisking occasionally.

Make Glaze: Chop chocolate and in a metal bowl set over a saucepan of barely simmering water melt it with remaining glaze ingredients, stirring until smooth. Remove bowl from heat.

Remove side of springform pan and with a long serrated knife halve cake horizontally. Arrange bottom half, cut side up, on a plate and top with custard, spreading it to edge. Put remaining cake half, cut side down, on custard and pour glaze on top, spreading glaze to edge and letting it drip down side. *Boston cream pie may be made 1 day ahead and chilled, loosely covered.*

Garnish pie with fruit and blossoms. SERVES 8.

Photo opposite

WALNUT BAKLAVA SPIRALS

— · —

1 pound walnut pieces (about 4 cups)

⅓ cup sugar

2 teaspoons finely grated fresh lemon zest

2 teaspoons finely grated fresh orange zest

1 teaspoon ground cinnamon

¼ teaspoon ground cloves

sixteen 17- by 12-inch *phyllo* sheets
(about 1 pound)

2 sticks (1 cup) unsalted butter

For Syrup
1 large navel orange

1 large lemon

½ cup water

1½ cups honey

¾ cup sugar

a 3-inch cinnamon stick

3 whole cloves

Finely chop walnuts with a knife or by pulsing in a food processor. In a bowl stir together walnuts, sugar, zests, and spices. Cover stack of *phyllo* with 2 overlapping sheets of plastic wrap and then a damp kitchen towel. Melt butter.

Assemble 2 Baklava Rolls, 1 at a Time: On a work surface arrange a 20-inch-long sheet of wax paper with long side facing you and arrange 1 *phyllo* sheet on paper. Brush *phyllo* with some butter and sprinkle evenly with ⅓ cup walnut mixture. Top *phyllo* sheet with 4 more layers each of *phyllo*, butter, and walnut mixture. Turn wax paper and layered *phyllo* so that a short side faces you and, using wax paper as an aid, loosely roll up *phyllo* into a roll, 12 inches long and about 3 inches wide. Wrap roll in wax paper and chill while preparing outer *phyllo* layers.

On another 20-inch-long sheet of wax paper, with long side facing you, arrange a *phyllo* sheet and brush with some butter. Top *phyllo* sheet with 2 more layers of *phyllo*, brushing each with some butter. Remove wax paper from chilled walnut roll and arrange roll on top of short end of buttered *phyllo*. Using wax paper as an aid, tightly roll buttered *phyllo* around walnut roll. Brush outside of *baklava* roll with some butter and wrap wax paper around it. Chill roll while making second *baklava* roll in same manner and chill both 15 minutes.

Preheat oven to 375° F.

Remove wax paper from chilled rolls and with a sharp knife cut each roll crosswise into 6 slices, about 2 inches thick. Fit spirals, cut sides up, into cups of a muffin tin.

Reduce temperature to 325° F. and immediately bake *baklava* spirals in middle of oven 45 to 50 minutes, or until golden.

Make Syrup while Baklava is Baking: With a vegetable peeler, remove four 2½- by ½-inch strips zest from orange and 4 from lemon. Squeeze enough orange juice to measure ½ cup and enough lemon juice to measure 1½ tablespoons. In a saucepan bring zests, juices, and remaining syrup ingredients to a boil, stirring until sugar is dissolved, and simmer syrup, skimming foam if necessary, until reduced to about 2¼ cups, about 10 minutes. Pour syrup through a fine sieve into a large measuring cup and discard solids.

Transfer baked spirals in muffin tin to a rack and immediately drizzle about 2 tablespoons hot syrup over each. *Let spirals stand in muffin tin, loosely covered at room temperature, at least 12 hours for flavors to develop and up to 5 days. Chill remaining syrup, covered, up to 5 days. Bring syrup to room temperature before serving.*

Serve *baklava* spirals with remaining syrup.
SERVES 12.

PEAR AND STAR ANISE BREAD PUDDING

— ✳ —

2 tablespoons unsalted butter

2 whole star anise

¾ cup sugar

4 ripe pears (about 1½ pounds)

a 1-pound store-bought pound cake

1 cup heavy cream

2 cups whole milk

3 whole large eggs

3 large egg yolks

1 teaspoon vanilla

3 tablespoons *Poire Williams* (pear brandy) or Cognac

Preheat broiler.

Melt butter and brush a shallow baking pan with about one third butter. In an electric coffee/spice grinder grind star anise to a powder and in a small bowl toss with sugar. Peel and quarter pears. Core pears and cut each quarter lengthwise into 5 wedges. Arrange about one third pears in one layer in baking pan and brush with remaining butter. Sprinkle pears in pan with 1 tablespoon sugar mixture and broil 2 to 3 inches from heat until golden and caramelized, about 5 minutes. Cool pears in pan on a rack.

Preheat oven to 350° F. and butter a 2-quart soufflé dish or baking dish.

Cut pound cake into large pieces and in a food processor pulse until coarse crumbs. In a bowl whisk together cream, milk, whole eggs, yolks, vanilla, *Poire Williams* or Cognac, and remaining sugar mixture until combined well. In soufflé dish or baking dish layer one third crumbs, half of uncooked pears, and one third custard mixture. Repeat layering and top with a third layer of crumbs and remaining custard mixture. Arrange broiled pears decoratively on top.

Let pudding stand at room temperature 15 minutes or chill, covered, up to 1 day. Bake pudding in middle of oven 1 hour, or until set and puffed, and cool on a rack 30 minutes. Serve pudding warm or at room temperature. SERVES 6 TO 8.

BUTTERSCOTCH PUDDINGS

— ✳ ⊕+

2¾ cups whole milk

2½ tablespoons cornstarch

¾ stick (6 tablespoons) unsalted butter

1 cup sugar

¼ cup light corn syrup

3 tablespoons water

1½ teaspoons cider vinegar

1½ teaspoons vanilla

In a heavy saucepan bring 2½ cups milk to a simmer. In a measuring cup stir together remaining ¼ cup milk and cornstarch until smooth and whisk into simmering milk. Simmer mixture, whisking constantly, until thickened, about 2 minutes, and remove pan from heat.

Cut butter into pieces. In a 3-quart heavy saucepan bring sugar, corn syrup, and water to a boil over moderate heat, stirring until sugar is dissolved. Boil mixture, without stirring, swirling pan occasionally, until a golden caramel. Remove pan from heat and add butter and vinegar (mixture will bubble and steam), swirling pan until butter is melted.

Pour milk mixture through a sieve into butterscotch mixture and whisk until combined well. Whisk in vanilla and pour pudding into four ⅔-cup ramekins or heatproof stemmed glasses. *Chill puddings, uncovered, until set, at least 1 hour, and covered, up to 2 days.* SERVES 4.

ORANGE FLANS WITH CANDIED ZEST

5 navel oranges
½ cup water
½ cup Grand Marnier
2 cups sugar
4 cups milk
8 large egg yolks
4 whole large eggs
1 teaspoon orange-flower water*
    or 1 teaspoon vanilla (optional)
½ teaspoon salt

*available at specialty foods shops

Line a plate with wax paper. With a vegetable peeler remove zest from 2 oranges in strips and cut strips into long, very thin shreds with a sharp knife. In a saucepan of boiling water blanch shreds 1 minute and drain. In a small heavy saucepan boil ½ cup water, Grand Marnier, blanched zest, and 1 cup sugar, stirring and washing down any sugar crystals clinging to side of pan with a brush dipped in cold water, 5 minutes. Transfer candied zest with a slotted spoon to wax-paper-lined plate. *Let candied zest stand, uncovered, 2 hours, or until dry.* Cook syrup over moderate heat, without stirring, until a deep caramel and divide among eight ¾-cup ramekins, tilting them to coat bottoms evenly. *Candied zest and caramel may be made (and ramekins coated) 1 day ahead and kept separately, covered, at room temperature.*

Preheat oven to 325° F.

With a vegetable peeler remove zest in strips from remaining 3 oranges (reserve oranges for garnish). In a heavy saucepan simmer milk, remaining cup sugar, and zest strips 5 minutes. In a bowl gently whisk together yolks, whole eggs, orange-flower water or vanilla, and salt until just combined. Discard zest strips and add milk mixture to egg mixture in a stream, stirring.

Pour custard through a fine sieve into a large measuring cup or heatproof pitcher and divide among ramekins. Put ramekins in a baking pan and add enough hot water to pan to reach halfway up sides of ramekins. Bake flans, covered with a baking sheet, in middle of oven 1 hour, or until just set but still trembling slightly. (Flans will continue to set as they cool.) Remove ramekins from pan and cool flans, uncovered, to room temperature. *Chill flans, covered, 2 hours. Flans may be made up to this point 1 day ahead and chilled, covered.*

To unmold flans, run a thin knife around edge of each flan. Invert a plate over each ramekin and invert flans onto plates.

Cut pith from reserved oranges with a sharp knife and cut sections from membranes. Garnish flans with candied zest and orange sections. SERVES 8.

Photo opposite

HAWAIIAN TAPIOCA WITH CARAMELIZED PINEAPPLE

6 cups water
½ cup pearl tapioca

For Caramelized Pineapple
1 pineapple (about 3½ pounds)
½ cup sugar
2 tablespoons cider vinegar
2 tablespoons dark rum

one 14-ounce can well-shaken unsweetened coconut milk (about 1¾ cups)
4 large egg yolks
½ cup sugar
1 tablespoon dark rum

In a saucepan bring water to a boil and stir in pearl tapioca. Simmer tapioca until translucent, about 30 minutes, and drain in a sieve.

Caramelize Pineapple while Tapioca is Cooking: Peel pineapple and cut lengthwise into 6 wedges. Cut core from wedges and cut wedges crosswise into ¼-inch-thick slices. In a 12-inch heavy skillet simmer pineapple, sugar, vinegar, and rum over moderate heat, carefully turning pineapple occasionally, until most liquid is evaporated and pineapple is slightly translucent (reduce heat as liquid is evaporated), about 25 minutes. Cool pineapple.

In a 2-quart heavy saucepan bring coconut milk to a simmer. In a bowl whisk together yolks and sugar. Add hot coconut milk in a slow stream, whisking, and transfer custard to pan. Stir in tapioca and rum and cook custard over moderately low heat, stirring constantly, until slightly thickened and an instant-read thermometer registers 170° F. (do not boil).

Divide tapioca custard among six ½-cup heatproof glasses or ramekins. Decoratively arrange pineapple pieces on custards. *Custards may be made 2 days ahead and chilled, covered.* Serve tapioca warm or chilled. **SERVES 6.**

PLUM CRISP

For Topping
1 stick (½ cup) cold unsalted butter
¼ cup granulated sugar
¼ cup packed light brown sugar
½ cup all-purpose flour
½ cup old-fashioned rolled oats such as Quaker
½ teaspoon ground ginger
¼ teaspoon freshly grated nutmeg
¼ teaspoon cinnamon
¼ teaspoon salt

2 pounds firm-ripe plums
¼ cup granulated sugar

ACCOMPANIMENT: vanilla ice cream

Preheat oven to 350° F. Butter a 1½-quart shallow baking dish or pie plate.

Make Topping: Cut butter into bits and chill about 5 minutes. In a bowl stir together remaining topping ingredients. Add butter and with your fingertips blend mixture until it resembles coarse meal. Chill topping while preparing plums.

Halve plums and discard pits. Cut each plum half into 4 wedges and in a bowl toss with sugar. Decoratively arrange plums in baking dish or pie plate, sprinkling any sugar remaining in bowl over them, and sprinkle with topping. *Crisp may be made up to this point 1 day ahead and chilled, covered.* Bake crisp 50 to 60 minutes, or until golden, and cool slightly.

Serve crisp warm or at room temperature with ice cream. **SERVES 6 TO 8.**

BANANA CHIFFON PIE

For Crust

5 tablespoons unsalted butter
thirty-five 1½-inch vanilla wafer cookies
   (about 5 ounces)
½ cup chopped pecans (about 2 ounces)
2 tablespoons sugar

For Filling

¾ cup packed light brown sugar
4 large egg yolks
1 cup whole milk
2 firm just-ripe bananas
2 tablespoons fresh lemon juice
1 teaspoon vanilla
1 envelope unflavored gelatin
   (about 1 tablespoon)
2 tablespoons water
1 tablespoon dark rum
¾ cup well-chilled heavy cream

For Topping

3 firm just-ripe bananas
   (with green-yellow peels)
2 tablespoons fresh lemon juice

Make Crust: Preheat oven to 350° F.

Melt butter and cool. In a food processor finely grind cookies and pecans with sugar and add butter, pulsing until combined well. Press crumb mixture onto bottom and up side of a 10-inch deep-dish (1½-quart) glass pie plate. Bake crust in middle of oven 15 minutes, or until crisp and golden around edge, and cool on a rack.

Make Filling: In a large bowl whisk together brown sugar, yolks, and a pinch salt until combined well. In a heavy saucepan bring milk just to a boil and add to yolk mixture in a stream, whisking. Transfer custard to saucepan and cook over moderately low heat, stirring constantly with a wooden spoon, until thickened and an instant-read thermometer registers 170° F. (do not boil). Transfer custard to a metal bowl and cool.

In a food processor purée bananas with lemon juice and vanilla until smooth and stir into custard. In a small saucepan sprinkle gelatin over water and rum and let stand 1 minute to soften gelatin. Heat gelatin mixture over low heat, stirring occasionally, until gelatin is dissolved and stir into banana custard. Set bowl in a larger bowl of ice and cold water and cool custard, stirring constantly, just until consistency of raw egg white. Remove bowl from ice water. In a bowl with an electric mixer beat cream until it just holds stiff peaks and fold into banana custard.

Pour filling into crust. *Chill pie, uncovered, 1 hour. Cover pie with plastic wrap and chill at least 3 hours more, or until set, and up to 1 day.*

Make Topping: Cut bananas into ¼-inch-thick slices and in a small bowl toss with lemon juice.

Decoratively arrange banana slices, overlapping them, on top of pie to completely cover filling. SERVES 8 TO 10.

BLACK WALNUT PIE

For Shell

1¼ cups unbleached all-purpose flour

⅓ cup chilled vegetable shortening

3 tablespoons ice water

For Filling

3 tablespoons unsalted butter

3 large eggs

⅓ cup packed light brown sugar

1 cup pure maple syrup

1 teaspoon cider vinegar

½ teaspoon vanilla

1 cup black walnuts* or other walnuts

ACCOMPANIMENT: whipped cream

*available at some specialty foods shops and by mail order from American Spoon Foods, tel. (888) 735-6700

Make Shell: In a bowl stir together flour and a pinch salt and with a pastry blender or your fingertips blend in shortening until mixture resembles meal. Add ice water and toss mixture until water is incorporated. Form dough into a ball. *Chill dough, wrapped tightly in plastic wrap, 30 minutes.* On a lightly floured surface roll out dough into a 10-inch round. Transfer dough to an 8-inch pie plate, trimming edge, and crimp edge decoratively. *Chill shell 1 hour.*

Preheat oven to 375° F.

Make Filling: Melt butter. In a large bowl with an electric mixer beat eggs until frothy. Add brown sugar and beat until smooth. Beat in syrup, vinegar, vanilla, and a pinch salt until smooth and beat in butter.

Chop walnuts and spread evenly on bottom of shell. Pour filling over walnuts and bake pie in lower third of oven 35 minutes. (Center of pie will not be completely set; it will continue to set as pie cools.)

Cool pie on a rack to room temperature. *Pie may be made 1 day ahead and chilled, covered. Bring pie to room temperature before serving.*

Serve pie with whipped cream. **SERVES 6 TO 8.**

Photo opposite

LEMON BUTTERMILK PIE

pastry dough (page 33)

½ stick (¼ cup) unsalted butter

1 cup sugar

1½ cups well-shaken buttermilk

4 large egg yolks

¼ cup all-purpose flour

1 teaspoon vanilla

1½ teaspoons finely grated fresh lemon zest

¼ teaspoon salt

freshly grated nutmeg to taste

On a lightly floured surface roll out dough ⅛ inch thick and fit into a 9-inch (1-quart) glass pie plate. Crimp edge decoratively. *Chill shell 30 minutes.*

Preheat oven to 350° F.

Melt butter and cool. In a bowl whisk together butter and remaining ingredients and pour filling into shell. Bake pie in lower third of oven 20 minutes. Reduce temperature to 325° F. and bake pie 20 to 25 minutes more, or until filling is set and golden. Cool pie on a rack. *Pie may be made 1 day ahead and chilled, covered.* Serve pie at room temperature or chilled. **SERVES 8.**

BLUEBERRY AND NECTARINE BUCKLE

For Topping

½ stick (¼ cup) cold unsalted butter

½ cup sugar

⅓ cup all-purpose flour

½ teaspoon cinnamon

½ teaspoon freshly grated nutmeg

For Batter

2 nectarines

1½ sticks (¾ cup) unsalted butter, softened

¾ cup sugar

1 teaspoon vanilla

1⅓ cups all-purpose flour

½ teaspoon salt

¼ teaspoon baking powder

3 large eggs

2 cups picked-over blueberries

ACCOMPANIMENT: vanilla ice cream

Make Topping: Cut butter into bits. In a small bowl with your fingertips or a pastry blender blend together butter, sugar, flour, and spices until mixture resembles coarse meal. Chill topping while making batter.

Preheat oven to 350° F. and butter a 10-inch round cake pan or a 2-quart baking pan.

Make Batter: Pit nectarines and cut into 1-inch wedges. In a large bowl with an electric mixer beat together butter and sugar and beat in vanilla. In a bowl stir together flour, salt, and baking powder. Beat flour mixture into butter mixture alternately with eggs, 1 at a time, beating well after each addition, and fold in blueberries and nectarines.

Spread batter in pan and sprinkle topping evenly over it. Bake buckle in middle of oven 45 to 50 minutes, or until a tester comes out clean and topping is crisp and golden.

Serve buckle with ice cream. SERVES 8.

GRASSHOPPER PIE

For Crust

about 30 chocolate wafer cookies

½ stick (¼ cup) unsalted butter

¼ cup sugar

For Filling

1½ teaspoons unflavored gelatin (less than 1 envelope)

1⅓ cups well-chilled heavy cream

¼ cup sugar

¼ cup green *crème de menthe*

¼ cup white *crème de cacao*

4 large egg yolks

GARNISH: grated chocolate (preferably mint-flavored)

Make Crust: Preheat oven to 450° F. and butter a 9-inch pie plate.

In a food processor finely grind enough cookies to measure 1½ cups crumbs. Melt butter. In a bowl stir together crumbs, sugar, and butter until mixture is combined well and pat onto bottom and up side of pie plate. Bake crust in middle of oven 5 minutes and cool on a rack.

Make Filling: Have ready a large bowl of ice and cold water. In a metal bowl sprinkle gelatin over ⅓ cup heavy cream and let stand 1 minute to soften gelatin. Whisk in sugar, liqueurs, and yolks. Set bowl over a saucepan of simmering water and cook mixture, whisking constantly, until it registers 160° F. on an instant-read thermometer. Set bowl in bowl of ice water and stir mixture until cool and thickened. In another bowl with an electric mixer beat remaining cup heavy cream until it holds stiff peaks and fold into mint mixture gently but thoroughly.

Pour filling into crust. *Chill pie, covered loosely, until set, about 4 hours, and up to 1 day.*

Sprinkle pie with grated chocolate. SERVES 8.

BANANA GINGER TRIFLES

For Custard

3 tablespoons crystallized ginger
½ cup sugar
2½ teaspoons cornstarch
2 large eggs
1¼ cups milk
½ cup heavy cream

20 chocolate wafer cookies
4 firm-ripe bananas
juice of ½ lemon
¼ cup banana liqueur

GARNISH: crystallized ginger

Make Custard: Finely chop ginger. In a bowl whisk together sugar and cornstarch and whisk in eggs and a pinch salt until combined well. In a heavy saucepan bring milk and cream just to a boil. Add milk mixture to egg mixture in a slow stream, whisking, and transfer to saucepan. Bring custard to a boil over moderate heat, whisking constantly, and boil, whisking, 1 minute. Stir in ginger and cool custard completely, stirring occasionally to prevent skin from forming. *Custard may be made 3 days ahead and chilled, covered.*

Assemble Trifles: In a food processor coarsely grind cookies. Peel 1 banana and cut into ⅛-inch-thick slices. Lightly brush slices with some lemon juice to prevent discoloration. Into a 1-cup stemmed glass, spoon ¼ cup custard and sprinkle evenly with about 2½ tablespoons cookie crumbs. Drizzle 1½ teaspoons liqueur over crumbs. Arrange some banana slices decoratively around inside of glass, pressing lightly to make adhere, and layer remaining banana slices on crumbs. Sprinkle about 2½ tablespoons cookie crumbs evenly over bananas and drizzle with 1½ teaspoons liqueur. Top crumbs with about

¼ cup custard and some ginger. Make 3 more trifles in same manner. *Chill trifles, covered loosely with plastic wrap, at least 3 hours and up to 1 day.* MAKES 4 INDIVIDUAL TRIFLES.

Photo below

LAVENDER CRÈME BRÛLÉES

— · —

2 cups heavy cream

4 teaspoons dried untreated lavender flowers*

4 large egg yolks

1/3 cup plus 2 tablespoons granulated sugar

1 tablespoon packed light brown sugar

*available at specialty foods shops and by mail order from Dean & Deluca, tel. (800) 221-7714

Preheat oven to 350° F.

In a small saucepan bring cream and lavender to a simmer. Remove pan from heat and let cream infuse 15 minutes. Pour cream through a sieve into a bowl and discard lavender. Return cream to pan and reheat until hot.

In a bowl whisk together yolks, 1/3 cup granulated sugar, and a pinch salt and add hot cream in a slow stream, whisking just until combined. Skim off any froth and divide custard among four 1/2-cup ramekins. Arrange ramekins in a shallow baking pan and carefully pour enough hot water into pan to reach halfway up sides of ramekins. Loosely cover pan with foil and bake custards in middle of oven until just set but still trembling slightly, 30 to 35 minutes. Transfer ramekins to a rack and cool custards. *Chill custards, loosely covered with plastic wrap, at least 4 hours and up to 1 day.*

Preheat broiler.

In a small bowl stir together brown sugar and remaining 2 tablespoons granulated sugar and sprinkle mixture evenly over custards. Fill shallow baking pan with ice and transfer ramekins to pan, nestling ramekins into ice. Broil custards about 1 inch from heat until sugar is caramelized, 1 to 2 minutes. (Alternatively, caramelize custards with a blowtorch, moving flame evenly back and forth over sugar.) **SERVES 4.**

INDIAN PUDDING WITH APPLES AND RAISINS

— · —

4 cups whole milk

1/2 cup yellow cornmeal

1/2 cup raisins

2 Granny Smith apples

1/2 stick (1/4 cup) unsalted butter

1/4 cup sugar

1/4 cup unsulfured molasses

1 teaspoon cinnamon

1/2 teaspoon salt

1/4 teaspoon freshly grated nutmeg

1/4 teaspoon ground allspice

1 large egg

Preheat oven to 325° F. and butter a 2-quart gratin or other shallow baking dish.

Fill bottom of a double boiler halfway with water and bring to a simmer. In top of double boiler bring milk to a simmer and set over bottom. Add cornmeal to milk in a stream, stirring constantly, and cook, stirring, 5 minutes. Add raisins and cook, stirring, 10 minutes (mixture will thicken slightly). Transfer mixture to a bowl and cool slightly. Peel and core apples. Cut apples into 1/2-inch cubes and stir into cornmeal mixture.

In a small saucepan melt butter. Remove pan from heat and stir in all remaining ingredients except egg. Cool butter mixture 5 minutes. Lightly beat egg and stir into butter mixture until combined well. Pour egg mixture into cornmeal mixture and stir until combined well.

Pour pudding into baking dish and bake in middle of oven 1 1/4 to 1 1/2 hours, or until a tester comes out clean. Cool pudding on a rack. *Pudding may be made 2 days ahead and chilled, covered.* Serve pudding warm or at room temperature. **SERVES 8.**

GINGERBREAD
WITH PENUCHE ICING

For Gingerbread

2 cups all-purpose flour
½ teaspoon baking powder
½ teaspoon baking soda
1 teaspoon ground ginger
½ teaspoon cinnamon
½ teaspoon freshly grated nutmeg
½ teaspoon salt
½ cup whole milk
½ cup sour cream
1 stick (½ cup) unsalted butter, softened
⅓ cup granulated sugar
⅓ cup packed light brown sugar
2 large eggs
⅓ cup molasses

For Icing

1½ cups packed light brown sugar
⅓ cup heavy cream
1 stick (½ cup) unsalted butter

Make Gingerbread: Preheat oven to 350° F. Butter a 9- by 5- by 3-inch loaf pan and line bottom with wax paper. Butter paper.

Into a bowl sift together flour, baking powder, baking soda, spices, and salt. In a small bowl stir together milk and sour cream.

In a large bowl with an electric mixer beat together butter and sugars until light and fluffy and beat in eggs and molasses. Add flour mixture and milk mixture alternately in batches, beginning and ending with flour mixture and beating after each addition until just combined. Pour batter into loaf pan, spreading evenly.

Bake cake in middle of oven 50 minutes, or until a tester comes out clean. Cool cake in pan on a rack 10 minutes and invert onto rack. Remove wax paper and cool cake completely.

Make Icing: In a saucepan bring brown sugar, cream, and 6 tablespoons butter to a boil over moderate heat, stirring until butter is melted, and boil, stirring occasionally, until a candy thermometer registers 238° F. Transfer mixture to a heatproof bowl and stir in remaining 2 tablespoons butter until smooth. Cool mixture 5 minutes. With an electric mixer beat mixture until glossy and almost thick enough to spread (icing will continue to thicken as it cools), about 1 minute.

Working quickly, with a metal cake spatula or knife frost top and sides of cake. Smooth icing if necessary by dipping spatula or knife into very hot water and running over icing. *Cake keeps, covered, at room temperature 1 day.* SERVES 8.

PEACH "PIZZA"

— · —

1 thawed puff pastry sheet (from a 17¼-ounce
   package frozen puff pastry sheets)
¼ cup sugar
½ teaspoon cinnamon
¼ teaspoon freshly grated nutmeg
5 to 6 peaches
2 tablespoons unsalted butter

Preheat oven to 400° F.

On a lightly floured surface roll out pastry into
a 12½-inch square and brush off excess flour. Using
a 12-inch plate or other round as a guide, with a
sharp knife cut out a round and carefully transfer to
a pizza pan (not black), at least 12 inches in diameter, or a baking sheet. Leaving a ¾-inch border,
prick pastry round all over with a fork. *Freeze pastry round on pan or baking sheet until firm, at
least 10 minutes and, covered with plastic wrap,
up to 3 days.* Bake pastry round in middle of oven
8 minutes, or until slightly puffed and lightly colored.
Transfer crust in pan or on baking sheet to a rack.
Gently flatten pastry inside border.

In a small bowl stir together sugar and spices.
Peel and halve peaches. Discard pits and cut each
peach half into 3 wedges. Halve wedges crosswise
and arrange in one layer on crust. Melt butter. Brush
peaches with butter and sprinkle with sugar mixture.

Bake "pizza" in middle of oven 20 minutes, or
until crust is golden brown and most of peach juices
are cooked off. Transfer pizza in pan or on baking
sheet to rack and cool slightly. *Pizza may be made
8 hours ahead and kept, covered, at room temperature. Reheat pizza before serving.* Cut pizza
into wedges with a pizza wheel or a long sharp
knife. SERVES 12.

Photo on page 10

CZECH NOODLE
AND APPLE PUDDING

— · —

2⅔ cups milk
¼ teaspoon salt
¼ pound wide egg noodles (about
   2½ cups), broken
5 tablespoons unsalted butter, softened
⅓ cup granulated sugar
3 large eggs, separated
1½ teaspoons vanilla
1 pound apples
confectioners' sugar for dusting pudding

Preheat oven to 350° F. and butter an 11-inch oval
gratin dish or other 1½-quart shallow baking dish.

In a saucepan bring milk to a boil. Add salt and
noodles and simmer 8 minutes, or until noodles are
tender. Remove pan from heat and cool noodles
slightly.

In a bowl with an electric mixer beat together
butter and granulated sugar until light and fluffy.
Add yolks and beat until light and pale. Gently stir
in warm noodles with milk and vanilla. Peel and core
apples and slice ⅛ inch thick (there should be about
2½ cups).

In a bowl with cleaned beaters beat whites until
they just hold stiff peaks and fold into noodle custard gently but thoroughly. Spoon half of noodle
mixture into baking dish and arrange apple slices in
an even layer over it. Spoon remaining noodle mixture over apples and bake pudding in middle of
oven 30 to 35 minutes, or until golden and cooked
through. Cool pudding on a rack 10 minutes. Dust
pudding with confectioners' sugar and serve immediately. SERVES 8.

Photo opposite

CINNAMON RAISIN RICE PUDDING

4 cups water
¼ teaspoon salt
1 cup long-grain white rice (not converted)
3 cups milk
½ cup sugar
⅛ teaspoon cinnamon
1½ teaspoons vanilla
¼ cup raisins

ACCOMPANIMENT: heavy cream

In a saucepan bring water with salt to a boil and stir in rice. Simmer mixture, covered, over low heat, stirring occasionally, 35 minutes, or until rice is very tender. Add milk, sugar, and cinnamon and simmer, uncovered, stirring frequently, 20 to 25 minutes, or until most of milk is absorbed. Stir in vanilla and raisins. Transfer pudding to a bowl and cool, its surface covered with plastic wrap. *Pudding may be made 2 days ahead and chilled, covered.*

Serve pudding at room temperature or chilled with cream. SERVES 6.

Photo right

Apricot Soufflés

Mint Chocolate Chip Ice-Milk Sandwiches

Peach Cheesecake

Raspberry Tea Gelées with Watermelon

Citrus Yogurt Custard Tart

Malted Chocolate Banana Frappé

Pineapple Tart

Mixed Berries in Cocoa Meringue Nests

Kumquat, Grape, and Kiwifruit Soup with Orange Muscat

Frozen Mocha Mousse

Cocoa Angel Food Cake with Orange Glaze

Cranberry Applesauce

Frozen Plum Meringue Cake

Banana Chocolate-Chip Soufflés

Chocolate Raspberry Roulade

LIGHT

Lighter than most sweets, these are ideal after a rich meal, or whenever you're looking for something a bit less filling. We hasten to add, however, that while **some** of our goodies are low in calories and fat (the ice-milk sandwiches; raspberry tea gelées; chocolate raspberry roulade; kumquat, grape, and kiwifruit soup; banana chocolate chip soufflés; and pineapple tart all meet such criteria), this was not our objective. From a frothy chocolate banana frappé to airy apricot soufflés, here are "lighter" options for every occasion.

APRICOT SOUFFLÉS

6 ounces dried apricots (about 1½ cups)
1½ cups water
¾ cup sugar plus additional for
    coating ramekins
1 tablespoon fresh lemon juice
1 tablespoon dark rum (optional)
½ teaspoon vanilla
5 large egg whites
¼ teaspoon cream of tartar

In a heavy saucepan simmer apricots, water, and ½ cup sugar, covered, 20 minutes. Transfer hot mixture to a food processor and purée until very smooth. Force purée through a fine sieve into a heatproof bowl and stir in lemon juice, rum, vanilla, and a pinch salt. Cool purée completely. *Purée may be made 2 days ahead and chilled, covered. Bring purée to room temperature before proceeding.* Transfer purée to a large bowl.

Preheat oven to 350° F. Generously butter six 7-ounce ramekins (3½ inches in diameter by 1¾ inches high) and coat with additional sugar, knocking out excess sugar.

In another large bowl with an electric mixer beat whites with a pinch salt until foamy. Beat in cream of tartar and beat whites until they hold soft peaks. Gradually beat in remaining ¼ cup sugar and beat meringue until it just holds stiff peaks. Whisk about one fourth meringue into purée to lighten and fold in remaining meringue gently but thoroughly. Arrange ramekins on a baking sheet and ladle batter into ramekins. Bake soufflés in middle of oven 20 to 25 minutes, or until puffed, golden brown, and just set in center. Serve soufflés immediately. SERVES 6.

Photo on page 131

MINT CHOCOLATE CHIP ICE-MILK SANDWICHES

about 2 cups mint chocolate chip ice milk
    (recipe follows), softened slightly
24 cocoa snaps (page 133)

Sandwich about 2½ tablespoons ice milk between 2 snaps, pressing snaps together gently, and put sandwich on a tray in freezer. Make 11 more sandwiches in same manner. *Freeze sandwiches on tray, covered, about 1 hour, or until hard. Ice-milk sandwiches may be made 1 week ahead and kept frozen, individually wrapped in plastic wrap.* MAKES 12 ICE-MILK SANDWICHES.

Photo opposite

MINT CHOCOLATE CHIP ICE MILK

½ cup sugar
1 tablespoon cornstarch
2⅓ cups low-fat milk
2 large egg yolks
1 tablespoon green or white *crème de menthe*
1 ounce fine-quality bittersweet chocolate
(not unsweetened)

In a saucepan whisk together sugar and cornstarch and whisk in milk. Bring milk mixture to a boil over moderate heat, stirring frequently, and boil, stirring constantly, 1 minute. Remove pan from heat.

In a small heatproof bowl lightly beat yolks. Stir about one fourth milk mixture into yolks and pour into remaining milk mixture, whisking constantly. Cook custard over low heat, stirring constantly, until slightly thickened and an instant-read thermometer registers 160° F. (do not let boil). Stir in *crème de menthe* and transfer to a bowl. *Chill custard about 1 hour, or until cool.*

Chop chocolate. In a small heavy saucepan melt chocolate over low heat, stirring occasionally, and cool slightly. Transfer chocolate to a small heavy-duty plastic bag. Gently squeeze chocolate to 1 corner and snip a small hole in corner to form a makeshift pastry bag. Freeze milk mixture in an ice-cream maker and with motor running add chocolate in a thin stream during last few minutes of freezing time. *Ice milk keeps, frozen in an airtight container, 1 week.* **MAKES ABOUT 3½ CUPS ICE MILK.**

COCOA SNAPS

½ cup all-purpose flour
½ cup sugar
¼ cup unsweetened cocoa powder
½ teaspoon baking powder
¼ teaspoon salt
2 tablespoons unsalted butter, softened
1 large egg

In a bowl whisk together flour, sugar, cocoa powder, baking powder, and salt and with your fingertips blend in butter until incorporated. In a small bowl lightly beat egg and stir into cocoa mixture until combined well. *Chill dough, covered, until firm, about 1 hour.*

Preheat oven to 400° F. and lightly grease a large baking sheet.

Spoon level tablespoons of dough onto a sheet of wax paper and cut each in half. With floured hands roll each piece of dough into a ball and arrange, evenly spaced, on baking sheet. With a floured metal spatula flatten each ball into a disk about 2 inches in diameter and bake in middle of oven 7 to 8 minutes, or until set but not hard. Cool cookies on racks (cookies will continue to crisp as they cool). *Cookies may be made 2 days ahead and kept in an airtight container at room temperature.* **MAKES ABOUT 26 COCOA SNAPS.**

PEACH CHEESECAKE

For Crust
½ stick (¼ cup) unsalted butter
thirty-two 1½-inch vanilla wafers (4½ ounces)
⅓ cup slivered almonds (about 2 ounces)
2 tablespoons sugar

For Filling
¾ cup plain yogurt
4 medium firm-ripe peaches (about 1 pound)
    or two 16-ounce cans sliced peaches
an 8-ounce package Neufchâtel cheese,
    softened
½ cup sugar
2 large eggs
3 tablespoons all-purpose flour
¼ teaspoon almond extract
2 tablespoons peach schnapps or peach brandy

Preheat oven to 350° F.

Make Crust: Melt butter and cool. In a food processor finely grind wafers and almonds with sugar and add butter, pulsing until combined well. Press mixture onto bottom and halfway up side of a 9-inch springform pan. Bake crust in middle of oven 10 to 15 minutes, or until crisp and golden, and cool completely in pan on a rack.

Make Filling: In a sieve lined with a paper towel and set over a bowl drain yogurt 30 minutes.

While yogurt is draining, if using fresh peaches, peel and cut into ¾-inch slices; if using canned, drain and pat dry on paper towels. In a bowl with an electric mixer beat together Neufchâtel cheese and sugar until smooth and add eggs 1 at a time, beating well after each addition. Beat in yogurt and add flour, almond extract, and schnapps or brandy, beating until combined well. Arrange peaches in one layer in crust and pour cheese mixture over them.

Bake cheesecake in middle of oven about 30 minutes, or until set and top is pale golden, and cool completely in pan on a rack. *Cheesecake may be made 1 day ahead and chilled, covered.* Run a thin knife around side of pan and carefully remove side. **SERVES 6 TO 8.**

RASPBERRY TEA GELÉES
WITH WATERMELON

a 2¼-pound piece watermelon
½ cup sugar
2 cups water plus 1 cup ice water
4 raspberry tea bags
2 envelopes unflavored gelatin
2 tablespoons fresh lemon juice
12 small fresh mint leaves

GARNISH: fresh mint sprigs

Cut rind from watermelon and cut enough flesh into ¼-inch dice, removing seeds, to measure 3 cups. Transfer watermelon to a bowl and chill.

In a saucepan bring sugar and 2 cups water to a boil over moderately high heat and boil, stirring, until sugar is dissolved. Add tea bags and remove pan from heat. Steep tea 5 minutes and remove tea bags, carefully squeezing any liquid in them into pan.

In a small bowl sprinkle gelatin over ¼ cup ice water and let stand 1 minute to soften gelatin. Stir gelatin mixture into hot tea and cook over low heat until gelatin is completely dissolved. Remove pan from heat and stir in remaining ¾ cup ice water and lemon juice. *Chill tea mixture 45 minutes, or until thickened to consistency of raw egg white.* Stir in watermelon and mint leaves. Rinse six 1-cup molds with cold water, shaking out excess water (do not dry), and spoon melon mixture into molds. *Chill gelées until set, about 2 hours, and up to 2 days.*

Dip each mold into a bowl of warm water to loosen and invert *gelées* onto plates. Garnish *gelées* with mint sprigs. **SERVES 6.**

CITRUS YOGURT CUSTARD TART

For Crust

½ stick (¼ cup) unsalted butter

eleven 5- by 2½-inch graham crackers

2 tablespoons sugar

2 teaspoons finely grated fresh orange zest

For Filling

1½ cups vanilla yogurt

¾ cup milk

3 large egg yolks

⅓ cup sugar

2 tablespoons fresh orange juice

2 tablespoons fresh lemon juice

2 tablespoons fresh lime juice

1 envelope unflavored gelatin
(about 1 tablespoon)

2 teaspoons finely grated fresh lemon zest

2 large navel oranges

1 large grapefruit

Make Crust: Preheat oven to 350° F.

Melt butter and cool. In a food processor finely grind graham crackers with sugar and add butter and zest, pulsing until combined well. Press mixture onto bottom and up side of a 10-inch tart pan with a removable rim. Bake crust in middle of oven 10 to 15 minutes, or until crisp and golden, and cool completely in pan on a rack.

Make Filling: In a large sieve lined with a paper towel and set over a bowl drain yogurt 30 minutes and discard liquid.

While yogurt is draining, in a heavy saucepan bring milk to a boil and remove pan from heat. In a bowl whisk together yolks and sugar until smooth and whisk in hot milk in a stream. Transfer milk mixture to saucepan and cook over moderately low heat, stirring constantly with a wooden spoon, until thickened and an instant-read thermometer registers 170° F. (do not boil). Transfer custard to a metal bowl and cool.

In a small saucepan stir together juices. Sprinkle gelatin over juice mixture and let stand 1 minute to soften gelatin. Cook gelatin mixture over low heat, stirring occasionally, until gelatin is dissolved and stir into custard with zest. Set bowl in a larger bowl of ice and cold water and cool custard. Stir in yogurt.

Pour filling into crust, spreading evenly. *Chill tart, uncovered, until set, at least 4 hours, and covered, up to 1 day.*

Working over a bowl, with a sharp knife cut peel and pith from oranges and grapefruit and cut sections free from membranes, letting sections fall into bowl. Drain fruit.

Serve tart with fruit. **SERVES 6 TO 8.**

MALTED CHOCOLATE BANANA FRAPPÉ

1 banana

½ pint chocolate sorbet

1 cup skim milk

¼ cup malted milk powder

Peel banana and put on a plate. *Freeze banana 1 hour.* Soften sorbet slightly. In a blender purée banana with sorbet, milk, and powder until smooth but still thick. **SERVES 2.**

PINEAPPLE TART

For Tart Shell
vegetable-oil cooking spray
three 2½-inch-square graham crackers
1½ tablespoons granulated sugar
four 17- by 12-inch *phyllo* sheets
2 tablespoons unsalted butter

For Filling
1 large pineapple (about 4¼ pounds)
½ vanilla bean
¼ cup packed light brown sugar
¼ cup granulated sugar

Make Shell: Preheat oven to 375° F. and lightly coat an 11-inch tart pan with a removable fluted rim with vegetable-oil cooking spray.

In a food processor finely grind graham crackers with sugar. Stack *phyllo* sheets between 2 overlapping sheets plastic wrap and then cover with a damp kitchen towel. Melt butter.

Working quickly, line tart pan with 1 *phyllo* sheet, allowing edges to overhang evenly, and with a pastry brush dot *phyllo* on bottom of tart pan with butter in 4 or 5 places. Sprinkle *phyllo* in bottom of tart pan evenly with one third crumb mixture and top with another *phyllo* sheet, arranging it at right angles to first *phyllo* sheet so overhang is even all around. Dot *phyllo* with butter and sprinkle with half of remaining crumb mixture. Continue layering in same manner, ending with *phyllo*.

Trim *phyllo* overhang with scissors to 1 inch beyond rim of tart pan and roll toward center, forming a shallow edge just inside tart pan. Brush shell with remaining butter and bake in middle of oven 12 minutes, or until golden and crisp. Cool shell in pan on a rack. *Shell may be made 1 day ahead and kept, loosely covered, in tart pan in a cool, dry place.*

Make Filling: Peel pineapple and halve lengthwise. Core halves and cut crosswise into ¼-inch-thick slices. Halve vanilla bean lengthwise and scrape seeds into a 12-inch heavy skillet. Add vanilla pod, pineapple, and sugars and simmer over moderate heat, carefully turning pineapple occasionally (try to keep slices whole), until most liquid is evaporated and pineapple is slightly translucent (reducing heat as liquid is evaporated), about 25 minutes. Cool mixture slightly and discard vanilla pod.

Arrange pineapple in overlapping concentric circles in shell and top with any syrup remaining in skillet. *Tart may be made 1 day ahead and kept, loosely covered, at room temperature.* SERVES 8.

Photo above

MIXED BERRIES IN COCOA MERINGUE NESTS

For Meringue Nests

3 large egg whites

¼ teaspoon cream of tartar

⅔ cup sugar

2 tablespoons unsweetened cocoa powder

For Vanilla Cream

1 cup vanilla low-fat yogurt

4 ounces Neufchâtel cheese, softened

3 tablespoons sugar

1 teaspoon vanilla

2 cups mixed fresh berries

Make Nests: Preheat oven to 250° F. Line a baking sheet with foil or parchment paper and trace four 4-inch circles on foil or paper.

In a large bowl with an electric mixer beat whites with cream of tartar and a pinch salt on moderately low speed until they are very frothy and begin to hold soft peaks. Increase speed to moderately high and gradually beat in sugar. Gradually increase speed to high, beating until meringue is thick and glossy. Sift cocoa powder over meringue and with a large rubber spatula fold in gently but thoroughly. Transfer meringue to a pastry bag fitted with a ½-inch plain tip and, beginning along inside edge of a traced circle, gently pipe meringue onto foil or parchment, filling in circle (do not press hard on pastry bag). Form 3 more rounds in same manner. Pipe 2 or 3 layers of meringue on top of outer edge of each round to create shallow nests. Bake meringue nests in middle of oven 1½ hours, or until firm and dry. Cool nests on foil or parchment on a rack and carefully peel off foil. *Meringue nests may be made 1 day ahead and kept, tightly wrapped in plastic wrap, at room temperature.*

Make Vanilla Cream: In a sieve lined with a paper towel and set over a bowl drain yogurt 30 minutes and discard liquid. In a food processor blend yogurt, cheese, sugar, and vanilla just until smooth and transfer to a bowl. *Chill vanilla cream, covered, until cold, at least 1 hour, and up to 1 day.*

Put ½ cup berries in each nest and top with a dollop of vanilla cream. **SERVES 4.**

KUMQUAT, GRAPE, AND KIWIFRUIT SOUP WITH ORANGE MUSCAT

½ cup kumquats

1½ cups water

½ cup sugar

½ cup orange Muscat such as Essensia

2 tablespoons fresh lemon juice

½ pound black grapes (about 1½ cups)

3 kiwifruits

Cut kumquats into thin slices and remove seeds. In a saucepan simmer water, sugar, and kumquats 10 minutes and stir in Muscat and lemon juice. Simmer soup 3 minutes. *Chill soup, covered, until cold, at least 2 hours, and up to 3 days.*

Halve grapes and remove seeds. Cut halves into very thin slices. Peel kiwifruits and halve lengthwise. Cut halves into thin slices. Stir grapes and kiwifruits into soup. **SERVES 6.**

Photo on back jacket

FROZEN MOCHA MOUSSE

— · —

3 ounces semisweet chocolate

1 cup milk

3 large egg yolks

¼ cup unsweetened Dutch-process cocoa powder such as Droste

¼ cup light corn syrup

1 tablespoon instant espresso powder*

1 cup water (2 tablespoons hot)

2 tablespoons Kahlúa or other coffee-flavored liqueur

1 teaspoon unflavored gelatin (less than 1 envelope)

2 tablespoons Just Whites (powdered egg whites)**

⅓ cup sugar

GARNISH: semisweet chocolate shavings

available at specialty foods shops, some supermarkets, and by mail order from Adriana's Caravan, tel. (800) 316-0820

**available at some supermarkets and by mail order from New York Cake and Baking Distributors, tel. (800) 942-2539.*

Chop chocolate. In a heavy saucepan bring milk to a boil and remove pan from heat. In a heatproof bowl whisk together yolks, cocoa powder, and corn syrup until smooth and whisk in hot milk in a stream. Transfer mixture to saucepan and cook over moderately low heat, stirring constantly with a wooden spoon, until thickened and an instant-read thermometer registers 170° F. (do not boil). Pour custard through a sieve into a metal bowl and add chocolate, stirring frequently until smooth. Set bowl in a larger bowl of ice and cold water and cool custard, stirring occasionally.

In a small saucepan dissolve espresso powder in 2 tablespoons hot water and add liqueur. Sprinkle gelatin over espresso mixture and let stand 1 minute to soften gelatin. Cook mixture over low heat, stirring occasionally, until gelatin is dissolved and stir into chocolate custard.

In bowl of a standing electric mixer sprinkle Just Whites over 6 tablespoons water and let stand, stirring occasionally with a whisk until powder is dissolved and mixture is frothy, about 5 minutes. In a small heavy saucepan bring sugar and remaining ½ cup water to a boil over moderate heat, stirring until sugar is dissolved, and boil until syrup registers 240° F. on a candy thermometer. While syrup is boiling, beat Just Whites until they just form soft peaks. Beat in hot syrup in a stream (try to avoid pouring onto beaters and side of bowl) and beat meringue until completely cool, thick, and glossy. With a large rubber spatula stir one third meringue into mocha mixture to lighten and fold in remaining meringue gently but thoroughly.

Pour mousse into a 1½-quart metal loaf pan (about 10 by 4½ by 3 inches). *Freeze mousse, uncovered, until frozen, about 4 hours, and covered with plastic wrap, up to 2 days.*

Dip loaf pan into a large bowl of warm water and run a thin knife around side of pan. Dry pan. Invert a platter over pan and invert mousse onto it.

Sprinkle mousse with chocolate shavings and cut into 1-inch-thick slices. SERVES 8 TO 10.

COCOA
ANGEL FOOD CAKE
WITH ORANGE GLAZE

For Cake
  1 cup self-rising cake flour
  ⅓ cup sifted unsweetened Dutch-process
    cocoa powder such as Droste
    (sift before measuring)
  1¼ cups granulated sugar
  1½ cups egg whites (from 10 to 11 large eggs)
  ¼ teaspoon salt
  2 teaspoons vanilla

For Orange Glaze
  2 cups confectioners' sugar
  3 tablespoons strained fresh orange juice
  1 tablespoon orange-flavored liqueur

Make Cake: Preheat oven to 325° F.

In a small bowl whisk together flour, cocoa powder, and ½ cup granulated sugar. In a large bowl with an electric mixer beat whites with salt on medium speed until white, opaque, and beginning to hold their shape. Gradually add remaining ¾ cup granulated sugar, beating at high speed until whites hold soft (not stiff), slightly glossy peaks. Beat in vanilla.

Sift about one third cocoa mixture over whites and fold in gently but thoroughly, scraping bottom of bowl to prevent lumps. Sift and fold in remaining cocoa mixture, half at a time, in same manner and pour batter into an ungreased 10-inch tube pan (about 4 inches deep) with a removable bottom. With a knife make a series of side-by-side chops in batter to remove air bubbles and smooth top. Bake cake in middle of oven 40 to 45 minutes, or until firm to the touch. Invert cake over neck of a bottle and cool completely.

Run a thin knife around edge of cake and remove side of pan. Run knife under bottom of cake and around center tube to loosen cake and invert cake onto a rack.

Make Glaze: Sift confectioners' sugar into a small saucepan and stir in orange juice and liqueur to make a smooth paste. Heat glaze over moderate heat until just warm to the touch.

Quickly pour warm glaze over cake, spreading evenly over top with a spatula and allowing excess to drip down outside. (Alternatively, spoon glaze into a heavy-duty plastic bag and squeeze into 1 corner. Snip a small hole in corner and streak glaze over cake from center outward.)

While glaze is still wet (to avoid cracking), transfer cake to a plate. When glaze is set, cover cake loosely with plastic wrap or place under a cake dome and keep at room temperature until ready to serve. *If cake is kept more than 1 day (before or after serving), it should be wrapped in plastic wrap and frozen. Bring cake to room temperature before serving.* SERVES 10.

Photo above

CRANBERRY APPLESAUCE

4 apples (about 2 pounds)

1 lemon

1 cup picked-over fresh cranberries

½ cup sugar

¼ cup apple juice or water

a 3-inch cinnamon stick

2 tablespoons unsalted butter

Peel, core, and chop apples. With a vegetable peeler remove a 3-inch strip zest from lemon. In a heavy saucepan cook apples, cranberries, sugar, and apple juice or water with zest and cinnamon stick over moderate heat, stirring, 15 minutes, or until apples are very soft, and discard zest and cinnamon stick. Force apple mixture through medium disk of a food mill into a bowl and stir in butter. *Applesauce keeps, covered and chilled, 1 week.* Serve applesauce warm or chilled. **MAKES ABOUT 3 CUPS.**

Photo below

FROZEN PLUM MERINGUE CAKE

For Meringue Layers

¾ cup hazelnuts (about 4 ounces)

1 cup sugar

1 tablespoon cornstarch

4 large egg whites

¼ teaspoon cream of tartar

For Filling

1 pound Italian prune plums (about 20)

½ cup sugar

1 tablespoon fresh lemon juice

1 teaspoon finely grated fresh lemon zest

2 tablespoons kirsch

½ gallon vanilla frozen yogurt

Make Meringue Layers: Preheat oven to 350° F. Line 2 baking sheets with foil or parchment paper and, using bottom of a 9½-inch springform pan as a guide, trace 1 circle on each sheet of foil or parchment.

In a shallow baking pan toast hazelnuts in middle of oven until they begin to turn pale golden, 7 to 10 minutes. Wrap nuts in a kitchen towel and rub to remove any loose skins (do not worry about skins that do not come off). Cool nuts completely.

Reduce temperature to 250° F.

In a food processor finely grind hazelnuts with ½ cup sugar and cornstarch. In a large bowl with an electric mixer beat whites with cream of tartar and a pinch salt until they hold soft peaks. Gradually add remaining ½ cup sugar, beating until whites hold stiff, glossy peaks. Fold in hazelnut mixture gently but thoroughly and transfer meringue to a pastry bag fitted with a ½-inch plain tip. Beginning along inside edge of a traced circle, pipe meringue onto foil or parchment, filling in circle, and with an offset spatula gently smooth top. Form another round in same manner. Bake meringues in upper and lower thirds of oven, switching position of sheets halfway through baking, 1½ hours total, or until firm and dry. Cool meringues completely on sheets on racks and carefully peel off foil. *Meringue layers may be made 1 day ahead and kept, tightly wrapped in plastic wrap, at room temperature.*

Make Filling: Halve and pit plums. In a heavy saucepan simmer plums, sugar, lemon juice, and zest, stirring occasionally, 15 minutes, or until plums are very soft. Force plum mixture through a sieve into a bowl, scraping with a rubber spatula, and stir in kirsch. Set bowl in a larger bowl of ice and cold water and cool mixture completely, stirring occasionally. *Plum mixture may be made 1 day ahead and chilled, covered.* Soften frozen yogurt slightly. In a large bowl swirl together plum mixture and frozen yogurt.

Assemble Cake: Working with one meringue layer at a time, place bottom of 9½-inch springform pan over each layer and with a small knife carefully trim each to fit in pan. Place 1 meringue layer, smooth side down, in bottom of assembled springform pan and spoon yogurt filling onto it, smoothing top. Put remaining meringue layer, smooth side down, on top of filling, pressing gently. *Freeze cake, uncovered, until filling is hard, about 4 hours. Cake may be made 2 days ahead and frozen, covered with plastic wrap.* Let cake soften in refrigerator 30 minutes before serving. **SERVES 10 TO 12.**

BANANA CHOCOLATE-CHIP SOUFFLÉS

3 large egg whites
⅓ cup sugar
2 firm-ripe bananas (each about 6 ounces)
2½ tablespoons miniature semisweet chocolate chips

Preheat oven to 450° F. and lightly butter six ¾-cup ramekins (3½ inches in diameter by 1½ inches high).

In a bowl with an electric mixer beat whites until they just hold soft peaks and gradually beat in sugar until meringue holds stiff peaks. Coarsely grate bananas onto meringue and gently fold with chocolate chips into meringue.

Arrange ramekins on a baking sheet and divide mixture evenly among them, mounding it in centers. Run a knife around sides of ramekins, freeing mixture to aid rising, and bake soufflés in middle of oven until puffed and golden brown, about 15 minutes. Serve soufflés immediately. **SERVES 6.**

Photo above

CHOCOLATE RASPBERRY ROULADE

½ cup plain low-fat yogurt

½ teaspoon vanilla

1 tablespoon plus 4 teaspoons confectioners' sugar

½ cup heavy cream

chocolate-covered meringue (recipe follows)

1½ cups picked-over raspberries

cocoa cake roll (page 143)

1 tablespoon Chambord (optional)

ACCOMPANIMENT: raspberries

In a small bowl stir together yogurt, vanilla, and 1 tablespoon confectioners' sugar. In a large bowl with an electric mixer beat cream with 2 teaspoons confectioners' sugar until it just holds stiff peaks. Crumble meringue into ½-inch pieces and gently fold into whipped cream. Gently fold in raspberries and yogurt mixture until just combined.

Unroll cake roll on kitchen towel and brush inside with Chambord. Gently spoon whipped cream mixture lengthwise along center of cake and roll cake around filling so that long edges just come together. Place *roulade*, seam side down, on a platter. *Chill roulade 1 hour to facilitate slicing.*

Just before serving, dust *roulade* with remaining 2 teaspoons confectioners' sugar. Serve *roulade* with raspberries. SERVES 8 TO 10.

Photo below

CHOCOLATE-COVERED MERINGUE

2 large egg whites
¼ teaspoon cream of tartar
½ cup sugar
1 ounce fine-quality bittersweet chocolate
  (not unsweetened)

Preheat oven to 325° F. and line a baking sheet with parchment paper or foil.

In a bowl with an electric mixer beat whites on high speed until foamy. Add cream of tartar and beat until whites hold soft peaks. Add sugar and beat until meringue holds stiff, glossy peaks. Spread meringue about ½ inch thick on baking sheet (shape does not matter) and bake in middle of oven 45 minutes, or until crisp. Turn off oven. *Let meringue stand in oven 1 hour.* Remove meringue from oven and cool completely on baking sheet on a rack.

Carefully peel off parchment or foil and put meringue, flat side up, on a work surface. Chop chocolate and in a small heavy saucepan melt over low heat, stirring occasionally. Spread chocolate on meringue in a thin layer and chill until chocolate is set, about 10 minutes. *Meringue may be made 1 week ahead and kept in a sealable plastic bag at cool room temperature.*

COCOA CAKE ROLL

¼ cup water
⅓ cup unsweetened Dutch-process cocoa
  powder such as Droste
1 teaspoon vanilla
3 large egg yolks
⅔ cup sugar
½ cup cake flour (not self-rising)
½ teaspoon salt
4 large egg whites
½ teaspoon cream of tartar

Preheat heat oven to 425° F. Grease a 17- by 10½- by 1-inch jelly roll pan and line with wax paper or parchment paper. Butter paper and dust with flour, knocking out excess flour.

In a small saucepan bring water to a boil. Remove pan from heat and into water stir cocoa powder and vanilla until smooth.

In a large bowl with an electric mixer beat together yolks and ⅓ cup sugar on high speed until pale and thick, about 5 minutes. Add cocoa mixture and beat until mixture is thick again, 3 to 5 minutes. Add flour and salt and beat 1 minute. (If using a standing electric mixer, transfer mixture to a large shallow bowl better suited to folding.)

In a bowl with cleaned beaters beat whites on high speed until foamy. Add cream of tartar and beat until whites hold soft peaks. Add remaining ⅓ cup sugar and beat until meringue holds stiff, glossy peaks.

Stir about one fourth whites into cocoa mixture to lighten and fold in remaining whites gently but thoroughly. Spoon batter into a large pastry bag fitted with a ½-inch plain tip and, holding bag with tip about ½ inch from surface of jelly-roll pan, pipe lengthwise in side-by-side strips, filling pan. (Alternatively, gently spoon batter into pan.) Bake cake 8 minutes, or until it springs back when touched lightly in center with your finger. Cool cake in pan, covered with a damp kitchen towel, on a rack.

Invert cake onto towel and gently peel off wax paper or parchment paper. Beginning with a long side, roll up cake in towel jelly-roll fashion.

Jam-Filled Butter Cookies ▪ Goat Cheese Chocolate Truffles

Macadamia and Hazelnut Brittle

Gingered Lemon Squares ▪ Chocolate Crackle Cookies

Anise Pine-Nut Cookies ▪ Semolina Shortbread Cookies

Spice Cookies ▪ Chocolate-Dipped Coconut Macaroons

Almond- and Ginger-Stuffed Dates

Peanut Butter Cookies ▪ Peanut Butter Swirl Brownies

Chocolate Linzer Bars ▪ Pecan Lace Cookies

Fig Pinwheels ▪ Almond Macaroons

Chocolate Almond Clusters

Big Oatmeal Cinnamon Cookies ▪ Chocolate Banana Squares

Cranberry Pistachio Biscotti ▪ Orange Almond Biscotti

Champagne Truffles ▪ Geometric Crystallized Ginger Cookies

Chocolate-Dipped Apricots

BITES

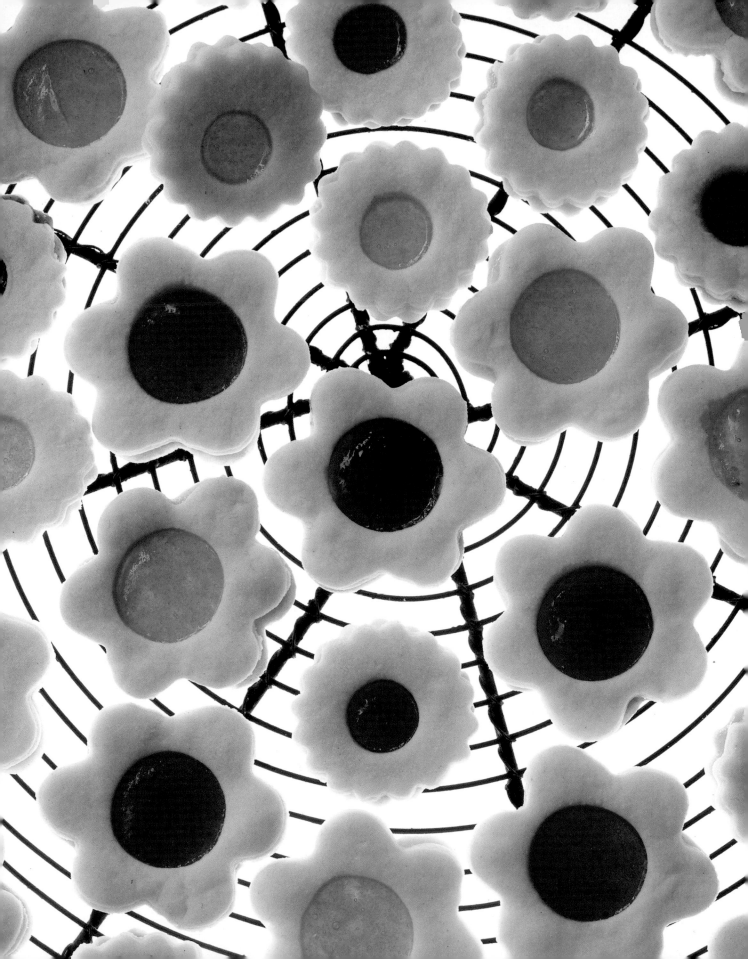

Bites—one or two bites—of something sweet is often just enough. Our cookies and confections come in every shape and size. Some, like our elegant Pecan Lace Cookies and Champagne Truffles, are ideal for formal occasions (both appear in our Champagne Dessert Party); while others, like Big Oatmeal Cinnamon Cookies and Peanut Butter Cookies need nothing fancier than a cold glass of milk. And don't overlook bar cookies—our Chocolate Linzer Bars and Gingered Lemon Squares are stylish as well as easy, and will serve a large gathering. Many of these goodies (like our brittle, chocolate-covered nuts and fruit, and *biscotti*) will keep for weeks and also make lovely gifts.

JAM-FILLED BUTTER COOKIES

1½ sticks (¾ cup) cold unsalted butter
1¾ cups all-purpose flour
½ cup confectioners' sugar
1 large egg yolk
2 tablespoons ice water
½ teaspoon light rum or vanilla
⅔ cup jam such as apricot, raspberry, or strawberry

Cut butter into bits. Into a bowl sift together flour and confectioners' sugar. Add butter and with a pastry blender or your fingertips blend until it resembles meal. In a small bowl whisk together yolk, ice water, and rum or vanilla and add to flour mixture, stirring until mixture forms a dough. On a work surface smear dough with heel of hand in a forward motion several times and form dough into a ball. Dust dough with flour. *Chill dough, wrapped in wax paper, 30 minutes.*

Preheat oven to 325° F. Grease 2 baking sheets. Halve dough. On a floured surface roll out 1 of halves ⅛ inch thick and cut into rounds with a 1½-inch scalloped cutter. Gather scraps. Reroll scraps and cut out more rounds. Roll out remaining half of dough and cut out more rounds. With a ½-inch plain round cutter cut out centers of half of rounds to form rings. Bake rounds and rings in batches on baking sheets in middle of oven 12 minutes, or until pale golden. Transfer cookies with a metal spatula to racks and cool.

In a small saucepan heat jam, stirring until melted, and with a rubber spatula force jam through a fine sieve into a bowl. Lightly spread bottom of each round with some jam and top with 1 ring. Drop a scant ¼ teaspoon remaining jam in center of each cookie. *Let cookies stand on racks 1 hour. Cookies keep, layered between sheets of wax paper in an airtight container and chilled, 2 days.* MAKES ABOUT 80 COOKIES.

Photo on page 145

GOAT CHEESE CHOCOLATE TRUFFLES

6 ounces fine-quality bittersweet chocolate (not unsweetened)

6 ounces (about ¾ cup) fresh goat cheese* (also known as goat *fromage blanc*)

2 tablespoons confectioners' sugar

½ teaspoon vanilla extract

⅛ teaspoon pure lemon extract

¼ cup unsweetened cocoa powder for coating truffles

available at some specialty foods shops and by mail order from Fromagerie Belle Chèvre, tel. (800) 735-2238

Chop chocolate and in a metal bowl set over a saucepan of barely simmering water melt it, stirring until smooth. Remove bowl from heat and cool chocolate slightly. In a bowl whisk together cheese, confectioners' sugar, and extracts until light and fluffy and whisk in melted chocolate until combined well. *Chill truffle mixture, covered, 1 hour, or until firm.*

Sift cocoa powder into a small shallow bowl. Form heaping teaspoons of truffle mixture into balls and roll in cocoa powder to coat. *Chill truffles on a baking sheet lined with wax paper 30 minutes, or until firm. Truffles keep in an airtight container, chilled, 3 days.* **MAKES ABOUT 25 TRUFFLES.**

Photo right

MACADAMIA AND HAZELNUT BRITTLE

¾ cup macadamia nuts (about 4 ounces)

½ cup hazelnuts (about 2½ ounces)

1 cup sugar

⅓ cup light corn syrup

½ teaspoon baking soda

½ stick (¼ cup) unsalted butter

Butter a shallow baking pan.

Coarsely chop nuts. In a 2½- to 3-quart heavy saucepan bring sugar and corn syrup to a boil over moderate heat, without stirring, and boil until a candy thermometer registers 255° F. Add nuts, stirring, and boil until thermometer registers 300° F. Remove pan from heat and stir in baking soda (mixture will bubble and steam). Stir in butter until well combined. Immediately pour mixture into baking pan, tilting pan to cover bottom. Cool brittle completely and break into large pieces. *Brittle keeps in an airtight container at room temperature 2 weeks.* **MAKES 1 POUND BRITTLE.**

GINGERED LEMON SQUARES

For Crust

¼ cup whole almonds with skins
1 stick (½ cup) cold unsalted butter
¼ cup confectioners' sugar
1 cup all-purpose flour

For Filling

2 large eggs
¾ cup granulated sugar
¼ cup fresh lemon juice
2 tablespoons all-purpose flour
½ teaspoon baking powder
1 teaspoon ground ginger

confectioners' sugar for dusting squares

Preheat oven to 350° F.

Make Crust: In a small baking pan lightly toast almonds in oven until fragrant, 7 to 10 minutes, and cool completely. Cut butter into pieces. In a food processor finely grind almonds with confectioners' sugar and flour. Add butter and pulse until mixture just resembles coarse meal. Pat mixture into bottom of an 8-inch square baking pan and bake in middle of oven 15 to 20 minutes, or until pale golden. Cool crust completely in pan on a rack.

Make Filling: In a bowl with an electric mixer beat eggs until thick and pale and beat in granulated sugar and lemon juice. Continue to beat mixture 8 minutes. Sift in remaining ingredients and a pinch salt and stir until combined well.

Pour filling over crust and bake in middle of oven 20 to 25 minutes, or until filling is set and pale golden. Cool confection in pan on rack and dust with confectioners' sugar. Cut confection into 2-inch squares. *Lemon squares keep covered and chilled 2 days.* **MAKES 16 SQUARES.**

Photo below

CHOCOLATE CRACKLE COOKIES

½ cup all-purpose flour

½ cup granulated sugar

¼ cup unsweetened Dutch-process cocoa powder

½ teaspoon baking powder

¼ teaspoon salt

2 tablespoons unsalted butter, softened

1 large egg

2 tablespoons confectioners' sugar plus additional for dusting hands

Preheat oven to 400° F. and lightly grease 2 baking sheets.

In a metal bowl stir together flour, granulated sugar, cocoa powder, baking powder, and salt and blend in butter with fingertips. In a small bowl lightly beat egg and stir into mixture until combined well. Spread dough in a thin layer in bowl and freeze 10 minutes, or until firm.

Spoon level teaspoons of dough onto a sheet of wax paper. Put 2 tablespoons confectioners' sugar in a small bowl and dust hands with additional. Form each piece of dough into a ball and roll in confectioners' sugar. Arrange balls about 2 inches apart on baking sheets and bake in upper and lower thirds of oven, switching position of sheets halfway through baking, 8 to 10 minutes total, or until cookies are just set. Transfer cookies to racks and cool. *Cookies keep in an airtight container at room temperature 5 days.* MAKES ABOUT 30 COOKIES.

Photo on page 41

ANISE PINE-NUT COOKIES

¾ cup pine nuts

½ stick (¼ cup) unsalted butter, softened

¼ cup vegetable shortening

⅓ cup confectioners' sugar

¼ cup granulated sugar

1 teaspoon vanilla

1 cup plus 2 tablespoons all-purpose flour

½ teaspoon salt

¼ teaspoon baking powder

½ teaspoon anise seeds

Preheat oven to 325° F. and grease 2 large baking sheets.

In a shallow baking pan lightly toast pine nuts, stirring occasionally, until pale golden, 10 to 12 minutes, and cool completely. In a bowl with an electric mixer beat together butter, shortening, and sugars until light and fluffy and beat in vanilla. In another bowl whisk together flour, salt, and baking powder and add to butter mixture, beating until just combined. In a small food processor or blender finely grind anise seeds with ½ cup pine nuts and add to dough, beating until combined well.

Drop teaspoons of dough about 2 inches apart onto baking sheets and top each cookie with several remaining whole pine nuts. Bake cookies in upper and lower thirds of oven, switching position of sheets halfway through baking, 18 to 20 minutes total, or until golden. Cool cookies on sheets 2 minutes and with a metal spatula carefully transfer (cookies are very delicate) to racks to cool completely. *Cookies keep in an airtight container 4 days.* MAKES ABOUT 55 COOKIES.

Photo on page 119

SEMOLINA
SHORTBREAD COOKIES

— · —

2 sticks (1 cup) unsalted butter, softened
2/3 cup sugar
1 1/4 cups all-purpose flour
2/3 cup semolina*
1/2 teaspoon salt

*available at Italian markets, some supermarkets, and by mail order from Balducci's, tel. (800) 225-3822

In a large bowl with an electric mixer beat together butter and sugar until light and fluffy. Add remaining ingredients and beat until combined well. Halve dough and roll out each half between sheets of wax paper into a 13-inch round (about 1/4 inch thick). Remove top sheet of wax paper from each round and with a 3-inch round cutter cut rounds, leaving *all* dough on wax paper. Replace top sheets of wax paper and stack dough on a baking sheet. *Chill dough until firm, about 20 minutes.*

Preheat oven to 375° F.

Transfer dough, still between sheets of wax paper, to a work surface and remove top sheets of wax paper. With a metal spatula transfer rounds to ungreased baking sheets, arranging them about 1 inch apart. Bake cookies in upper and lower thirds of oven, switching position of sheets halfway through baking, about 15 minutes total, or until pale golden. Transfer cookies to racks and cool completely. While cookies are baking, reroll scraps and make more cookies in same manner. *Cookies keep in airtight containers at room temperature 1 week.* MAKES ABOUT 45 COOKIES.

SPICE COOKIES

— · —

1 1/2 cups all-purpose flour
1 teaspoon baking powder
1/2 teaspoon salt
3/4 teaspoon coarsely ground black pepper
1 teaspoon ground ginger
3/4 teaspoon ground cinnamon
1/4 teaspoon ground cloves
a pinch cayenne
1 stick (1/2 cup) unsalted butter, softened
1 cup sugar
1 large egg

Into a bowl sift together flour, baking powder, salt, pepper, and spices. In a large bowl with an electric mixer beat together butter and sugar until light and fluffy. Add egg and beat until combined well. Beat in flour mixture until combined well. Halve dough and roll out each half between sheets of wax paper into a 10-inch round (about 1/4 inch thick). Remove top sheet of wax paper from each round and with a 3-inch scalloped leaf-shaped cutter cut cookies, leaving *all* dough on wax paper. Replace top sheets of wax paper and stack dough on a baking sheet. *Chill dough until firm, about 20 minutes.*

Preheat oven to 350° F.

Transfer dough, still between sheets of wax paper, to a work surface and remove top sheets of wax paper. With a metal spatula transfer leaf shapes to ungreased baking sheets, arranging them about 1 inch apart. Bake cookies in upper and lower thirds of oven, switching position of sheets halfway through baking, 10 to 12 minutes total, or until edges begin to turn pale golden. Transfer cookies to a rack and cool. While cookies are baking, reroll scraps and make more spice cookies in same manner. *Cookies keep in airtight containers at room temperature 2 weeks.* MAKES ABOUT 42 COOKIES.

CHOCOLATE-DIPPED COCONUT MACAROONS

4 large egg whites
1⅓ cups sugar
½ teaspoon salt
1½ teaspoons vanilla
2½ cups sweetened flaked coconut
¼ cup plus 2 tablespoons all-purpose flour
8 ounces fine-quality bittersweet chocolate
(not unsweetened)

Preheat oven to 300° F. and butter 2 baking sheets.

In a heavy saucepan stir together whites, sugar, salt, vanilla, and coconut. Sift in flour and stir until combined well. Cook mixture over moderate heat, stirring constantly, 5 minutes. Increase heat to moderately high and cook mixture, stirring constantly, 3 to 5 minutes more, or until thickened and begins to pull away from bottom and side of pan. Transfer dough to a bowl and cool slightly. *Chill dough, its surface covered with plastic wrap, until just cold, about 30 minutes.* Drop heaping teaspoons of dough about 2 inches apart onto baking sheets and bake in batches in middle of oven 20 to 25 minutes, or until pale golden. Transfer macaroons to a rack and cool.

Chop chocolate and in a small metal bowl set over a saucepan of barely simmering water melt it, stirring until smooth. Remove bowl from heat. With fingertips dip macaroons 1 at a time into chocolate, coating them halfway and hold macaroons over chocolate a few seconds to let excess chocolate drip back into bowl. Transfer dipped macaroons to a foil-lined tray. *Chill macaroons 30 minutes, or until chocolate is set. Macaroons keep, layered between sheets of wax paper in an airtight container and chilled, 3 days. Bring macaroons to room temperature before serving.* MAKES ABOUT 30 MACAROONS.

Photo right

ALMOND- AND GINGER-STUFFED DATES

½ cup whole almonds with skins
3 tablespoons chopped crystallized ginger
24 pitted whole dates

Lightly toast almonds and cool completely. Halve 12 almonds lengthwise and reserve. In a food processor finely grind remaining almonds and ginger until mixture holds together when pinched. Transfer mixture to a small bowl and knead until it holds together. Mold rounded teaspoons of almond mixture around reserved almond halves to form 24 almond shapes. Working with 1 date at a time, make an incision along length of date. Open date carefully and fill with a molded almond, pressing date gently around almond (filling will not be completely enclosed). *Dates keep in an airtight container, chilled, 2 days.* MAKES 24 CONFECTIONS.

PEANUT BUTTER COOKIES

½ cup vegetable shortening
1 cup chunky peanut butter
1 cup packed light brown sugar
1 large egg
1½ cups all-purpose flour
½ teaspoon baking soda
½ teaspoon salt

Preheat oven to 400° F.

In a bowl beat together shortening, peanut butter, and brown sugar until light and fluffy and beat in egg. Stir in flour, baking soda, and salt.

Form tablespoons of dough into balls, transferring to ungreased baking sheets. With tines of a fork flatten cookies, making a crosshatch pattern, and bake in batches in middle of oven 8 to 10 minutes, or until golden. Transfer cookies to racks and cool completely. *Cookies keep in an airtight container at room temperature 5 days.* MAKES ABOUT 36 COOKIES.

Photo below

PEANUT BUTTER SWIRL BROWNIES

2½ sticks (1¼ cups) unsalted butter, softened
1 cup chunky peanut butter
½ cup packed light brown sugar
3 large eggs
8 ounces cream cheese, softened
4 ounces unsweetened chocolate
2 cups granulated sugar
1 teaspoon vanilla
⅞ cup all-purpose flour

Preheat oven to 350° F. and butter a 13- by 9-inch baking pan.

In a bowl beat together ½ stick butter, peanut butter, and brown sugar and beat in 1 egg and cream cheese, a little at a time, beating until smooth.

Chop chocolate. In a saucepan melt 1 stick of remaining butter with chocolate over low heat, stirring until smooth, and cool. In another bowl beat together remaining stick butter and granulated sugar until light and fluffy and beat in remaining 2 eggs, 1 at a time, beating well after each addition. Stir in chocolate mixture and vanilla. Sift in flour and stir until combined well.

Pour chocolate batter into baking pan and drop dollops of peanut butter mixture on top. With a knife swirl batters to marble. Bake brownies in middle of oven 45 to 50 minutes, or until they pull away slightly from sides of pan and a tester comes out with crumbs adhering. Cool brownies before cutting into squares. *Brownies keep, layered between sheets of wax paper in an airtight container at cool room temperature, 5 days.* MAKES ABOUT 24 BROWNIES.

Photo left

CHOCOLATE LINZER BARS

1¼ cups hazelnuts
¾ cup sugar
1½ sticks (¾ cup) unsalted butter, softened
½ teaspoon salt
1 teaspoon vanilla
1 large egg yolk
1½ cups all-purpose flour
½ teaspoon baking soda
1 cup raspberry jam
2 ounces semisweet chocolate or
    ½ cup chocolate chips

Preheat oven to 350° F. Grease and flour a 13- by 9-inch baking pan, knocking out excess flour.

In another shallow baking pan toast hazelnuts in 1 layer in middle of oven until they begin to turn pale golden, about 7 minutes. Wrap hazelnuts in a kitchen towel and rub to remove any loose skins (do not worry about skins that do not come off). Cool nuts completely and in a food processor finely grind with ¼ cup sugar. In a large bowl with an electric mixer beat together hazelnut mixture, butter, remaining ½ cup sugar, salt, and vanilla until combined well. Add egg yolk and beat until smooth. Sift in flour and baking soda and beat just until a dough forms.

Press dough into bottom of prepared baking pan and bake in middle of oven 25 to 30 minutes, or until pale golden. Leaving a ¼-inch border, spread jam evenly on hot crust and bake 10 minutes more, or until jam is bubbling gently. Cool confection completely in pan on a rack.

Chop semisweet chocolate, if using. In a small bowl set over a saucepan of barely simmering water melt chopped chocolate or chocolate chips, stirring until smooth, and remove bowl from heat. Transfer chocolate to a small heavy-duty plastic bag and gently squeeze chocolate to 1 corner. Snip a small hole in corner and pipe chocolate over jam in a back and forth motion to form thin stripes. *Let confection stand until chocolate is set, about 20 minutes. Cut confection into 1½- by ¾-inch bars. Bars keep, layered between sheets of wax paper in an airtight container and chilled, 5 days.* MAKES ABOUT 100 SMALL BARS.

PECAN LACE COOKIES

1 cup pecan pieces
1 stick (½ cup) unsalted butter
½ cup packed brown sugar
⅓ cup light corn syrup
½ cup all-purpose flour
½ teaspoon salt

Preheat oven to 375° F.

In a food processor coarsely grind pecans. In a saucepan heat butter, brown sugar, and corn syrup, stirring occasionally, until sugar is dissolved. Remove pan from heat and stir in nuts, flour, and salt until combined well.

Working in batches of 4, drop heaping tablespoons of dough about 4 inches apart onto an ungreased baking sheet. Bake cookies in middle of oven 6 minutes, or until golden.

Working quickly, remove cookies, 1 at a time, with a thin metal spatula from sheet and immediately drape over a rolling pin to create a curved shape. (If cookies become too brittle to drape on rolling pin, return sheet to oven a few seconds to allow them to soften.) Cool cookies completely on rolling pin and transfer to an airtight container. Make more cookies with remaining batter in same manner. *Cookies keep in airtight containers at room temperature 2 days.* MAKES ABOUT 30 COOKIES.

Photo on page 12

FIG PINWHEELS

— · —

For Filling
    1 pound fresh figs
    ½ cup water

For Dough
    ¼ cup hazelnuts
    1¼ cups all-purpose flour
    1 cup cornmeal
    2 tablespoons finely grated fresh lemon zest
    ½ teaspoon salt
    1½ sticks (¾ cup) unsalted butter, softened
    1 cup sugar
    2 large egg yolks
    ½ teaspoon vanilla

Make Filling: Quarter figs and in a small saucepan simmer in water, stirring occasionally, until the consistency of jam, about 40 minutes. Remove pan from heat and with a fork mash remaining large pieces. Transfer filling to a bowl and cool. *Chill filling, covered, at least 1 hour and up to 2 days.*

Make Dough: In a food processor finely grind nuts and in a bowl whisk together with flour, cornmeal, zest, and salt. In a large bowl with an electric mixer beat together butter and sugar until light and fluffy. Add yolks and vanilla and beat until combined well. Add flour mixture, beating just until combined.

Divide dough into thirds and roll out each piece between sheets of wax paper into a 12- by 7-inch rectangle (about ⅛ inch thick). Remove top sheet of wax paper from 1 rectangle and, leaving a ¼-inch border, thinly spread top of rectangle with about one third filling. Beginning on a long side and using wax paper as an aid, roll up rectangle into a tight log. Make 2 more logs in same manner. *Freeze logs until firm, at least 20 minutes, and up to 1 week.*

Preheat oven to 375° F. and line 2 large baking sheets with wax paper.

Cut logs into ½-inch-thick slices and arrange about ½ inch apart on baking sheets. Bake cookies in batches in middle of oven 15 minutes, or until golden brown. Transfer cookies to racks and cool. *Cookies keep in airtight containers at room temperature 5 days.* MAKES ABOUT 72 COOKIES.

ALMOND MACAROONS

— · —

    1 cup blanched almonds
    ⅔ cup granulated sugar
    1 large egg white
    ¼ teaspoon almond extract
    confectioners' sugar for dusting dough
    16 whole almonds with skins

Preheat oven to 350° F. and lightly butter a baking sheet.

In a food processor finely grind blanched almonds with granulated sugar. Add egg white, almond extract, and a pinch salt and pulse until combined. Form dough into 16 balls, each about 1 inch in diameter, and arrange about 2 inches apart on baking sheet. Slightly flatten balls and lightly dust with confectioners' sugar. Gently press 1 whole almond into each cookie.

Bake macaroons in middle of oven 10 minutes, or until pale golden. Transfer macaroons to a rack and cool completely. *Macaroons keep in an airtight container at room temperature 4 days.* MAKES 16 MACAROONS.

Photo on page 47

CHOCOLATE ALMOND CLUSTERS

2 cups whole blanched almonds
1 cup sugar
¼ cup water
9 ounces fine-quality bittersweet chocolate
(not unsweetened)

Preheat oven to 350° F. and line a tray with parchment paper.

Toast almonds in a baking pan in 1 layer in middle of oven until golden, 7 to 10 minutes.

In a small heavy saucepan heat sugar and water over moderately low heat, stirring slowly with a fork, until sugar is melted and pale golden. Cook caramel, without stirring, swirling pan, until golden. Remove pan from heat and stir in almonds. Form clusters of about 5 nuts with a spoon and drop onto sheets of parchment paper (use caution when handling hot caramel). If caramel becomes too thick to form clusters, reheat over moderate heat to soften slightly. Cool clusters.

Chop chocolate and in a metal bowl set over a saucepan of barely simmering water melt three fourths chocolate, stirring until smooth. Remove bowl from heat and add remaining chocolate in 2 or 3 batches, stirring until smooth and allowing each batch to melt before adding next.

With a fork submerge 1 cluster in chocolate. Hold cluster over chocolate a few seconds to let excess chocolate drip back into bowl and transfer to parchment paper. Repeat procedure with remaining clusters. *Let clusters stand until chocolate is set, about 20 minutes. Clusters keep, in airtight containers and chilled, 2 weeks.* MAKES ABOUT 35 CLUSTERS.

BIG OATMEAL CINNAMON COOKIES

2½ cups all-purpose flour
1 teaspoon baking soda
1 teaspoon salt
½ teaspoon baking powder
½ teaspoon cinnamon
2 sticks (1 cup) unsalted butter, softened
1 cup granulated sugar
½ cup packed light brown sugar
2 large eggs
2 cups old-fashioned rolled oats
such as Quaker

Preheat oven to 375° F. and grease 2 large baking sheets.

In a small bowl whisk together flour, baking soda, salt, baking powder, and cinnamon. In a large bowl with an electric mixer beat together butter and sugars until light and fluffy. Add eggs 1 at a time, beating well after each addition, and beat in flour mixture and oats until just combined.

Drop heaping 2 tablespoons of dough about 3 inches apart onto sheets. Bake cookies in batches if necessary in upper and lower thirds of oven, switching position of sheets halfway through baking, about 12 minutes total, or until pale golden. Cool cookies on sheets on racks 5 minutes and transfer to racks to cool completely. *Cookies keep in airtight containers at room temperature 5 days.* MAKES ABOUT 20 COOKIES.

CHOCOLATE BANANA SQUARES

For Crust
    1 cup all-purpose flour
    1 stick (½ cup) unsalted butter
    ⅓ cup granulated sugar

For Banana Topping
    2½ pounds ripe bananas
    ¼ cup packed light brown sugar
    2 tablespoons unsalted butter, softened
    1 tablespoon fresh lemon juice

    3 ounces fine-quality bittersweet chocolate

Preheat oven to 375° F. and butter a 9-inch square baking pan.

Make Crust: In a food processor pulse crust ingredients until a dough just forms. Pat dough evenly onto bottom of baking pan and bake in middle of oven 25 minutes, or until pale golden.

Make Banana Topping: Cut bananas into ¼-inch-thick slices and in a large bowl toss with brown sugar, butter, and lemon juice.

Transfer topping to crust, spreading evenly. Bake confection in upper third of oven 40 minutes, or until pale golden, and cool completely in pan on a rack. Cut confection into 1½-inch squares.

Chop chocolate and in a small metal bowl set over a saucepan of barely simmering water melt it, stirring until smooth. Transfer melted chocolate to a small heavy-duty plastic bag and gently squeeze chocolate to 1 corner. Snip a small hole in corner and pipe chocolate over banana squares in a back and forth motion to form thin stripes. Let squares stand until chocolate is set, about 15 minutes. *Squares keep, layered between sheets of wax paper in airtight containers at room temperature, 2 days.* MAKES ABOUT 36 SQUARES.

CRANBERRY PISTACHIO BISCOTTI

    1⅓ cups dried cranberries (about 4 ounces)
    2½ cups unbleached all-purpose flour
    1 cup sugar
    ½ teaspoon baking soda
    ½ teaspoon baking powder
    ½ teaspoon salt
    4 large eggs
    1 teaspoon vanilla
    1 cup shelled natural pistachios

Preheat oven to 325° F. and butter and flour a large baking sheet, knocking out excess flour.

In a bowl cover cranberries with hot water and let soak 5 minutes. Drain cranberries well and pat dry. In bowl of a standing electric mixer fitted with paddle attachment blend flour, sugar, baking soda, baking powder, and salt until combined well. Add 3 eggs and vanilla, beating until a dough is formed, and with a wooden spoon stir in cranberries and pistachios.

Turn out dough onto a lightly floured surface. Knead dough several times and halve it. Working on baking sheet, with floured hands form each half into a flattish log 13 inches long and 2 inches wide and arrange logs at least 3 inches apart on sheet. Beat together remaining egg and 1 teaspoon water and brush logs with egg wash.

Bake logs in middle of oven 30 minutes and transfer sheet to a rack to cool slightly, 10 minutes. On a cutting board diagonally cut logs into ¾-inch-thick slices and arrange *biscotti*, cut sides down, on sheet. Bake *biscotti* in middle of oven 10 minutes. Remove sheet from oven and turn *biscotti* over with a spatula. Bake *biscotti* 10 minutes more, or until pale golden and transfer to racks to cool. *Biscotti keep in airtight containers at room temperature 1 week.* MAKES ABOUT 36 BISCOTTI.

Photo right

ORANGE ALMOND BISCOTTI

1½ cups whole almonds with skins
2 cups unbleached all-purpose flour
1 cup sugar
1 teaspoon baking soda
¼ teaspoon salt
3 whole large eggs
1 large egg yolk
1 teaspoon vanilla
1 tablespoon finely grated fresh orange zest

Preheat oven to 300° F. and butter and flour a large baking sheet, knocking out excess flour.

Toast almonds and coarsely chop. In bowl of an electric mixer fitted with paddle attachment blend flour, sugar, baking soda, and salt until combined well. In a small bowl whisk together 2 whole eggs, yolk, vanilla, and zest and add to flour mixture, beating until a dough is formed. With a wooden spoon stir in almonds.

Turn out dough onto a lightly floured surface. Knead dough several times and halve it. Working on baking sheet, with floured hands form each piece of dough into a flattish log 12 inches long and 2 inches wide and arrange logs at least 3 inches apart on sheet. Beat together remaining whole egg and 1 teaspoon water and brush logs with egg wash.

Bake logs in middle of oven 50 minutes and transfer sheet to a rack to cool slightly, 10 minutes. On a cutting board diagonally cut logs crosswise into ½-inch-thick slices and arrange *biscotti*, cut sides down, on sheet. Bake *biscotti* in middle of oven 15 minutes. Remove sheet from oven and turn *biscotti* over with a spatula. Bake *biscotti* 15 minutes more, or until pale golden and transfer to racks to cool. *Biscotti keep in airtight containers at room temperature 1 week.* MAKES ABOUT 48 BISCOTTI.

Photo below

CHAMPAGNE TRUFFLES

For Truffle Mixture

12 ounces fine-quality bittersweet chocolate (not unsweetened)

1 stick (½ cup) unsalted butter

a split (1½ cups) Champagne

1 teaspoon cornstarch

⅓ cup heavy cream

⅛ teaspoon salt

For Coating and Decorating Truffles

12 ounces fine-quality bittersweet chocolate (not unsweetened)

2 ounces fine-quality white chocolate such as Lindt

Make Truffle Mixture: Line an 8- or 9-inch square baking pan with plastic wrap, leaving a 3-inch overhang on ends.

Chop chocolate and in a food processor finely grind. Cut butter into pieces. In a small bowl whisk together 2 teaspoons Champagne and cornstarch until smooth. In a saucepan boil remaining Champagne until reduced to about ⅓ cup. Stir cornstarch mixture and whisk into Champagne in pan. Add butter, cream, and salt and simmer, whisking constantly, 3 minutes. Add cream mixture to ground chocolate and blend until smooth. Transfer mixture to baking pan, spreading evenly. *Chill truffle mixture until firm, about 6 hours.*

Invert truffle mixture onto work surface and peel off plastic wrap. Cut truffle mixture into 49 squares and with palms of your hands, press and roll squares into balls, transferring to a tray. (Mixture is very sticky; wash hands frequently and rinse in cold water.) *Chill balls until firm, at least 2 hours.*

Coat Truffles: Line a tray with wax paper. Chop bittersweet chocolate and in a metal bowl set over a saucepan of barely simmering water melt it, stirring until smooth. Remove bowl from heat and with 2 forks quickly submerge 1 ball in chocolate. Hold truffle over chocolate a few seconds to let excess chocolate drip back into bowl and transfer to tray. Repeat procedure with remaining balls. *Chill truffles until set, about 2 hours.*

Decorate Truffles: Chop white chocolate and in a metal bowl set over a saucepan of barely simmering water melt it, stirring until smooth. Transfer melted chocolate to a small heavy-duty plastic bag and gently squeeze chocolate to 1 corner. Snip a small hole in corner and pipe chocolate in decorative patterns over truffles.

Chill truffles until set, about 2 hours. Truffles keep, layered between sheets of wax paper in an airtight container and chilled, 2 weeks. Let truffles come to room temperature before serving. **MAKES 49 TRUFFLES.**

Photo below

GEOMETRIC CRYSTALLIZED GINGER COOKIES

1½ cups all-purpose flour
1 teaspoon ground cinnamon
¾ teaspoon ground ginger
¼ teaspoon baking soda
⅛ teaspoon freshly ground black pepper
1 stick (½ cup) unsalted butter, softened
¾ cup packed brown sugar
1 teaspoon vanilla
¼ teaspoon salt
1 large egg
¼ cup finely chopped crystallized ginger
royal icing (recipe follows)

Preheat oven to 350° F.

Into a bowl sift together flour, cinnamon, ground ginger, baking soda, and pepper. In another bowl with an electric mixer beat together butter, brown sugar, vanilla, and salt until combined well. Add egg and beat until smooth. Slowly beat in flour mixture and crystallized ginger until just combined.

Halve dough and transfer 1 piece to a large ungreased baking sheet. With a well-floured rolling pin roll out dough on sheet into an ⅛-inch-thick rectangle and trim edges to straighten. Bake dough in middle of oven until pale golden, about 10 minutes. Immediately transfer large cookie to a work surface and with a long sharp knife cut into random geometric shapes. Transfer cookies to racks to cool. Make more ginger cookies with remaining dough in same manner.

Transfer icing to a pastry bag fitted with a small plain tip and pipe decorative patterns onto cookies. Let cookies stand until icing is set. *Cookies keep, layered between sheets of wax paper in airtight containers at room temperature, 1 week.*

ROYAL ICING

4 teaspoons Just Whites
(powdered egg whites)*
¼ cup warm water
⅛ teaspoon cream of tartar
2 cups confectioners' sugar

available at some supermarkets and by mail order from New York Cake and Baking Distributors, tel. (800) 942-2539

In bowl of a standing electric mixer sprinkle Just Whites over ¼ cup warm water and let stand, stirring occasionally with a whisk, until egg powder is dissolved and mixture is frothy, about 5 minutes. Add cream of tartar and beat until foamy. Gradually beat in confectioners' sugar and beat until icing is thick and glossy, about 5 minutes.

CHOCOLATE-DIPPED APRICOTS

4 ounces fine-quality bittersweet chocolate
(not unsweetened)
2 cups dried apricots (about 8 ounces)

Line a tray with parchment paper. Chop chocolate and in a metal bowl set over a saucepan of barely simmering water melt it, stirring until smooth. Remove bowl from heat and with fingertips dip 1 apricot into chocolate to coat three fourths of it. Hold apricot over chocolate a few seconds to let excess chocolate drip back into bowl and transfer to tray. Repeat procedure with remaining apricots. *Chill apricots until chocolate is set, about 30 minutes. Apricots keep, layered between sheets of wax paper in airtight containers and chilled, 2 weeks.* MAKES ABOUT 45 APRICOTS.

Sweet Potato Maple Pie with Pecan Crust

Raspberry Swirl Parfaits ▪ Chestnut Bavarian Cream

Halloween Candied Lady Apples

Frozen Cranberry Soufflé with Spun Sugar Cranberry Wreath

Red, White, and Blue Cheesecake

Pumpkin Flan with Maple Caramel ▪ Lemon Pecan Crescents

Little Chocolate Cherry Cakes ▪ Hazelnut Shortbread

Valentine Meringue Hearts

Passover Chocolate Nut Cake with Grilled Oranges

Mother's Day "Mochaccino" Cups

Star-Spangled Orange Buttermilk Cupcakes

Easter Ricotta Pie ▪ Father's Day Mint Chocolate Cream Pie

Rhubarb Lemon Cake Roll ▪ Individual Mincemeat Pithiviers

Rocky Road Cream Cheese Fudge ▪ Maple Walnut Fudge

HOLID

AYS

H olidays and traditional sweets go hand-in-hand, and you'll find plenty of yummy favorites in this chapter—*two* fudge recipes for Christmas, a creamy Easter ricotta pie, even little candied apples for your Trick-or-Treaters.... Then, for the more adventurous, we have created a selection of unusual offerings. Why not try our Pumpkin Flan with Maple Caramel this Thanksgiving? Or, delight mom on her day with "Mochaccino" Cups, a fanciful chilled mocha finale served in your china coffee cups? Our holiday desserts may look extra-special, but they really aren't complicated. And, most of them can be made ahead of time!

SWEET POTATO MAPLE PIE WITH PECAN CRUST

For Crust

- 1 cup pecan pieces
- 2 tablespoons sugar
- ¾ stick (6 tablespoons) cold unsalted butter
- 1¼ cups all-purpose flour
- ½ teaspoon salt
- 3 tablespoons ice water
- pie weights or raw rice for weighting crust

For Filling

- 2 pounds sweet potatoes (about 3 medium)
- 3 large eggs
- 1 cup half-and-half
- ¾ cup pure maple syrup
- 1½ teaspoons maple extract
- 1 teaspoon ground cinnamon
- 1 teaspoon ground ginger
- ¼ teaspoon ground cloves
- ½ teaspoon salt

ACCOMPANIMENTS
whipped cream
pure maple syrup

Preheat oven to 425° F.

Make Crust: In a food processor coarsely grind pecans with sugar and transfer to a bowl. Cut butter into pieces. In food processor blend together butter, flour, and salt until mixture resembles meal and add to pecan mixture. Add ice water and toss until water is incorporated. Press dough onto bottom and up side of a 9-inch (1-quart) deep-dish pie plate and crimp edge decoratively. Prick crust all over with a fork. *Chill crust 30 minutes. Crust may be made 2 weeks ahead and frozen, wrapped well in plastic wrap.* Line crust with foil and fill with pie weights or rice. Bake crust in middle of oven 7 minutes. Carefully remove foil and pie weights or rice and bake crust 5 minutes more. Cool crust on a rack.

Reduce temperature to 350° F.

Make Filling: Peel sweet potatoes and cut into 1-inch cubes. In a steamer set over boiling water steam potatoes, covered, 20 to 25 minutes, or until very tender. Force potatoes through a ricer into a large bowl or in a large bowl beat with an electric mixer until smooth. In another large bowl lightly beat eggs and whisk in sweet-potato purée and remaining filling ingredients, whisking until smooth. *Filling may be made 2 days ahead and chilled, covered.*

Pour filling into crust. Bake pie in middle of oven 40 to 45 minutes, or until just set in middle, and cool on rack.

Serve pie topped with whipped cream and drizzled with maple syrup. **SERVES 8 TO 10.**

Photo on page 161

RASPBERRY SWIRL PARFAITS

two 10-ounce packages frozen raspberries
  in light syrup, thawed
½ cup walnuts
3 large eggs
2½ tablespoons sugar
2½ tablespoons honey
¾ cup well-chilled heavy cream
GARNISH: fresh raspberries

In a food processor purée raspberries, including syrup. Force purée through a fine sieve into a heavy saucepan, pressing hard on solids, and boil purée, stirring occasionally, until reduced to about 1 cup. Cool purée and chill.

Lightly toast walnuts and cool completely. Chop walnuts. Have ready a large bowl of ice and cold water. In a metal bowl with a hand-held electric mixer beat together eggs, sugar, and honey until combined well. Set bowl over a pan of simmering water and beat mixture until pale, thick, and an instant-read thermometer registers 160° F. Set bowl over bowl of ice water and beat until cold. In another bowl with cleaned beaters beat cream until it just holds stiff peaks and fold with walnuts into egg mixture gently but thoroughly. Alternately spoon raspberry purée and cream mixture into six 6-ounce glasses and swirl with a wooden skewer. *Freeze parfaits, covered, at least 8 hours and up to 2 days. Let parfaits stand at room temperature 15 minutes before serving.*

Garnish parfaits with raspberries. **SERVES 6.**

Photo right

CHESTNUT BAVARIAN CREAM

—·—

1 envelope unflavored gelatin

2 tablespoons water

¾ cup milk

4 large eggs

½ cup sugar

a 7.4-ounce jar vacuum-packed whole chestnuts

2 tablespoons Frangelico

1½ teaspoons vanilla

1 cup well-chilled heavy cream

ACCOMPANIMENT: 2 cups hot fudge sauce (page 99)

In a small bowl sprinkle gelatin over water and let stand 1 minute to soften gelatin.

In a small heavy saucepan bring milk to a simmer and remove pan from heat. In a bowl whisk together eggs and sugar and add milk in a stream, whisking. In saucepan cook custard over moderately low heat, whisking, until slightly thickened and an instant-read thermometer registers 170° F. (do not boil). Pour custard through a fine sieve into cleaned bowl and add gelatin mixture, whisking until gelatin is dissolved. In a blender purée 18 chestnuts with Frangelico, vanilla, and custard, scraping down side frequently with a rubber spatula, until smooth. Transfer mixture to a metal bowl set in a larger bowl of ice and cold water. Cool mixture, stirring occasionally with spatula, until thick and cold but not completely set and remove bowl from ice water.

Coarsely chop remaining chestnuts and reserve some for garnish. In a bowl with an electric mixer beat cream until it just holds stiff peaks and fold into custard gently but thoroughly with chestnuts. Pour Bavarian cream into a 1-quart bowl and sprinkle with reserved chestnuts. *Chill Bavarian cream, covered, until firm, at least 3 hours, and up to 1 day.*

Serve Bavarian cream with sauce. **SERVES 8 TO 10.**

HALLOWEEN CANDIED LADY APPLES

—·—

16 Popsicle sticks* or sixteen 6-inch bamboo skewers

16 lady apples (about 2 pounds)

½ cup blanched almonds (about 3 ounces; optional)

2 cups sugar

available by mail order from New York Cake and Baking Distributors, tel. (800) 942-2539

Preheat oven to 350° F. and line a baking sheet with parchment paper.

If using bamboo skewers, cut each to measure 4½ inches. Remove stems from apples and insert sticks or skewers into stem ends. Arrange apples on baking sheet.

Finely chop almonds. Toast almonds in a shallow baking pan in middle of oven, stirring occasionally, until golden, about 10 minutes. Transfer almonds to a small bowl and cool.

In a dry large heavy saucepan cook sugar over moderately low heat, stirring slowly with a fork, until melted and pale golden. Cook caramel, without stirring, swirling pan, until deep golden. Remove saucepan from heat and working quickly, submerge 1 apple in caramel, tilting pan if necessary. Lift apple, scraping bottom against side of pan to remove excess caramel. Lightly roll coated apple in almonds and transfer to baking sheet. Make more candied apples in same manner and let stand until coating is hardened. *Candied apples may be made 1 day ahead and kept, loosely covered, at cool room temperature.* **MAKES 16 CANDIED APPLES.**

FROZEN
CRANBERRY SOUFFLÉ

For Cranberry Mixture
>   2½ cups picked-over cranberries
>   ⅔ cup sugar
>   ⅔ cup water

For Meringue
>   ¾ cup sugar
>   ⅓ cup water
>   4 large egg whites

>   2½ cups well-chilled heavy cream

For Spun Sugar Wreath
>   ⅓ cup light corn syrup
>   ¼ cup sugar
>   ½ cup picked-over cranberries
>   GARNISH: fresh mint sprigs

Make Cranberry Mixture: In a heavy saucepan bring cranberry mixture ingredients to a boil, stirring until sugar is dissolved, and simmer, stirring occasionally, 5 minutes, or until thickened. Cool mixture completely.

Make Meringue: In a small heavy saucepan bring sugar and water to a boil, stirring until sugar is dissolved. Boil syrup, washing down any sugar crystals clinging to side of pan with a brush dipped in water, until a candy thermometer registers 248° F. and remove pan from heat. While syrup is boiling, in large bowl of a standing electric mixer beat whites with a pinch salt until they hold soft peaks. With motor running, add hot syrup in a stream, beating, and beat meringue on medium speed until completely cool, about 8 minutes.

Fold cranberry mixture into meringue gently but thoroughly. In a bowl with cleaned beaters beat cream until it just holds stiff peaks and fold into cranberry meringue mixture gently but thoroughly. Spoon soufflé into a 2½-quart (8-inch diameter) freezer-proof glass bowl, smoothing top. *Freeze soufflé, its surface covered with plastic wrap, at least 8 hours and up to 3 days.*

Make Spun Sugar Wreath: In a small heavy saucepan bring corn syrup and sugar to a boil over moderate heat, stirring until sugar is dissolved, and boil syrup, without stirring, until a golden caramel and a candy thermometer registers 320° F. While syrup is boiling, lightly oil a 12-inch-square sheet of foil and on it arrange cranberries in a 6-inch-wide wreath shape. Remove pan from heat and cool syrup 30 seconds. Dip a fork into syrup and drizzle syrup over cranberries, repeating until cranberries are covered with syrup and a solid wreath is formed. (If syrup becomes too thick to drizzle from fork, reheat over moderate heat until right consistency.) Cool wreath completely. *Wreath may be made 2 hours ahead (preferably not on a damp day) and kept in a cool, dry place.*

Pry wreath gently from foil and arrange on soufflé. Garnish wreath with mint sprigs. **SERVES 8.**

Photo above

RED, WHITE, AND BLUE CHEESECAKE

For Crust

    28 chocolate wafers

    1 stick (½ cup) unsalted butter

For Filling

    four 8-ounce packages cream cheese, softened

    1½ cups sugar

    2 tablespoons all-purpose flour

    5 large eggs

    ½ cup sour cream

    1 teaspoon finely grated fresh orange zest

    1 teaspoon finely grated fresh lemon zest

    ½ teaspoon salt

    1½ teaspoons vanilla

    about 1½ cups picked-over raspberries

    about 1½ cups picked-over blueberries

Make Crust: In a blender or food processor finely grind wafers. Melt butter and in a bowl stir together with cookie crumbs until combined well. Pat mixture onto bottom and ½ inch up side of a 9½-inch spring-form pan. *Chill crust 30 minutes.*

Preheat oven to 325° F. Line bottom and sides of a shallow baking pan with foil.

Make Filling: In a bowl with an electric mixer beat cream cheese until light and fluffy. Gradually beat in sugar and beat until combined well. Beat in flour and add eggs 1 at a time, beating well after each addition. Beat in remaining filling ingredients until combined well.

Pour filling into crust. Set cheesecake in baking pan and bake in middle of oven 1 hour and 10 minutes. (Cheesecake will not be completely set; it will set as it cools.) Turn oven off and let cheesecake stand in oven with oven door ajar about 6 inches until cooled completely. *Chill cheesecake, covered, at least 6 hours and up to 2 days.*

Remove side of pan. Arrange raspberries on top of cheesecake in a star shape and arrange blueberries around star to completely cover top of cheesecake. **SERVES 10 TO 12.**

Photo opposite

PUMPKIN FLAN WITH MAPLE CARAMEL

    ¾ cup pure maple syrup
       (preferably dark amber)

    1⅓ cups canned solid-pack pumpkin

    1 cup sweetened condensed milk

    2 cups whole milk

    ⅓ cup sugar

    3 whole large eggs

    5 large egg yolks

    1 teaspoon vanilla

    1 teaspoon cinnamon

    ¼ teaspoon freshly grated nutmeg

    ⅛ teaspoon ground allspice

    ¼ teaspoon salt

Preheat oven to 325° F.

In a small heavy saucepan boil syrup, stirring occasionally, until a candy thermometer registers 230° F., about 8 minutes (maple syrup will bubble up). Immediately pour syrup into a 1½-quart shallow baking dish, tilting to coat bottom, and let harden.

In a large bowl whisk together remaining ingredients until smooth and pour through a sieve over hardened syrup. Put dish in a larger baking pan and add enough hot water to pan to reach halfway up side of dish. Bake flan in middle of oven until just set, about 1 hour and 10 minutes. Remove flan from water bath and cool on a rack. *Chill flan, covered, at least 4 hours and up to 1 day.* Run a thin knife around edge of dish and invert a platter over it. Quickly invert flan onto platter. **SERVES 8 TO 10.**

LEMON PECAN CRESCENTS

— · —

1 cup pecan pieces
1 cup confectioners' sugar plus additional
  for sifting over cookies
2 sticks (1 cup) unsalted butter, softened
1 large egg yolk
1 tablespoon fresh lemon juice
1 teaspoon vanilla
2 cups all-purpose flour
1 teaspoon salt

Preheat oven to 350° F.

In a food processor finely grind pecans with ½ cup confectioners' sugar. Into a bowl sift ½ cup confectioners' sugar and with an electric mixer beat together with butter and nut mixture. Add yolk, lemon juice, and vanilla and beat until smooth. Add flour and salt and beat until combined.

Transfer dough to a pastry bag fitted with a ⅜-inch plain tip and pipe 2-inch crescents about 1 inch apart onto ungreased baking sheets. Bake cookies in batches in middle of oven 10 to 12 minutes, or until they just begin to turn golden. While still warm, transfer cookies with a metal spatula to a platter and sift confectioners' sugar over them to coat well. Cool cookies completely. *Cookies keep layered between sheets of wax paper in an airtight container at cool room temperature 1 week.* MAKES ABOUT 120 COOKIES.

LITTLE CHOCOLATE CHERRY CAKES

— · —

½ cup dried tart cherries*
¼ cup *eau-de-vie de framboise* or other
  raspberry liqueur
3 ounces fine-quality bittersweet chocolate
  (not unsweetened)
½ stick (¼ cup) unsalted butter
½ cup granulated sugar
½ teaspoon vanilla
2 large eggs
¼ cup plus 2 tablespoons all-purpose flour
¼ teaspoon salt
confectioners' sugar for sifting over cakes

*available at specialty foods shops and some supermarkets and by mail order from American Spoon Foods, tel. (888) 735-6700

Preheat oven to 350° F. and generously butter six ½-cup muffin cups.

In a small saucepan simmer cherries in liqueur, stirring, until all liquid is evaporated and let cool.

Chop chocolate and cut butter into pieces. In a small metal bowl set over a pan of barely simmering water melt chocolate and butter, stirring until smooth. Remove bowl from heat and whisk in granulated sugar and vanilla. Whisk in eggs 1 at a time, whisking well after each addition. Add flour and salt, stirring until just combined, and fold in cherries.

Divide batter among muffin cups and bake in middle of oven about 20 minutes, or until a tester comes out with crumbs adhering. Turn cakes out onto a rack and cool. *Cakes keep in an airtight container at room temperature 4 days.*

Cut out a 1¼-inch paper heart and center on top of 1 cake. Sift confectioners' sugar over cake and carefully remove heart. Decorate remaining cakes in same manner. MAKES 6 LITTLE CAKES.

Photo on back jacket

HAZELNUT
SHORTBREAD

— · —

1 cup hazelnuts

⅔ cup confectioners' sugar

2 sticks (1 cup) unsalted butter, softened

1½ cups all-purpose flour

½ teaspoon salt

2 tablespoons granulated sugar

Preheat oven to 375° F and butter a 10-inch round baking pan.

In a shallow baking pan toast hazelnuts in middle of oven until they begin to turn pale golden, 7 to 10 minutes. Wrap nuts in a kitchen towel and rub to remove any loose skins (do not worry about skins that do not come off). Cool nuts completely. In a food processor finely grind hazelnuts.

Into a bowl sift confectioners' sugar and with an electric mixer beat together with butter. Add nuts, flour, and salt and beat just until combined. Spread dough with a rubber spatula in buttered baking pan, smoothing top, and sprinkle with 1 tablespoon granulated sugar. Make a design in dough by lightly pressing with tines of a fork.

Bake shortbread in middle of oven 20 to 25 minutes, or until pale golden. Cool shortbread in baking pan on a rack 10 minutes. Sprinkle shortbread with remaining tablespoon granulated sugar and cut into decorative shapes. *Shortbread keeps, layered between sheets of wax paper in an airtight container and chilled, 1 week.* MAKES ABOUT 18 COOKIES.

VALENTINE
MERINGUE HEARTS

— · —

2 large egg whites

⅛ teaspoon cream of tartar

½ cup packed light brown sugar

1 teaspoon vanilla

1 cup super-premium or homemade ice cream

ACCOMPANIMENT: dark chocolate sauce (page 81) and/or raspberry sauce (page 81)

Preheat oven to 275° F. On a piece of paper draw a heart measuring 3 inches across. Using drawing as a template, put a sheet of parchment paper over drawing and with a pencil trace 4 times on parchment paper. Invert parchment paper onto a baking sheet.

In a bowl with an electric mixer beat whites with a pinch salt until foamy. Add cream of tartar and beat until whites hold soft peaks. Add brown sugar 1 tablespoon at a time, beating until sugar is dissolved, and beat in vanilla. Transfer meringue to a pastry bag fitted with a ½-inch star or plain tip and, beginning along inside edge of 1 traced heart, gently pipe meringue onto parchment, filling in heart. Make 3 more hearts in same manner. With remaining meringue pipe "kisses" (½-inch mounds with peaks) onto sheet. Bake meringues in middle of oven 45 minutes. Turn off oven and, with oven door ajar, dry meringues in oven 1 hour.

Soften ice cream slightly and carefully remove meringues from parchment. Sandwich about ½ cup ice cream between smooth sides of 2 hearts, gently pressing hearts together. With a small spatula or knife smooth sides of ice cream layer. Make another sandwich in same manner and wrap sandwiches in plastic wrap. *Freeze sandwiches until firm, at least 2 hours, and up to 3 days. "Kisses" keep in an airtight container at room temperature 3 days.*

Pour sauce onto 2 plates and arrange hearts and kisses on top. SERVES 2.

PASSOVER CHOCOLATE NUT CAKE

- – · –

For Cake

- 1 cup pecans
- 1 cup hazelnuts
- 1 cup almonds
- 1 cup walnuts
- 7 ounces fine-quality bittersweet chocolate (not unsweetened)
- ¾ cup sugar
- 8 large eggs, separated
- 1 teaspoon finely grated fresh lemon zest
- 1 tablespoon finely grated fresh orange zest

For Grilled Oranges

- 12 navel oranges
- ½ cup honey

Make Cake: Preheat oven to 350° F. Lightly grease a 9-inch springform pan and line bottom with parchment paper.

In a food processor in batches finely grind nuts, transferring to a bowl. Chop chocolate and in cleaned food processor finely grind with 6 tablespoons sugar. In a bowl with an electric mixer beat yolks until thick and pale and add chocolate mixture. Add zests and beat until just combined. In another bowl with cleaned beaters beat whites with remaining 6 tablespoons sugar until they hold soft peaks. Fold nuts and meringue alternately into chocolate mixture gently but thoroughly until just combined.

Pour batter into pan and bake in middle of oven 55 minutes, or until a tester comes out clean. Cool cake in pan on a rack and remove side of pan. *Cake may be made 1 day ahead and kept, covered with plastic wrap, at room temperature.*

Make Grilled Oranges: Working over a bowl, with a sharp knife cut peel and pith from oranges and cut sections free from membranes, allowing sections to drop into bowl. Add honey to orange sections and toss gently. Let oranges stand 10 minutes. Heat a ridged grill pan over high heat until hot and grill oranges in batches about 10 seconds on each side.

Serve cake with grilled oranges. **SERVES 10 TO 12.** Photo opposite

MOTHER'S DAY "MOCHACCINO" CUPS

- – · –

- 1 envelope unflavored gelatin
- 3 tablespoons instant espresso powder*
- 1 tablespoon unsweetened cocoa powder
- ½ cup sugar
- 2 tablespoons Kahlúa or Grand Marnier
- 2 cups well-chilled half-and-half
- 1 cup ice cubes
- ½ cup well-chilled heavy cream
- cinnamon for dusting desserts

*available at specialty foods shops and some supermarkets and by mail order from Adriana's Caravan, tel. (800) 316-0820

Chill 6 coffee cups on a tray in freezer.

In a blender blend together gelatin, espresso powder, cocoa powder, and ¼ cup sugar. Add liqueur and ½ cup half-and-half and blend until combined well. Let mixture stand in blender 1 minute to soften gelatin.

In a small saucepan heat 1 cup half-and-half and remaining ¼ cup sugar over moderate heat, stirring, until very hot (do not boil) and add to mocha mixture. Blend mixture on low speed 3 minutes. Add remaining ½ cup half-and-half and ice cubes and blend on high speed 3 minutes. Immediately pour mixture into cups. *Chill desserts at least 2 hours, or until set, and, covered, up to 2 days.*

In a bowl beat heavy cream just until thickened. Top desserts with whipped cream and lightly dust with cinnamon. **SERVES 6.**

STAR-SPANGLED ORANGE BUTTERMILK CUPCAKES

— · —

For Cupcakes

1½ cups cake flour (not self-rising)

½ teaspoon baking powder

¼ teaspoon baking soda

¼ teaspoon salt

1 stick (½ cup) unsalted butter, softened

1 cup granulated sugar

2 large eggs

1 tablespoon finely grated fresh orange zest

1 teaspoon vanilla extract

½ cup well-shaken buttermilk

For Icing

4 ounces cream cheese, softened

1 cup confectioners' sugar

½ teaspoon pure orange extract

GARNISH: red or blue sanding sugar* (Note: to make stars you will need a 1½- to 2-inch star-shaped cookie cutter*)

*available by mail order from New York Cake and Baking Distributors, tel. (800) 942-2539

Make Cupcakes: Preheat oven to 375° F. and line twelve ½-cup muffin cups with paper liners. Lightly butter edges of muffin pan around cups.

Into a bowl sift together flour, baking powder, baking soda, and salt and sift again into another bowl. In a large bowl with an electric mixer beat butter until creamy and gradually beat in sugar until light and fluffy. Beat in eggs 1 at a time, and beat in zest and vanilla. Add flour mixture and buttermilk alternately in batches, beginning and ending with flour mixture and beating after each addition until just combined. Spoon batter into muffin cups, filling them about two thirds full. Bake cupcakes in middle of oven until golden and a tester comes out clean,

about 15 minutes. Cool cupcakes in pan on a rack 10 minutes and turn out onto racks to cool completely.

Make Icing: In a bowl with an electric mixer beat cream cheese until creamy. Sift in confectioners' sugar and beat until smooth. Beat in orange extract.

Spread icing evenly over cupcakes, smoothing tops. Gently push a 1½- to 2-inch star cutter into icing of 1 cupcake and spoon about ¼ teaspoon sanding sugar into cutter, tilting cupcake to distribute sugar evenly into star points. Remove cutter and wipe clean. Decorate remaining cupcakes in same manner. **MAKES 12 CUPCAKES.**

EASTER RICOTTA PIE

— · —

½ cup golden raisins

½ cup dried tart cherries*

¼ cup light rum

For Shell

1 stick (½ cup) cold unsalted butter

2 cups all-purpose flour

3 tablespoons sugar

½ teaspoon baking powder

½ teaspoon salt

3 large egg yolks

3 tablespoons ice water

1½ pounds whole-milk ricotta cheese (about 3 cups)

4 whole large eggs

1¼ cups sugar

1 teaspoon vanilla extract

¼ teaspoon almond extract

1 teaspoon finely grated fresh lemon zest

1 teaspoon finely grated fresh orange zest

2 tablespoons all-purpose flour

½ cup heavy cream

*available at specialty foods shops and by mail from American Spoon Foods, tel. (888) 735-6700

In a bowl stir together raisins, cherries, and rum. *Macerate fruit, covered, stirring occasionally, at room temperature at least 8 hours and up to 1 day.*

Make Shell: Cut butter into pieces and in a food processor pulse with flour, sugar, baking powder, and salt until most of mixture resembles coarse meal. Add yolks and water and pulse until mixture just forms a dough. On a lightly floured surface roll out dough into a 14- to 15-inch round (about ⅛ inch thick) and fit into a 10-inch springform pan. Press dough onto bottom and up side of pan and trim to about ½ inch below rim. *Chill shell until firm, about 1 hour and, covered, up to 1 day.*

Preheat oven to 350° F.

In a large bowl with an electric mixer beat together remaining ingredients (except macerated fruit) until smooth, about 5 minutes. Stir in fruit until combined well and pour filling into shell.

Bake pie in middle of oven 1½ hours, or until set and deep golden brown. Cool pie in pan on a rack. *Chill pie, loosely covered, until firm, at least 4 hours, and up to 2 days before unmolding.* SERVES 10 TO 12.

FATHER'S DAY MINT CHOCOLATE CREAM PIE

For Shell

5 tablespoons unsalted butter
six 5- by 2½-inch graham crackers
6 saltine crackers
3 tablespoons granulated sugar

For Filling

3 ounces unsweetened chocolate
½ stick (¼ cup) unsalted butter
⅔ cup granulated sugar
3 tablespoons cornstarch

3 tablespoons *crème de menthe* (preferably white)
3 large eggs
1 teaspoon vanilla
½ cup well-chilled heavy cream

For Topping

½ cup well-chilled heavy cream
1 tablespoon plain yogurt or sour cream
1 tablespoon confectioners' sugar

GARNISH: grated semisweet chocolate

Make Shell: Preheat oven to 375° F.

Melt butter and cool slightly. In a food processor finely grind crackers and granulated sugar. Add butter and blend until combined well. Press crumb mixture onto bottom and up side of a 9-inch glass pie plate. Bake shell in middle of oven 8 minutes, or until light brown, and cool completely on a rack.

Make Filling: Have ready a large bowl of ice and cold water. Chop chocolate and in a small heavy saucepan melt it and butter over low heat, stirring until smooth. Remove pan from heat. In a large metal bowl whisk together granulated sugar and cornstarch and whisk in *crème de menthe* and eggs, whisking until smooth. Whisk in chocolate mixture and transfer custard to saucepan. Bring custard to a simmer over moderately low heat, whisking constantly, and transfer to cleaned bowl. Set in bowl of ice water and stir in vanilla. Stir custard just until thick and cool and remove bowl from ice water. In another bowl with an electric mixer beat cream until it holds stiff peaks and fold into custard gently but thoroughly.

Pour filling into pie shell. *Chill pie until set, about 2 hours and, covered, up to 1 day.*

Make Topping: Beat heavy cream with yogurt or sour cream and confectioners' sugar until it just holds stiff peaks.

Spread topping evenly over pie and garnish with grated chocolate. SERVES 8.

RHUBARB LEMON CAKE ROLL

For Filling
1 pound rhubarb (about 4 thick stalks)
½ cup granulated sugar
1 teaspoon unflavored gelatin
(less than 1 envelope)
1 tablespoon cold water

For Lemon Cake
4 large eggs, separated
½ cup granulated sugar
2 teaspoons finely grated fresh lemon zest
1 teaspoon vanilla
¼ teaspoon salt
¼ cup all-purpose flour
¼ cup cornstarch
confectioners' sugar for dusting towel

For Lemon Syrup
2 tablespoons granulated sugar
1 tablespoon fresh lemon juice
1 tablespoon water

For Lemon Glaze
½ cup confectioners' sugar
1 tablespoon fresh lemon juice

ACCOMPANIMENT: white chocolate toasted almond
semifreddo (page 76)

Make Filling: Chop rhubarb and in a heavy saucepan cook with sugar over moderate heat, stirring frequently, 20 to 25 minutes, or until a thick purée is formed (about 1½ cups). In a very small bowl sprinkle gelatin over water and let stand 1 minute to soften gelatin. Add gelatin mixture to rhubarb and cook over low heat 1 minute, or until gelatin is dissolved. Transfer filling to a metal bowl and set in a bowl of ice and cold water. Cool filling, stirring occasionally, until thickened.

Make Lemon Cake: Preheat oven to 350° F. Grease a 15½- by 10½- by 1-inch jelly-roll pan and line bottom with foil. Grease foil and dust with flour, knocking out excess flour.

In a bowl with an electric mixer beat yolks, ¼ cup granulated sugar, zest, and vanilla until thick, pale, and mixture forms a ribbon when beaters are lifted.

In a large bowl with cleaned beaters beat whites with salt until they hold soft peaks. Gradually beat in remaining ¼ cup granulated sugar and beat until whites hold stiff peaks.

Stir one third whites into yolk mixture to lighten and fold in remaining whites gently but thoroughly. Sift flour and cornstarch over batter and fold in gently until batter is just combined.

Spread batter evenly in pan and bake in middle of oven 6 to 9 minutes, or until pale golden and springy to the touch. On a work surface dust a kitchen towel generously with confectioners' sugar. Invert cake onto towel and gently peel off foil. Beginning with a long side, loosely roll up cake in towel and cool 30 minutes.

Make Syrup: In a very small saucepan bring syrup ingredients to a simmer, stirring until sugar is dissolved. Keep syrup warm.

Assemble Cake: Carefully unroll cake and brush with half of syrup. Spread cake with filling and carefully reroll cake. Transfer cake to a platter, seam side down, and brush with remaining syrup. *Chill roll, loosely covered, at least 2 hours and up to 8 hours.*

Make Glaze: In a small bowl stir together sugar and lemon juice to make a pourable glaze.

Diagonally trim ends of cake. Transfer glaze to a small heavy-duty plastic bag and gently squeeze glaze to 1 corner. Snip a small hole in corner and pipe glaze decoratively over cake.

Serve cake with *semifreddo*. SERVES 6 TO 8.
Photo opposite

INDIVIDUAL MINCEMEAT PITHIVIERS

— · —

For Mincemeat

1 tart apple
⅓ cup packed brown sugar
⅓ cup raisins
3 tablespoons dried cranberries
3 tablespoons pecan or walnut pieces
  (optional)
2 tablespoons brandy or rum
1 tablespoon unsalted butter
1 teaspoon vanilla
1 teaspoon cider vinegar
1 teaspoon finely grated fresh orange zest
½ teaspoon cinnamon
¼ teaspoon ground allspice
¼ teaspoon freshly grated nutmeg
¼ teaspoon salt

2 thawed puff pastry sheets (from one
  17¼-ounce package frozen puff pastry)
1 large egg

Make Mincemeat: Peel, core, and cut apple into ¼-inch dice. In a small heavy saucepan cook all mincemeat ingredients over low heat, stirring, 15 minutes and cool completely. *Mincemeat may be made 1 week ahead and chilled in an airtight container.*

On a work surface unfold 1 pastry sheet. Using a 3-inch round cutter as a guide, with tip of a small sharp knife cut out 9 rounds and arrange about 1 inch apart on an ungreased baking sheet. Put a heaping tablespoon mincemeat in center of each round. Make 9 more rounds with remaining pastry sheet in same manner and cut out a small (¼-inch) hole in center of each round. In a small bowl lightly beat egg. Brush dough around mincemeat rounds with some egg, being careful not to let it drip down sides. Arrange a center-cut round on top of each mincemeat round and seal edges by firmly pressing together.

Holding knife tip down, draw back of knife from edge toward center of each pastry at ½-inch intervals to form a scalloped edge. Brush pastry tops with some egg. *Pastries may be frozen on a wax paper-lined baking sheet 2 hours, then kept frozen in sealable heavy-duty plastic bags up to 6 weeks. Do not thaw pastries before baking.*

Preheat oven to 400° F.

Bake *pithiviers* in middle of oven 15 to 20 minutes, or until golden brown. Serve *pithiviers* warm or at room temperature. **MAKES 9 PITHIVIERS.**

ROCKY ROAD CREAM CHEESE FUDGE

— · —

1½ cups walnut pieces
6 ounces unsweetened chocolate
8 ounces cream cheese, softened
1 teaspoon vanilla
⅛ teaspoon salt
a 1-pound box confectioners' sugar (4 cups)
½ cup packed light brown sugar
1½ cups miniature marshmallows

Line bottom and sides of an 8-inch square baking pan with wax paper.

Coarsely chop walnuts. Chop chocolate and in a metal bowl set over a pan of barely simmering water melt it, stirring until smooth. Remove bowl from heat and cool chocolate slightly. In a bowl with an electric mixer beat cream cheese with vanilla and salt until smooth. Gradually beat in sugars and beat in chocolate until combined well. Stir in walnuts and marshmallows and press fudge into pan. *Chill fudge 1 hour, or until firm.* Turn fudge out of pan, discarding wax paper, and cut fudge into squares. *Fudge keeps layered between sheets of wax paper in an airtight container at cool room temperature 1 week.* **MAKES ABOUT 2½ POUNDS FUDGE.**

Photo opposite

MAPLE WALNUT FUDGE

1 cup walnut pieces
1 cup packed light brown sugar
1 cup granulated sugar
1 cup pure maple syrup
2 tablespoons light corn syrup
¾ cup half-and-half
¼ teaspoon salt
2 tablespoons unsalted butter
1 teaspoon vanilla

GARNISH: walnut pieces

Line bottom and sides of an 8-inch square baking pan with foil and butter foil.

Chop walnuts. In a large heavy saucepan stir together sugars, syrups, half-and-half, and salt and cook over moderate heat, stirring and washing down any sugar crystals clinging to side of pan with a brush dipped in water, until sugar is completely dissolved. Bring mixture to a boil and boil, without stirring, until a candy thermometer registers 238° F. Remove pan from heat. Add butter and vanilla, without stirring, and let mixture cool until a candy thermometer registers 130° F. Beat mixture with a wooden spoon until it begins to lose its gloss, lightens in color, and thickens. (Do not overbeat or it will become too thick to spread.) Quickly stir in chopped walnuts and immediately spread fudge in baking pan. Score top with a knife into squares and top each square with a walnut piece. Cool fudge 15 minutes, or until it begins to harden. Cut fudge into squares and cool completely. *Fudge keeps layered between sheets of wax paper in an airtight container at cool room temperature 2 weeks.* MAKES ABOUT 2 POUNDS FUDGE.

Photo right

Lemon Verbena Pound Cake with Strawberries

Apricot Butter Cookies ▪ Bakewell Tart

Carrot and Pineapple Cake ▪ Cornmeal Raisin Cake

Mango Ginger Triangles with Lime Cream

Orange Poppy-Seed Cake with Berries and Crème Fraîche

Dried Fruit and Pomegranate Seed Upside-Down Cake

Miniature Currant Pies ▪ Banana Coffeecake

Jelly Doughnuts ▪ Honey Pecan Sticky Buns

Blueberry Scones ▪ Moravian Sugar Cake

Peach Cinnamon Streusel Muffins

Cranberry Cupcakes with Maple Cream-Cheese Frosting

Peanut Butter Fairy Cakes ▪ Cheesecake Phyllo Purses

Anise Lemon Madeleines ▪ Hazelnut Featherlight Cake

ANYT

IME

Anytime is a good time for sweets, and here is a collection of goodies that invites a cozy pot of tea or fresh-brewed coffee. Brunch, served with our satisfying Honey Pecan Sticky Buns, promises to be a success, while teatime calls for daintier delights, like Anise Lemon Madeleines, or Blueberry Scones with whipped cream and fruit preserves. (But there are no hard-and-fast rules!) Our Cornmeal Raisin Cake, ideal for noshing whenever the mood strikes, is still delicious days after baking, especially when toasted, buttered, and spread with marmalade. And don't forget to try our Peanut Butter Fairy Cakes and Peach Cinnamon Streusel Muffins—they make terrific lunchbox treats.

LEMON VERBENA POUND CAKE WITH STRAWBERRIES

For Cake

- 1 cup cake flour (not self-rising)
- ½ teaspoon baking powder
- ¼ teaspoon salt
- 3 tablespoons finely chopped fresh lemon verbena* or 1 tablespoon finely grated fresh lemon zest
- 1 tablespoon finely grated fresh lemon zest
- 1 stick (½ cup) unsalted butter, softened
- 1 cup granulated sugar
- 3 large eggs
- ¾ teaspoon vanilla
- 2 tablespoons milk
- 2 tablespoons fresh lemon juice

For Glaze

- ½ cup plus 1 tablespoon confectioners' sugar
- 1 tablespoon fresh lemon juice

ACCOMPANIMENT: strawberries

*available at specialty produce markets and some farmers markets

Make Cake: Preheat oven to 325° F. Butter and flour a 1-quart *kugelhupf* pan, knocking out excess flour.

In a bowl whisk together flour, baking powder, salt, verbena (or zest), and zest. In another bowl with an electric mixer beat together butter and granulated sugar until light and fluffy. Beat in eggs 1 at a time, beating well after each addition, and beat in vanilla. Beat in half of flour mixture. Beat in milk and lemon juice and beat in remaining flour mixture until just combined.

Spoon batter into pan, smoothing top, and bake in middle of oven 45 to 55 minutes, or until golden brown and a tester comes out clean. Cool cake in pan on a rack 15 minutes and invert onto rack set over a baking sheet to cool completely.

Make Glaze while Cake is Cooling: In a small bowl gradually whisk confectioners' sugar into lemon juice until smooth and thick.

When cake is completely cool, drizzle glaze over cake and let it drip down sides. *Cake may be made 1 day ahead and chilled, covered. Bring cake to room temperature before serving.*

Serve cake with strawberries. SERVES 8 TO 10.

Photo on page 179

APRICOT
BUTTER COOKIES

For Apricot Purée
¾ cup dried apricots (about ¼ pound)
¼ cup granulated sugar
⅔ cup water
1 tablespoon dark rum

For Dough
2½ cups all-purpose flour
1 teaspoon baking powder
2 sticks (1 cup) unsalted butter, softened
½ cup granulated sugar
¼ cup packed brown sugar
1 teaspoon vanilla
1 large egg

For Icing
1 cup confectioners' sugar
2 teaspoons fresh lemon juice

Make Purée: In a small saucepan simmer apricots, granulated sugar, and water 15 to 18 minutes, or until liquid is reduced by half. Add rum and cool mixture slightly. In a blender purée mixture and transfer to a bowl.

Make Dough: In a bowl whisk together flour, baking powder, and a pinch salt. In a large bowl with an electric mixer beat together butter, granulated sugar, and brown sugar until light and fluffy and beat in vanilla and egg until combined well. Add flour mixture and beat until just combined. Form dough into a log. *Chill log, wrapped in wax paper, 1 hour.*
Preheat oven to 350° F.

Divide log into 8 pieces. Working with 1 piece of dough at a time, on a sheet of plastic wrap form into 8-inch ropes, wrapping plastic wrap around ropes to keep dough from sticking. On 2 ungreased baking sheets pat ropes into 8- by 1½-inch rectangles. Make a canal down center of each rectangle with your finger and spread apricot purée in canals. Bake rectangles in batches in middle of oven 18 to 20 minutes, or until edges are golden. Transfer rectangles to racks to cool.

Make Icing: In a small bowl whisk together confectioners' sugar, lemon juice, and enough water to make a thick but pourable icing.

Drizzle icing over rectangles and diagonally cut into 1-inch strips. *Cookies keep in an airtight container 1 week.* **MAKES ABOUT 32 COOKIES.**

Photo below

BAKEWELL TART

For Pastry Dough

    1 stick (½ cup) cold unsalted butter
    1¼ cups all-purpose flour
    ¼ teaspoon salt
    2 to 4 tablespoons ice water

    pie weights or raw rice for weighting shell

For Filling

    ¼ cup raspberry jam
    ½ cup all-purpose flour
    ¼ cup sliced almonds
    ⅛ teaspoon salt
    1 stick (½ cup) unsalted butter, softened
    ½ cup granulated sugar
    1 whole large egg
    3 large egg yolks

For Icing

    1 cup confectioners' sugar
    1½ tablespoons water

Make Dough: Cut butter into bits and in a bowl with a pastry blender or in a food processor blend or pulse together with flour and salt until most of mixture resembles coarse meal with remainder in small (roughly pea-size) lumps. Drizzle 2 tablespoons ice water evenly over mixture and stir with a fork or pulse until incorporated. Test mixture by gently squeezing a small handful: When it has proper texture it should hold together without crumbling apart. If necessary, add more water, 1 tablespoon at a time, stirring or pulsing after each addition until incorporated, and test mixture again. (Do not overwork or add too much water; pastry will be tough.)

Turn mixture out onto a work surface and divide into 4 portions. With heel of hand smear each portion once in a forward motion to help distribute fat. Gather dough together and form it, rotating it on work surface, into a disk. *Chill dough, wrapped in plastic wrap, until firm, at least 1 hour, and up to 3 days.*

Preheat oven to 375° F.

On a lightly floured surface roll out dough into a 16- by 6-inch rectangle (about ⅛ inch thick) and fit into a 13½- by 4- by 1-inch tart pan with a removable fluted rim. Roll rolling pin over pan to trim shell flush with top of rim and with a fork prick bottom of shell all over. Line shell with foil and fill with pie weights or raw rice. Bake shell in middle of oven 10 minutes. Carefully remove foil and weights or rice and bake shell until pale golden, about 5 minutes more. Cool shell on a rack.

Make Filling: With a small offset spatula evenly spread jam on bottom of shell. In a food processor finely grind flour, almonds, and salt. In a bowl with an electric mixer beat together butter and granulated sugar until light and fluffy and beat in whole egg. Beat in yolks 1 at a time, beating well after each addition, and add flour mixture, beating until just combined. Spoon batter into tart shell, spreading evenly with spatula.

Bake tart in middle of oven about 30 minutes, or until puffed and golden. Cool tart in pan on a rack.

Make Icing: In a bowl stir together confectioners' sugar and water until combined well and transfer to a small heavy-duty plastic bag. Gently squeeze icing to 1 corner and snip a small hole in corner. Pipe icing onto tart in a back and forth motion to form stripes. Let tart stand at cool room temperature until icing is set, about 20 minutes. *Tart may be made 3 days ahead and kept tightly covered at cool room temperature.* SERVES 10.

CARROT AND PINEAPPLE CAKE

For Cake

1¾ cups cake flour (not self-rising)
1 teaspoon baking powder
¼ teaspoon baking soda
½ teaspoon salt
½ teaspoon ground allspice
4 large carrots
a 20-ounce can unsweetened crushed pineapple
2 large eggs
⅓ cup vegetable oil

For Frosting

an 8-ounce package cream cheese, softened
½ stick (¼ cup) unsalted butter, softened
1 cup confectioners' sugar
¾ cup unsweetened crushed pineapple
   reserved from making cake layer

Make Cake: Preheat oven to 350° F. Butter and flour an 8-inch springform pan, knocking out excess flour.

Into a bowl sift together flour, baking powder, baking soda, salt, and allspice. Coarsely shred carrots. Drain pineapple in a fine sieve. Transfer ¾ cup pineapple to a small bowl and reserve for icing. In a large bowl lightly beat eggs and whisk in oil, carrots, and 1¼ cups pineapple until combined. Stir flour mixture into carrot mixture until just combined. Spoon batter into pan, smoothing top, and bake in middle of oven until golden and a tester comes out clean, about 50 minutes. Cool cake in pan on a rack, 20 minutes. Remove side of pan and cool cake completely on rack.

Make Frosting: In a bowl with an electric mixer beat together cream cheese and butter until smooth. Beat in confectioners' sugar and reserved pineapple until frosting is just combined.

With a serrated knife horizontally halve cake. On a plate arrange bottom half, cut side up, and spread top with half of frosting. Put remaining cake half, cut side down, on frosting and spread top with remaining frosting. *Cake may be made 3 days ahead and chilled, covered. Bring cake to room temperature before serving.* SERVES 8.

CORNMEAL RAISIN CAKE

1½ sticks (¾ cup) cold unsalted butter
1¾ cups all-purpose flour
1¼ cups yellow cornmeal
½ cup sugar
1 tablespoon baking powder
1 teaspoon salt
1 whole large egg
1 large egg yolk
1 cup golden raisins
1 cup dark raisins
1 cup sour cream
⅔ cup milk
1 tablespoon fennel seeds

Preheat oven to 350° F. and butter a 9- by 5- by 3-inch loaf pan.

Cut butter into bits. In a food processor blend together butter, flour, cornmeal, sugar, baking powder, and salt until mixture resembles fine meal and transfer to a large bowl. Lightly beat whole egg and yolk and stir in with remaining ingredients until just combined. Spoon batter into pan, smoothing top.

Bake cake in middle of oven until golden and a tester comes out clean, about 1 hour and 15 minutes. Cool cake in pan on a rack 20 minutes. Run a thin knife around edge of pan and turn cake out onto rack. Invert cake and cool completely. *Cake keeps in an airtight container at room temperature 3 days.*

Serve cake slices plain or toasted and buttered. SERVES 12.

MANGO GINGER TRIANGLES

For Batter

- 2 mangoes (about 1½ pounds total)
- a 2-inch piece gingerroot
- 2¾ cups all-purpose flour
- 2 teaspoons baking powder
- 1 teaspoon salt
- ½ teaspoon baking soda
- 1 stick (½ cup) unsalted butter, softened
- 1½ cups granulated sugar
- 1 teaspoon vanilla
- 2 large eggs
- ½ cup milk

For Lime Cream

- an 8-ounce package cream cheese
- ⅔ cup confectioners' sugar
- 3 tablespoons fresh lime juice, or to taste
- ¼ cup heavy cream

Make Batter: Preheat oven to 350° F. Butter and flour a 13- by 9-inch baking pan, knocking out excess flour.

Peel and pit mangoes and cut enough flesh into ¼-inch dice to measure 2 cups. Peel and finely grate enough gingerroot to measure 1½ tablespoons. Into a bowl sift together flour, baking powder, salt, and baking soda. In a large bowl with an electric mixer beat together butter and granulated sugar until light and fluffy and beat in vanilla and eggs, beating until smooth. Beat in about 1 cup flour mixture until just combined. Beat in milk, mango, and gingerroot until combined. Beat in remaining flour mixture until just combined.

Spoon batter into pan, smoothing top, and bake in middle of oven until a tester comes out clean, about 40 minutes. Cool cake completely in pan on a rack and invert onto a work surface. *Cake may be made 2 days ahead and chilled, wrapped well in plastic wrap.*

Make Lime Cream: In a bowl with an electric mixer beat together cream cheese, confectioners' sugar, and lime juice until smooth. Add cream and beat until thick and smooth.

Trim cake and cut into 1½-inch squares. Diagonally halve squares to form triangles. Transfer lime cream to a pastry bag fitted with a ½-inch decorative tip and pipe a rosette onto each triangle. Transfer triangles to a tray. *Triangles may be made 8 hours ahead and chilled, loosely covered.* MAKES ABOUT 96 TRIANGLES.

ORANGE POPPY-SEED CAKE WITH BERRIES

For Cake

- 1½ cups cake flour (not self-rising)
- ¾ teaspoon salt
- 1 teaspoon baking soda
- ½ teaspoon baking powder
- ¼ cup poppy seeds
- 1½ sticks (¾ cup) unsalted butter, softened
- 1¼ cups granulated sugar
- 2 teaspoons finely grated fresh orange zest
- 4 large eggs, separated
- ⅔ cup sour cream
- 2 teaspoons vanilla
- ¼ teaspoon cream of tartar

For Syrup and Berry Mixture

- 1 large navel orange
- 1 cup fresh orange juice
- 1 cup plus 2 tablespoons Grand Marnier or other orange-flavored liqueur
- 3 tablespoons granulated sugar
- 3 cups picked-over mixed berries

confectioners' sugar for dusting cake

ACCOMPANIMENT: *crème fraîche*

Make Cake: Preheat oven to 350° F. Butter and flour a 10-inch springform pan, knocking out excess flour.

Into a bowl sift together flour, salt, baking soda, and baking powder and stir in poppy seeds. In a large bowl with an electric mixer beat together butter, 1 cup granulated sugar, and zest until light and fluffy. In a small bowl whisk together yolks, sour cream, and vanilla until combined well. Add flour mixture and yolk mixture to butter mixture alternately in batches, beginning and ending with flour mixture and beating well after each addition. In another bowl with cleaned beaters beat whites with a pinch salt until foamy. Add cream of tartar and beat whites until they hold soft peaks. Gradually beat in remaining ¼ cup granulated sugar, and beat until meringue holds stiff peaks. Stir about one third meringue into batter to lighten and fold in remaining meringue gently but thoroughly. Pour batter into pan, smoothing top. Bake cake in middle of oven 40 to 45 minutes, or until a tester comes out clean.

Make Syrup and Berry Mixture while Cake is Baking: With a zester remove enough zest from orange to measure ¼ cup. In a small saucepan stir together zest, juice, liqueur, and granulated sugar and cook over moderately high heat, stirring, until sugar is dissolved. Remove saucepan from heat and with a fork transfer zest to a bowl. Pour ⅓ cup syrup over zest and add berries, tossing until combined. *Macerate berries, covered and chilled, at least 2 hours and up to 1 day. Reserve remaining syrup, chilled.*

Transfer cake in pan to a rack and immediately poke top all over with a skewer. Generously brush top of cake with half of reserved syrup, letting some run down between cake and side of pan, and let cake stand 10 minutes. Run a thin knife around edge of pan and remove side of pan. Invert cake onto rack set over a baking sheet. Poke cake all over with skewer and brush generously with remaining syrup. Invert cake onto another rack and cool completely. *Cake may be made 1 day ahead and kept wrapped well in plastic wrap or in an airtight container at room temperature.*

Just before serving, sift confectioners' sugar over top of cake. Serve cake with macerated berries and *crème fraîche.* SERVES 8 TO 10.

Photo below

DRIED FRUIT AND POMEGRANATE SEED UPSIDE-DOWN CAKE

For Topping

⅔ cup dried apricots

⅓ cup pitted prunes

2 tablespoons dark raisins

2 tablespoons golden raisins

2 tablespoons dried cranberries

3 tablespoons pomegranate seeds
(from about ¼ of a pomegranate; optional)

3 tablespoons unsalted butter

¾ cup packed light brown sugar

For Cake Batter

1 cup all-purpose flour

½ teaspoon baking powder

¼ teaspoon salt

4 ounces almond paste (a scant ½ cup)

¾ cup granulated sugar

1 stick (½ cup) unsalted butter, softened

3 large eggs

For Pomegranate Seed Accompaniment (optional)

½ cup pomegranate seeds (from about
¾ of a pomegranate)

1 tablespoon granulated sugar

1 teaspoon orange-flower water*

ACCOMPANIMENT: orange whipped cream
(recipe follows)

*available at specialty foods shops

Make Topping: Cut half of apricots into quarters. In a large saucepan cover dried fruits with water by 1 inch. Simmer fruits, uncovered, until softened, about 15 minutes. In a colander drain fruits and cool. Cut pomegranate in half and with hands gently break in two. Bend back rinds and dislodge seeds from membranes into a bowl. In a seasoned 10-inch cast-iron skillet melt butter over moderate heat until foam subsides. Reduce heat to low. Sprinkle brown sugar evenly onto bottom of skillet and heat, without stirring, 3 minutes (not all brown sugar will be melted). Remove skillet from heat and arrange fruits evenly over brown sugar. Sprinkle 3 tablespoons pomegranate seeds around fruits.

Preheat oven to 350° F.

Make Cake Batter: Into a bowl sift together flour, baking powder, and salt. In a food processor blend together almond paste and granulated sugar until combined well. Add butter and blend until smooth. With motor running, add eggs 1 at a time, blending well after each addition. Transfer almond mixture to a bowl and stir in flour mixture until just combined.

Pour batter over topping in skillet, spreading evenly (do not disturb topping), and bake in middle of oven 35 to 40 minutes, or until golden brown and just beginning to pull away from side of skillet.

Immediately run a thin knife around edge of skillet. Invert a plate over skillet and invert cake onto plate (keeping plate and skillet firmly pressed together). Carefully lift skillet off cake and replace any fruit that is stuck to bottom of skillet if necessary.

Make Pomegranate Seed Accompaniment: In a bowl stir together pomegranate seeds, granulated sugar, and orange-flower water and chill, covered.

Serve cake warm with chilled pomegranate seeds and whipped cream. SERVES 8.

Photo opposite

ORANGE WHIPPED CREAM ⊕

1 cup well-chilled heavy cream

confectioners' sugar to taste

1 teaspoon finely grated fresh orange zest

In a bowl with an electric mixer beat together cream, confectioners' sugar, and zest until mixture holds soft peaks. MAKES ABOUT 1½ CUPS.

MINIATURE CURRANT PIES

— · —

For Pastry Dough

1½ sticks (¾ cup) cold unsalted butter
1½ cups all-purpose flour
¼ teaspoon salt
⅓ cup sour cream

For Filling

¾ cup dried currants
⅓ cup golden raisins
⅓ cup dark raisins
¼ cup granulated sugar
2 tablespoons brandy
1 teaspoon finely grated fresh orange zest
1 teaspoon finely grated fresh lemon zest

confectioners' sugar for sprinkling pies

Make Dough: Cut butter into bits. In a bowl with your fingertips or a pastry blender blend together flour, salt, and butter until mixture resembles coarse meal. Stir in sour cream with a fork until incorporated and form mixture into a ball. Halve dough and flatten each piece into a disk. *Chill disks, wrapped separately in plastic wrap, until firm, at least 1 hour, and up to 2 days.*

Make Filling: In a small saucepan stir together all filling ingredients and heat over moderate heat just until heated through. Transfer filling to a bowl and cool. *Filling may be made 2 days ahead and chilled, covered.*

Preheat oven to 400° F.

On a lightly floured surface roll out 1 piece dough into a 12- by 9-inch rectangle (less than ¼ inch thick). Using a sharp knife and a ruler cut rectangle into twelve 3-inch squares. Fit squares into 12 ungreased ⅛-cup mini-muffin cups (about 1¾ inches across top and 1 inch deep) and drop 2 teaspoons filling onto centers of squares. Fold all 4 corners of

squares over filling (filling will not be completely covered). Make 12 more pies in same manner. *Pies may be made up to this point 2 days ahead and chilled, covered.*

Bake pies in middle of oven until pale golden, about 20 minutes. Cool pies in pans on racks 10 minutes and transfer to racks.

Serve pies warm, sprinkled with confectioners' sugar. MAKES 24 MINIATURE PIES.

BANANA COFFEECAKE

— · —

For Topping

⅓ cup sliced almonds
¾ stick (6 tablespoons) unsalted butter
1 cup all-purpose flour
⅓ cup packed light brown sugar

For Cake Layer

3 ripe large bananas
2½ cups cake flour (not self-rising)
1 teaspoon baking powder
½ teaspoon baking soda
¼ teaspoon salt
1½ sticks (¾ cup) unsalted butter, softened
1 cup granulated sugar
3 large eggs
½ cup well-shaken buttermilk

Preheat oven to 350° F. Butter a 10- by 2-inch square baking pan and line bottom with wax paper. Butter paper and dust pan with flour, knocking out excess flour.

Make Topping: Toast almonds until golden. Cut butter into bits and in a food processor pulse together all topping ingredients until combined well and mixture resembles coarse meal.

Make Cake Layer: In a small bowl mash enough banana to measure 1½ cups. Into a bowl sift together flour, baking powder, baking soda, and salt. In a bowl with an electric mixer beat together butter and granulated sugar until light and fluffy. Beat in 1 cup mashed banana and beat in eggs 1 at a time, beating well after each addition. Beat in flour mixture and buttermilk alternately in batches, beginning and ending with flour mixture and beating after each addition until batter is smooth. Fold in remaining ½ cup mashed banana.

Spoon batter into pan, smoothing top, and sprinkle evenly with topping. Bake cake in middle of oven about 45 minutes, or until a tester comes out clean. Cool cake in pan on a rack 30 minutes. *Cake keeps, covered, at cool room temperature 2 days.* Run a thin knife around edges of pan and cut cake into 16 squares. Serve coffeecake warm or a room temperature. MAKES 16 SQUARES.

JELLY DOUGHNUTS

¼ cup milk

½ cup water

⅓ cup granulated sugar

a ¼-ounce package active dry yeast

¾ stick (6 tablespoons) unsalted butter

2 large eggs

¼ teaspoon salt

about 3¼ cups all-purpose flour

about ½ cup raspberry jelly

1 tablespoon water

about 5 cups vegetable oil

about 1 cup confectioners' or granulated sugar

In a small saucepan heat milk and water until warm (105° to 115° F.). Transfer mixture to a large bowl and stir in 1 teaspoon granulated sugar. Sprinkle yeast over mixture and let stand 10 minutes, or until foamy. Melt butter and lightly whisk into yeast mixture with remaining sugar, 1 egg, and salt. Stir in 3 cups flour, stirring until a dough is formed.

Turn out dough onto a well-floured surface and with floured hands knead dough, adding ¼ cup flour, 1 tablespoon at a time as necessary, until smooth and elastic, about 6 minutes. Lightly butter cleaned large bowl and transfer dough to bowl, turning to coat. *Let dough rise, loosely covered with plastic wrap, at room temperature until doubled in bulk, about 1½ hours.*

Punch down dough and on floured surface with a floured rolling pin roll out dough into a 15-inch round (about ¼ inch thick). Using a floured 2½- or 3-inch round cutter cut out rounds (you will have about 20). Gather scraps and cut out about 4 more rounds in same manner. Spoon about 1 teaspoon jelly onto centers of half of rounds. In a small bowl stir together remaining egg and water and brush onto dough around jelly. Arrange a plain round on top of each jellied round, pressing gently around jelly to seal. Line a tray with wax paper and transfer doughnuts to tray. *Let doughnuts rise, loosely covered with plastic wrap, at room temperature until puffed and almost doubled in bulk, about 1 hour.*

In a deep (at least 4 inches) 3-quart heavy saucepan heat about 2½ inches oil over moderate heat until a deep-fat thermometer registers 360° F. Working in batches of 2, transfer doughnuts to oil by gently flipping them 1 at a time onto a slotted spoon and sliding them into oil. Fry doughnuts 1½ minutes on each side, or until a deep brown (doughnuts will brown before they are cooked through). With slotted spoon transfer doughnuts as fried to a rack set over paper towels. Return oil to 360° F. between batches.

Line a baking sheet with wax paper and mound sugar on sheet. When doughnuts are cool enough to handle, roll in sugar to coat. Serve doughnuts warm. MAKES ABOUT 12 DOUGHNUTS.

HONEY PECAN STICKY BUNS

½ cup dried currrants
2 tablespoons brandy
¼ cup hot water
¾ cup packed light brown sugar
¼ cup honey
½ stick (¼ cup) unsalted butter
½ cup pecan pieces

For Dough
2 cups all-purpose flour
1 tablespoon baking powder
½ teaspoon salt
1¼ cups heavy cream

2 teaspoons cinnamon

In a small bowl soak currants in brandy and hot water 20 minutes, or until softened, and drain. In a saucepan heat ¼ cup brown sugar, honey, and butter over moderately low heat, stirring, until sugar is melted. Pour mixture into an 8½-inch round cake pan. Chop pecans and sprinkle on top of mixture.

Preheat oven to 425° F.

Make Dough: Into a bowl sift together flour, baking powder, and salt. Add cream and stir until a dough just forms.

On a lightly floured surface roll out dough into an 18- by 10-inch rectangle. Force remaining ½ cup brown sugar through a coarse sieve evenly over dough and sprinkle currants and cinnamon over brown sugar. Beginning with a long side, tightly roll up dough jelly-roll fashion. Cut roll into 1-inch-thick slices with a sharp knife and fit slices, cut sides up, in one layer in cake pan, pressing slices down gently.

Bake buns in middle of oven 20 minutes, or until a tester comes out clean. Run a thin knife around edge of pan. Invert a plate over cakepan and invert buns onto a plate. MAKES 18 BUNS.

BLUEBERRY SCONES

4 cups all-purpose flour
2 tablespoons baking powder
½ cup plus 2 tablespoons sugar
1 stick (½ cup) cold unsalted butter
1 large egg yolk
1 whole large egg
1 cup plus 3 tablespoons milk
1 cup picked-over blueberries

ACCOMPANIMENTS
lightly whipped cream
jam

Preheat oven to 425° F. and lightly butter 2 large baking sheets.

Into a large bowl sift together flour, baking powder, a pinch salt, and ½ cup sugar. Cut butter into bits and blend into flour mixture with your fingertips until mixture resembles coarse meal. In a small bowl whisk together yolk, whole egg, and 1 cup plus 2 tablespoons milk until just combined. Add milk mixture and blueberries to flour mixture, gently stirring until a dough just forms.

On a lightly floured surface form dough into a ball and flatten into a disk. With a floured rolling pin roll out dough 1 inch thick (about a 10 inch round) and with a 3-inch round cutter cut out rounds, transferring to baking sheets. Gather scraps and make more rounds in same manner. Brush tops of rounds with remaining tablespoon milk and sprinkle with remaining 2 tablespoons sugar.

Bake scones in upper and lower thirds of oven, switching position of sheets halfway through baking, 15 minutes total, or until golden. Transfer scones to a rack and cool.

Serve scones with cream and jam. MAKES ABOUT 10 SCONES.

MORAVIAN SUGAR CAKE

For Dough

1 russet (baking) potato (about ½ pound)
½ cup plus 2 tablespoons warm water (105°–115° F.)
a ¼-ounce package (2½ teaspoons) active dry yeast
¾ stick (6 tablespoons) unsalted butter
½ cup granulated sugar
1 large egg
1½ teaspoons salt
2½ to 3 cups unbleached all-purpose flour

¾ stick (6 tablespoons) cold unsalted butter
¾ cup packed light brown sugar
2 teaspoons cinnamon

Peel potato and cut into 1-inch pieces. In a small saucepan cover potato with water by 1 inch and simmer, covered, 10 to 15 minutes, or until very tender. Drain potato well and force through a ricer into a large bowl. Stir in 2 tablespoons warm water. In a small bowl sprinkle yeast over remaining ½ cup warm water and let stand 5 minutes, or until mixture is foamy. Melt butter and cool. Stir yeast mixture into mashed potato and stir in butter, granulated sugar, egg, and salt until combined well. Add 2½ cups flour and stir until combined well. Turn dough out onto a floured work surface and knead 8 to 10 minutes, adding as much of remaining ½ cup flour as necessary to form a smooth, elastic dough.

Butter a large bowl and transfer dough to bowl, turning to coat. *Let dough rise, covered with plastic wrap, at room temperature 1½ to 2 hours, or until doubled in bulk.* Punch down dough. *Dough may be made 1 day ahead and chilled, covered. Bring dough to room temperature before proceeding.*

Preheat oven to 400° F. and butter a 13- by 9-inch baking pan.

Press dough evenly in baking pan. *Let dough rise, covered with a kitchen towel, in a warm place 30 to 45 minutes, or until puffed.*

Cut butter into bits. Make indentations all over top of dough with your thumb and scatter butter over dough. In a small bowl stir together brown sugar and cinnamon and sprinkle evenly over dough. Bake sugar cake in middle of oven 20 to 25 minutes, or until dark brown and cooked through. Cool cake 5 minutes and cut into squares. **MAKES ABOUT 15 SQUARES.**

Photo below

PEACH CINNAMON STREUSEL MUFFINS

For Topping

2 tablespoons unsalted butter
⅓ cup all-purpose flour
⅓ cup packed light brown sugar
1 teaspoon cinnamon

For Muffins

2 cups all-purpose flour
½ cup packed light brown sugar
1 tablespoon baking powder
¾ teaspoon cinnamon
¼ teaspoon baking soda
½ teaspoon salt
½ stick (¼ cup) unsalted butter
1 cup sour cream
1 large egg
4 ripe peaches

Preheat oven to 400° F. and butter twelve ½-cup muffin cups.

Make Topping: Cut butter into bits and in a food processor pulse together with remaining topping ingredients until mixture resembles coarse meal.

Make Muffins: In a large bowl stir together flour, brown sugar, baking powder, cinnamon, baking soda, and salt. Melt butter and in a small bowl whisk together with sour cream and egg. Halve and pit peaches and chop enough to measure 1¾ cups. Stir sour cream mixture and chopped peaches into flour mixture until just combined.

Divide batter among muffin cups and sprinkle evenly with topping. Bake muffins in middle of oven 20 minutes, or until golden and a tester comes out clean. Cool muffins in pan on a rack 10 minutes and turn out onto rack. Serve muffins warm or at room temperature. *Muffins keep in an airtight container at cool room temperature 1 day.* MAKES 12 MUFFINS.

CRANBERRY CUPCAKES

¼ cup dried cranberries
6 tablespoons all-purpose flour
2 tablespoons cornstarch
½ teaspoon baking powder
¼ teaspoon cinnamon
a pinch freshly grated nutmeg
1 large egg
3 tablespoons unsalted butter, softened
⅓ cup sugar
¼ teaspoon vanilla
2 tablespoons milk

For Frosting

¼ cup (2 ounces) cream cheese, softened
1 tablespoon unsalted butter, softened
2 teaspoons pure maple syrup or honey

Preheat oven to 350° F. and line six ½-cup muffin cups with paper liners.

In a small heatproof bowl cover cranberries with boiling water and soak 5 minutes.

While cranberries are soaking, into a bowl sift together flour, cornstarch, baking powder, cinnamon, nutmeg, and a pinch salt. In a small bowl lightly beat egg. In a bowl with an electric mixer beat together butter and sugar until light and fluffy and beat in egg 1 tablespoon at a time, beating well after each addition. Beat in vanilla. Stir in flour mixture and milk alternately in several batches, beginning and ending with flour mixture and stirring after each addition until smooth.

Drain cranberries and pat dry. Finely chop cranberries and stir into batter. Divide batter among muffin cups and bake in middle of oven until a tester comes out clean, about 20 minutes.

Make Frosting: In a bowl beat together frosting ingredients until smooth and chill.

Turn cupcakes out onto a rack and cool 10 minutes. Frost cupcakes. MAKES 6 CUPCAKES.

PEANUT BUTTER FAIRY CAKES

For Cakes
1½ cups all-purpose flour
1½ teaspoons baking powder
1½ sticks (¾ cup) unsalted butter, softened
¾ cup granulated sugar
¾ teaspoon vanilla
3 large eggs

For Filling
⅓ cup well-chilled heavy cream
2 tablespoons granulated sugar
⅓ cup peanut butter, at room temperature

confectioners' sugar for sprinkling cakes

Make Cakes: Preheat oven to 400° F. Butter and flour twelve ⅓-cup muffin cups, knocking out excess flour.

Into a bowl sift together flour, baking powder, and a pinch salt. In another bowl with an electric mixer beat butter until pale. Add granulated sugar and beat until light and fluffy. Beat in vanilla and beat in eggs 1 at a time, beating well after each addition. With mixer on low speed, beat in flour mixture until just combined. Spoon batter evenly into cups and bake in middle of oven 15 minutes, or until pale golden and a tester comes out clean. Cool cakes in pan on a rack 5 minutes and turn out onto rack to cool completely.

Make Filling: In a small bowl with cleaned beaters beat heavy cream until it just holds stiff peaks. Gently fold in granulated sugar and peanut butter until just combined.

Cut about ⅓ inch off top of each cake and cut tops in half. Spoon 1 tablespoon cream mixture onto each cake and top with 2 cake pieces, tipping them to create "wings." Sprinkle cakes with confectioners' sugar. *Cakes keep in an airtight container at cool room temperature 2 days.* MAKES 12 FAIRY CAKES.

CHEESECAKE PHYLLO PURSES

For Filling
12 ounces cream cheese, softened
⅔ cup sugar
1 large egg yolk
1 teaspoon vanilla
1 tablespoon finely grated fresh lemon zest
1 tablespoon fresh lemon juice
¼ teaspoon salt

six 17- by 12-inch *phyllo* sheets
1 stick (½ cup) unsalted butter
⅓ cup graham cracker crumbs

Preheat oven to 375° F.

Make Filling: In a bowl with an electric mixer beat together cream cheese and sugar until smooth. Add remaining filling ingredients and beat until combined well.

Stack *phyllo* sheets between 2 overlapping sheets of plastic wrap and then cover with a damp kitchen towel. Melt butter. On a work surface arrange 1 *phyllo* sheet with a long side facing you and lightly brush with some butter. Top with a second *phyllo* sheet and lightly brush with some butter. Cut long side crosswise into four 12- by 4¼-inch rectangles and halve crosswise to make eight 6- by 4¼-inch rectangles.

Lay rectangles over ungreased 1¾- by 1-inch mini-muffin cups and drop ½ teaspoon graham cracker crumbs onto centers of rectangles. Top crumbs with 1 tablespoon filling. Bring all 4 corners of each rectangle together and press just above filling to seal. Make 16 more pastries in same manner, filling a total of 24 mini-muffin cups.

Bake *phyllo* purses in middle of oven until golden, 15 to 20 minutes. MAKES 24 PASTRIES.

ANISE LEMON
MADELEINES

— · —

2 teaspoons anise seeds

1 cup cake flour (not self-rising)

½ teaspoon baking powder

¼ teaspoon salt

1 stick (½ cup) unsalted butter, softened

¾ cup sugar

1½ tablespoons Sambuca or other anise-
flavored liqueur

1½ teaspoons finely grated fresh lemon zest

3 large eggs

Preheat oven to 325° F. Generously butter and flour a *madeleine* pan, knocking out excess flour.

In an electric coffee/spice grinder finely grind anise seeds. Into a bowl sift together flour, baking powder, and salt and stir in anise. In another bowl with an electric mixer beat together butter, sugar, liqueur, and zest until light and fluffy. Beat in eggs 1 at a time, beating well after each addition, and add flour mixture, beating until just combined.

Fill *madeleine* molds with batter and with a spatula level tops, scraping back and forth over molds and returning excess batter to bowl. (This will eliminate any air pockets and ensure that molds are not overfilled.) Wipe excess batter from edges of pan. Bake *madeleines* in middle of oven 20 minutes, or until edges are browned and tops are golden. Cool *madeleines* in pan on a rack 5 minutes. Loosen edges of *madeleines* and transfer to rack to cool completely. Clean *madeleine* pan and butter and flour again. Make more *madeleines* in same manner. *Madeleines keep in an airtight container at cool room temperature 4 days.* MAKES ABOUT 28 MADELEINES.

HAZELNUT
FEATHERLIGHT CAKE

— · —

6 large eggs, separated

1 tablespoon fresh lemon juice

1 cup sugar

½ cup all-purpose flour

2 teaspoons baking powder

2 teaspoons finely grated fresh orange zest

¼ teaspoon cream of tartar

½ teaspoon salt

2¾ cups finely ground hazelnuts

ACCOMPANIMENTS

whipped cream

raspberries

Preheat oven to 350° F.

In bowl of a standing electric mixer beat yolks with lemon juice until thick and pale and gradually beat in ¾ cup sugar, beating until combined well. Into a small bowl sift together flour and baking powder and stir into yolk mixture with zest. In a bowl with cleaned beaters beat whites until foamy. Add cream of tartar and salt and beat until whites hold soft peaks. Beat in remaining ¼ cup sugar and beat until whites hold stiff peaks. Fold meringue gently but thoroughly into yolk mixture. Sprinkle hazelnuts over batter and fold in gently but thoroughly.

Pour batter into an ungreased 10- by 4½-inch tube pan with a removable bottom, smoothing top, and bake in middle of oven 45 to 50 minutes, or until a tester comes out clean. Invert cake onto a rack and cool cake completely in pan. Run a thin knife around edge of pan and remove side of pan. *Cake may be made 2 days ahead and kept covered at room temperature.*

Serve cake with whipped cream and berries. SERVES 10 TO 12.

Photo opposite

INDEX

— · —

Page numbers in *italics* indicate color photographs
☾ indicates recipes that can be made in 45 minutes or less
☾+ indicates recipes that can be made in 45 minutes or less but require additional unattended time

TABLE SETTING ACKNOWLEDGEMENTS

Items not credited are privately owned.
All addresses are in New York City unless otherwise indicated.

FRONT JACKET

Profiteroles with Burnt Orange Ice Cream and Hot Fudge Sauce: "Follement" dessert plate designed by Christian Lacroix—Christofle, (800) 799-6886; "Ellipse" teaspoon—Pottery Barn, (800) 922-9934.

BACK JACKET (CLOCKWISE FROM UPPER LEFT)

Little Chocolate Cherry Cake; Grapefruit Campari Granita; Chocolate Raspberry Ganache Cake: All items in photographs are privately owned.
Kumquat, Grape, and Kiwifruit Soup: Soup bowl—Crate & Barrel, (800) 996-9960.

FRONTISPIECE

Old-Fashioned Cherry Vanilla Pie (page 2): See credits below for Fruit chapter.

TITLE PAGE

Pails of cherries (page 3): All items in photograph are privately owned.

TABLE OF CONTENTS

Red, White, and Blue Cheesecake (page 6): See credits below for Holidays chapter.
Fresh Peach Ice Cream (page 7): See credits below for Icy chapter.
Champagne Truffles; Raspberry Tea Gelée with Watermelon; Cappuccino Brownies (page 7): All items in photographs are privately owned.
Sliced Baked Apple (page 7): See credits below for Fruit chapter.

INTRODUCTION

Profiteroles with Burnt Orange Ice Cream and Hot Fudge Sauce (page 8): See credits above for Front Jacket.

A GARDEN DESSERT PARTY

Picnic Setting (pages 10 and 11): "Pemberton" solid teak bench and checked throw pillows—Smith & Hawken, (800) 776-3336; "Sorbetto" aqua oval platter—Vietri, (800) 277-5933; blue pillow, blue dessert plates, and cream-handled flatware—Pottery Barn, (800) 922-9934; "Tiber" sorbet spoon—Buccellati, (212) 308-5533.

A CHAMPAGNE DESSERT PARTY

Buffet Setting (pages 12 and 13): "Silver leaf" wall covering—Donghia Textiles, (800) 366-4442; Macassar ebony and silver leaf demi-lune console—Dakota Jackson, (212) 838-9444; "Laura" champagne flutes—William Yeoward Glass,

(800) 818-8484; "Tiber" sterling cake server—Buccellati, (212) 308-5533; linen napkins—Angel Zimick at Metropolitan Design Group, (212) 944-6110; footed glass trifle bowl—Crate & Barrel, (800) 996-9960.

CHOCOLATE

Bittersweet Chocolate Soufflé (page 15): Glass soufflé dish—Dean & DeLuca, 560 Broadway.
Bittersweet Chocolate Mousse in Phyllo (page 19): "Messalina" bone-china dessert plate—Villeroy & Boch, 974 Madison Avenue.
Turtle Brownies; Sambuca Brownies (page 21): Box—Kate's Paperie, 561 Broadway.
Chocolate Cream Pie (page 27): Stoneware pie plate—Pottery Barn, (800) 922-9934.

BERRIES

Strawberries with Molasses Sour Cream Sauce; Chocolate Crackle Cookies (page 41): "Flore" crystal coupes—Baccarat, 625 Madison Avenue. "Garance" Limoges salad/dessert plates—Bernardaud, (800) 884-7775. Sterling dessert spoons (from a set of 8), London, 1870—James II Galleries, 11 East 57th Street.
Raspberry Mango Trifle (page 44): See credits above for A Champagne Dessert Party.

FRUIT

Old-Fashioned Cherry Vanilla Pie (page 49): Vintage Adirondack chair—Rhubarb Home, 26 Bond Street. Vintage napkins—Paula Rubenstein Ltd., 65 Prince Street.
Baked Pear on Sugared Puff Pastry with Caramel Sauce (page 51): "Corona Banded" ironstone dessert plate—Pottery Barn, (800) 922-9934.
Peach and Strawberry Longcake (page 53): Collection of Americana from Gail Lettick's Pantry & Hearth Antiques, 121 East 35th Street.
Apple Walnut Upside-Down Cake (page 56): Glass cake stand—Bloomingdale's, 1000 Third Avenue.
Spiced Caramel Oranges (page 59): Glass compotes—Frank McIntosh Shop at Henri Bendel, 712 Fifth Avenue. "Carla" fabric by Athena Design, Inc. (available through decorator). For stores call (212) 268-9165.
Sliced Baked Apple (page 60): Molin ceramic dessert plates—Bloomingdale's, 1000 Third Avenue.
Honey Vanilla Poached Apricots (page 65): Glazed bowls (from a set of five nesting bowls)—Wolfman • Gold & Good Company, 117 Mercer Street. "Pastoral" cotton napkin by Necessities. For stores call (718) 797-0530.

ICY

Tropical Fruit Champagne Granita (page 69): Porcelain charger. For stores call Archipelago, (212) 334-9460.

Fresh Peach Ice Cream (page 73): Collection of Americana from Gail Lettick's Pantry & Hearth Antiques, 121 East 35th Street.

Cranberry Swirl Ice-Cream Cake (page 74): English sterling compote (as cake stand) by Crichton—S. Wyler, 941 Lexington Avenue. Handmade decoupage dessert plate; cachepot by Jered Holmes Ltd.—Hoagland's of Greenwich, 175 Greenwich Avenue, Greenwich, CT 06830, tel. (203) 869-2127. " Spangle" cotton fabric by Jean Churchill (available through decorator)—Cowtan & Tout, 979 Third Avenue.

Banana Peanut Semifreddo (page 77): "Epson" teaspoon—ABC Carpet & Home, 888 Broadway.

Three Grape Sorbets (page 79): Parfait glass—Crate & Barrel, (800) 996-9960.

California Gingered Fruit Salsa Sundae; Southern Peanut Butterscotch Sundae (page 80): "Eclipse" stainless-steel teaspoon—Pottery Barn, (800) 922-9934.

SHOWSTOPPERS

Lemon Raspberry Wedding Cake (pages 83 and 86): "Tiffany Weave" bone-china dessert plates; "Chrysanthemum" sterling cake knife—Tiffany & Co., 727 Fifth Avenue. Champagne flutes—Pottery Barn, (800) 922-9934. "Heartland" hand-blown glass cake stand—Simon Pearce, 500 Park Avenue (at 59th Street).

Pineapple Coconut Layer Cake (page 89): "Windham" sterling cake server—Tiffany & Co., 727 Fifth Avenue. Flowers—Zezé, 398 East 52nd Street.

Macadamia Rum Baked Alaska (page 92): Apilco porcelain platter—Bridge Kitchenware Corp., 214 East 52nd Street. Cotton matelassé fabric—ABC Carpet & Home, 888 Broadway. Flowers—Zezé, 398 East 52nd Street.

Swedish Meringue Cake (page 100): "Cavalier Check" cotton tablecloth—Country Swedish, 35 Post Road West, Westport, CT 06880. Flowers—Castle & Pierpont, 1441 York Avenue.

Chocolate Mousse and Raspberry Cream Dacquoise (page 103): "Vienne Gold" crystal wineglasses—Baccarat, Inc., 625 Madison Avenue. English silver-plate salver, Sheffield, circa 1870—S. Wyler, 941 Lexington Avenue. Italian embroidered tablecloth with filet lace inserts, circa 1900—Françoise Nunnallé Fine Arts, 105 West 55th Street. French nineteenth-century ormolu and Baccarat crystal candelabra—Bardith, 901 Madison Avenue.

Key Lime Mascarpone "Cannoli" with Mango Sauce (page 105): Gien "Tamarin" faience plates—Baccarat, 625 Madison Avenue. "Bamboo" sterling flatware—Tiffany & Co., 727 Fifth Avenue. "Laurel Green" water goblets. For stores call Sasaki (212) 686-5080. "Palma" cotton fabric (available through decorator)— Brunschwig & Fils, 979 Third Avenue. "Snowflake" wrought-iron chairs—Lexington Furniture Industries, (800) 544-4694.

HOMEY

Apple Pie with Walnut Streusel (page 111): Patrick Frey "Paniers Fleuris" Limoges dessert plates and "Sorgues" cotton napkin. For stores call Roseline Crowley, Inc., (203) 785-9376.

Cherry Cobbler (page 113): Enameled cast-iron oval au gratin. For stores call Le Creuset, (803) 943-4308. Vintage napkins—Paula Rubenstein Ltd., 65 Prince Street.

Boston Cream Pie (page 114): "Heartland" crystal cake plate— Simon Pearce, 500 Park Avenue (at 59th Street). Tiffany sterling cake server, circa 1880—Fortunoff, 681 Fifth Avenue.

Orange Flans with Candied Zest; Anise Pine-Nut Cookies (page 119): Gien "Olerys" faience plates—Baccarat, 625 Madison Avenue. "Melrose" plaid wool fabric (available through decorator)—Brunschwig & Fils, 979 Third Avenue.

Black Walnut Pie (page 122): Ceramic pie plate by BBP—Dean & DeLuca Inc., 560 Broadway. Hobnail glasses—Pottery Barn, (800) 922-9934. Cotton fabric—Waverly, (800) 423-5881.

Banana Ginger Trifles (page 125): Ceramic saucer—ABC Carpet & Home, 888 Broadway.

Czech Noodle and Apple Pudding; Cinnamon Raisin Rice Pudding (page 129): Chambray tablecloth—The Ralph Lauren Home Collection, (212)642-8700. Le Creuset enameled cast-iron gratin dish—Bloomingdale's, 1000 Third Avenue.

LIGHTER

Apricot Soufflé (page 131): "Masquerade" faience plates by Cassis & Co.—Kitchen Classics, Main Street, Bridgehampton, New York 11932, (800) 251-2421. "Folio" stainless-steel flatware— Pavillon Christofle, 680 Madison Avenue. Wineglasses by Laure Japy—Hoagland's, 175 Greenwich Avenue, Greenwich, Connecticut 06830. Chateau X hand-painted straw placemats by Jane Krolik—Tabletoppings by Frank McIntosh at Henri Bendel, 712 Fifth Avenue.

Pineapple Tart (page 136): Stack of three plates—Crate & Barrel, (800) 996-9960.

Cranberry Applesauce (page 140): Molin ceramic dessert plates— Bloomingdale's, 1000 Third Avenue. "Pavillon" crystal coupes— Baccarat, 625 Madison Avenue.

BITES

Goat Cheese Chocolate Truffles (page 147): "Vibrations" silver-plate and glass dish—Pavillon Christofle, 680 Madison Avenue.

Champagne Truffles (page 158): See credits on page 205 for A Champagne Dessert Party.

HOLIDAYS

Sweet Potato Maple Pie with Pecan Crust (page 161): Tin napkin rings; Shaker box—Gail Lettick's Pantry & Hearth, 121 East 35th Street. "Indigo Crewel" fabric (available through decorator)— Brunschwig & Fils, 979 Third Avenue.

Raspberry Swirl Parfaits (page 163): "Pyramide" glasses by Cristal D'Arques—Frank McIntosh at Henri Bendel, 712 Fifth Avenue.

Frozen Cranberry Soufflé (page 165): Crystal bowl—Tiffany & Co., 727 Fifth Avenue.

Red, White, and Blue Cheesecake (page 166): Fioriware "Star" ceramic dessert plates—Barneys New York, Madison Avenue at 61st Street. "Wainwright" stainless-steel flatware by Reed & Barton—The Ralph Lauren Home Collection, (212) 642-8700.

Passover Chocolate Nut Cake (page 171): Frosted floral dessert plate—Keesal & Mathews, 1244 Madison Avenue. English sterling-silver dessert fork—F. Gorevic & Son, Inc., 118 East 57th Street. Vintage glass cake stand—William-Wayne, 850 Lexington Avenue. One-of-a-kind ceramic Passover plate by Sara Mann—The Jewish Museum Design Shop, 1 East 92nd Street.

Rhubarb Lemon Cake Roll; White Chocolate Toasted Almond Semifreddo (page 174): Coalport porcelain plates, circa 1840—Bardith, 901 Madison Avenue. "Laura" hand-crafted sterling flatware—Buccellati, 46 East 57th Street. Flowers—Zezé, 398 East 52nd Street.

ANYTIME

Orange Poppy-Seed Cake with Berries (page 185): Raynaud/Céralene "Ramage" porcelain plate; Chambly silver-plate flatware—Barneys New York, Madison Avenue at 61st Street.

RECIPE CREDITS

Grateful acknowledgment is made to the following contributors for permission to reprint recipes previously published in *Gourmet* Magazine.

ESTATE OF LILLIAN LANGSETH-CHRISTENSEN
Rocky Road Cream Cheese Fudge (page 176); *Maple Walnut Fudge* (page 177). Copyright © 1989.

JAMES COHEN
Passover Chocolate Nut Cake (page 170). Copyright © 1994.

CAROL FIELD
Cranberry Pistachio Biscotti (page 156); *Orange Almond Biscotti* (page 157). Copyright © 1992.

DEBORAH MADISON
Dried Fruit and Pomegranate Seed Upside-Down Cake (page 187). From VEGETARIAN COOKING FOR EVERYONE by Deborah Madison. Copyright © 1997. Used by permission of Broadway Books, a division of Bantam Doubleday Dell Publishing Group.

NICK MALGIERI
Chocolate Raspberry Ganache Cake (page 108); *Cocoa Angel Food Cake with Orange Glaze* (page 139). Copyright © 1997.

MARIAN ELLIS MAY
Peach and Strawberry Longcake (page 52); *Fresh Peach Ice Cream* (page 73). Copyright © 1990.

LOU SEIBERT PAPPAS
Hazelnut Featherlight Cake (page 194). Copyright © 1990.

LESLIE GLOVER PENDLETON
Old-Fashioned Cherry Vanilla Pie (page 50); *Cherry Cobbler* (page 113). Copyright © 1997.

ESTATE OF RICHARD SAX
Czech Noodle and Apple Pudding (page 128); *Cinnamon Raisin Rice Pudding* (page 129) from CLASSIC HOME DESSERTS. Adapted by arrangement with Chapters/Houghton Mifflin Company. Copyright © 1994. All rights reserved.

HELEN WITTY
Black Walnut Pie (page 123). Copyright © 1992.

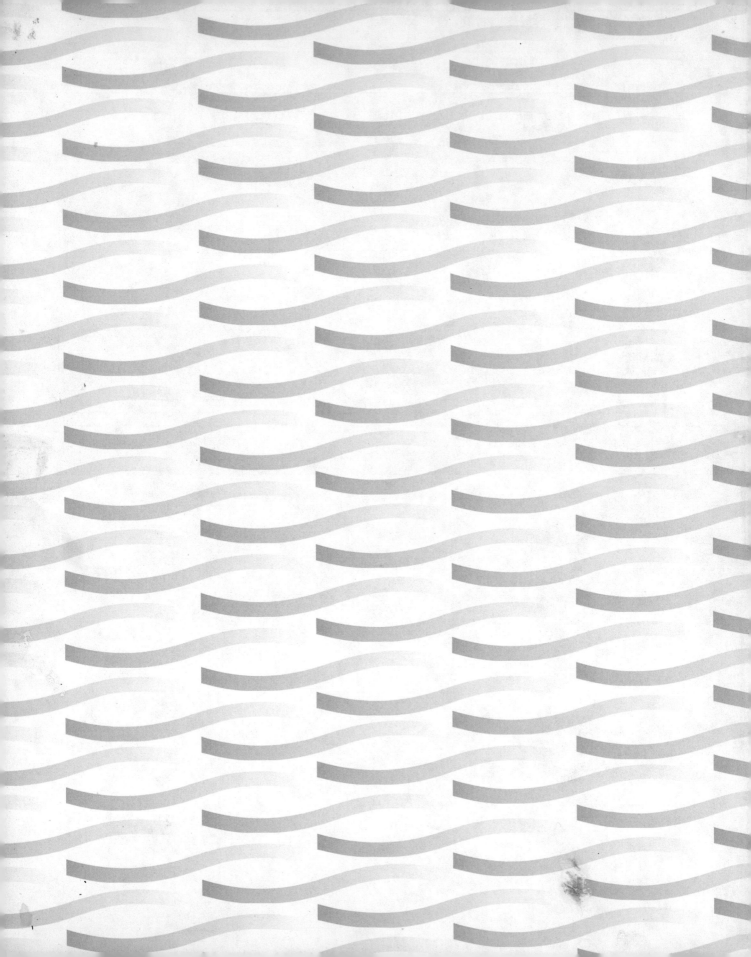